E-religion

A Critical Appraisal of Religious Discourse on the World Wide Web

E-religion
A Critical Appraisal of Religious Discourse on the World Wide Web

Anastasia Karaflogka

LONDON   OAKVILLE

Published by

UK: Equinox Publishing Ltd
Unit 6, The Village
101 Amies St.
London, SW11 2JW

US: DBBC
28 Main Street
Oakville, CT 06779

www.equinoxpub.com

British Library Cataloguing-in-Publication Data
A catalogue record for this book is available from the British Library.

Library of Congress Cataloging-in-Publication Data
Karaflogka, Anastasia.
  E-religion : a critical appraisal of religious discourse on the World
Wide Web / Anastasia Karaflogka.
      p. cm.
  Includes bibliographical references and index.
  ISBN 1-904768-83-0 (hb) -- ISBN 1-904768-84-9 (pbk.)
  1. Internet--Religious aspects. 2. Cyberspace--Religious aspects. I.
Title.
  BL37.K37 2006
  200.285'4678--dc22
                              2005032080

ISBN 978-1-90476-883-8 (hardback)
ISBN 978-1-90476-884-5 (paperback)

Typeset by CA Typesetting, www.sheffieldtypesetting.com
Printed and bound in Great Britain by Antony Rowe, Chippenham, Wiltshire

To my Father

Contents

Preface

The question of religion and its interaction with the Internet has only recently begun to be examined in a systematized way. For example, Wertheim (1999) suggests an understanding of cyberspace as a sacred space; Cobb (1998) considers the question of spiritual life in cyberspace; Davis (1998) addresses the mystical aspect of information communication technologies (ICTs); Bunt Brasher (2001) examines both the meaning of cyber-faith and the future of traditional religion. A broader view of issues regarding religion and the Internet is offered in the edited collection of Hadden and Cowan (2000).

The primary concern of this thesis is to contribute to the current research regarding the presence of religions in cyberspace, indicating the necessity for a paradigm shift in scholarly approaches to cyberspatial religious discourse. One of the aims of this paradigm shift is to develop at least a basic understanding of the "field's" ontology, by incorporating web epistemology and theory as integral to the study of cyberreligion in order to generate conceptual change and renewal.

Yet, any academic inquiry into a given subject requires a set of tools which would provide the necessary framework upon which the investigation will be based. Equally, regarding the exploration of the notion of religion and its relationship with ICTs, a specific collection of methodological devices is requisite.

Therefore, adding to the existing works, the scope of this thesis is to provide a critical methodological framework. The thesis' unique contribution is that it identifies the website as its "field" of study and, by considering the hidden socio-economic and political aspects that govern the Web's structure and operation, it offers a methodological apparatus for investigating the diverse religious phenomena as they appear on the World Wide Web, advancing thus the practical and theoretical understanding of the diverse cyberreligious landscapes.

Acknowledgements

"Religious Discourse and Cyberspace", at the end of the nineties, was only an idea of an undergraduate student fascinated by the mysterious awe of ICTs. Today, this idea has become the doctoral thesis of a graduate student still fascinated by ICTs; only this time the fascination is generated by knowing its present ontological character and anticipating its future evolution.

Although the original idea was the product of one person's wondering, thinking and inquiring processes, the materialisation of this doctoral thesis is the result of various factors. One major contribution came from AHRB, who financed my Religious Discourse and Cyberspace project, for which I am grateful.

This work would never have been transformed from a potentiality to an actuality without the munificent help and support of a number of people.

I wish to express my deepest gratitude to my supervisor, Professor Brian Bocking, not only for inspiring me through his constructive guidance but, most importantly, for his continuous encouragement throughout this endeavour and for his belief in me and my project. I am truly thankful and indebted to my friend Chris Gray for kindly perfecting my use of the English language and for supporting me with her friendship during all these years of my study.

My quest for the "Holy Grail" would have remained unfulfilled if Christos Boinis, Leonor Barata-Boinis (my children), Costas Kavadias and Costakis Kavadias had not offered the necessary "Excalibur" for such an expedition. Each one brought into my research life a different facet of "Excalibur", whether emotional, technical, or practical, and kept the panic attacks under control. To their presence I am beholden. I wish to thank Jon Gray, who, along with Costas Kavadias, oversaw the technical support and kept the "error margins" to a minimum.

I am particularly grateful to all my British and Greek friends who endured my "disappearance", tears and laughs; without them this quest would have been far more difficult to bring into being.

About the CD

The accompanying CD is a mirror of the book; however, the links are "live" in the sense that if the reader is connected to the Internet while using the CD then he or she will be able to access the websites, articles and other e-sources that are mentioned in the text. The readers, though, should know that the different Internet applications (Web, emails, chat rooms, etc.) are fluid and in constant flux, which implies that some links may be "dead" by the time of publication. There are a number of reasons for such an eventuality, as for example, the website(s) may have moved to a different Internet provider which means that the URL(s) have changed, or the website(s) may have been removed from the Web. Regarding religious websites, if the existing URL provides no access, then the reader could: (a) either use the title of the website (e.g. "Dominican Voodoo") to find the site or relevant information or, (b) visit the Internet archive (http://www.archive.org/) and find the site there. Searching the Internet is very time consuming and, as mentioned in Chapter 3 on Web epistemology, there are a number of issues that the researcher has to take into account.

1 Introduction

Introducing the Field/Study

Prologue

The advancement and contemporary development of information communication technologies (ICTs)[1] have created new media which have changed and will continue to change almost all human perceptions of daily activities in all areas of life, whether these be professional, financial, educational, commercial, social, political, cultural and/or religious.

From its conception, and up to the beginning of the 1990s, ICTs were a territory occupied solely by an elitist minority consisting of academics, the military and computer scientists. Today, their widespread usage suggests that the public now occupies the foreground of "online life", which in turn indicates that the "computer world now supports a new and real social space" (Cybernauts Awake! 1999) where people can "meet" to interact, to exchange ideas, knowledge, information and experience, to give substance to creative, imaginative and innovative new concepts and ideas and to re-locate, re-evaluate and deconstruct old concepts and ideas in a new setting.

This is the first time in history that a medium offers, theoretically,[2] unlimited access to an open space, thus providing the opportunity to all humankind to express itself to a global audience. The presence of humanity's vast diversity of cultures, languages, political and economic systems, institutions, ways of life, religions and individuals constitutes the Internet's identity and uniqueness, representing the experiences of all those who participate in the formation of that identity, differentness and diversity.

Internet: perceptions and perspectives

A historical exploration of the Internet, from its origin and through its development, reveals two contrasting ways in which the Net has been perceived, understood and interpreted. The first way is that the Internet originated from wealth, power and the armed forces of one of the richest, if not *the* richest, countries in the world, the USA. That, by definition, implies that it incorporates the value system, ideology, political and economic principles and approaches to advanced technologies of the US and more especially of its West coast. The relationship between the Net and society, seen through the eyes of the "virtual class" (i.e. the skilled workers and entrepreneurs of the information communication industries of the American West coast) is expressed by a particular ideology which Barbrook and Cameron (1995) have termed the "Californian Ideology": a "mix of cybernetics, free market economies and counter-culture libertarianism" which promotes and supports concurrently the "New Left utopia of the electronic agora and the New Right's vision of the electronic marketplace".[3] With an emphasis on a predetermined view of the inevitability and conquest of the hi-tech free market, Californian Ideology promotes a "Jeffersonian democracy"[4] in cyberspace (Barbrook and Cameron 1995) and ignores issues such as racism, poverty, gender inequalities and illiteracy, which exert influence on the participation process. Popular culture magazines, such as *Wired* and *Mondo 2000*,[5] advocate and forcefully promote in their pages the West coast's view of ICTs, which clearly equates New Edge technophilia with New Age spiritualism, and compares at the same time the "sixties' counter cultural 'guerrilla' political action and social consciousness with a particularly privileged, selfish, consumer-oriented, and technologically dependent libertarianism" (Sobchack 1993).

The second way is that despite its militaristic and elitist origins, the Internet has been a democratizing and emancipating medium giving voice to many different kinds of marginalized groups and individuals, who are now capable not only of publicizing their opinions and convictions, but also of organizing both their members and fellow sympathizers, and forming coalitions, alliances and collaborations. In this way they extend their presence from that of a confined and local one, to one which is wide open and global.[6]

Widespread usage

A number of factors may have contributed to the widespread adoption of the Internet, and these could be summarized as belonging to either functional or infrastructural causes. The functional category includes the elimination of distance between interlocutors, speed of communication and relatively low cost of connection.[7] Apart from factors relating to the Internet's general functionality, there are also infrastructural constituents, related to its technical development, which further aided its rapid proliferation. For instance, the design of a friendly user interface has been, according to Poster (1995a, 93), a critical factor for the success of the Internet, for it minimized—if not eliminated—the fear that humans feel toward machines and their interaction with them. Interface means a boundary across which two independent systems meet and communicate with each other.

Regarding computers there are three types of interface: First is the user interface, such as the keyboard, software menus and any other tools that enable communication between the user and the computer. Additionally, this could be expanded to include tools that are used to facilitate users' access to virtual reality. Second is the software interface, that is, the computer language that the different programs use to communicate with each other and with the hardware. Last is the hardware interface, such as the wires, plugs and sockets (i.e. hard discs, disc drives, screens, printers, keyboards etc.) that are used to communicate with each other (Source: Webopedia.com 2002). Furthermore, the development of the World Wide Web, which enables the transmission of multimedia files, not only enriched substantially the aesthetics of transmitted information, but radically also transformed the power of control of information flow by the mass media, such as newspapers and broadcasting corporations, by allowing every individual to become a publisher. However, it should be noted that the Web, as it exists today, is not as its creator envisioned it. Berners-Lee's design[8] was based on his conception of the Web as a "social place"; as a "creative and expressive tool" where anyone could add their views and/or comments on a website (Wright 1997). One need not imagine the repercussions of such an eventuality.[9]

Internet, the Web and cyberspace: perceptions and approaches

Another factor which may have contributed to the success of the Internet is the notion of cyberspace. The term cyberspace, as well as a number of terms with the prefix "cyber", have now become a part of the lives and vocabulary of cybernauts all over the world. Although today's cyberspace is a far cry from the one presented in its founder's books,[10] it has nevertheless become a celebrated term, used in every work on ICTs and computer mediated communication (CMC), generating considerable numbers of discourses about its subjectivity and its role and impact on netizens'[11] perception of technology, society, culture and themselves.

Cyberspace, as well as the Internet, has been defined and perceived in a number of different ways; its proponents fall into two main categories: enthusiastic supporters and sceptical critics. Their rhetoric has been termed by Hakken (1999, 17) as "computopian" and "computropian" respectively. Thus, while for some, cyberspace promotes active participation, interaction and cooperation among all citizens, for others, it diminishes the idea of a global village by increasing the chasm between rich and poor and by creating an exclusive "cyburbia"[12] for its netizens.

The principal claim of Internet supporters is that of democratization of society, which is generally understood to mean significant equality, both in terms of access to information, and in terms of communication, across established boundaries (Ess 1998). On the opposite side, and despite arguments supporting the view that human computer interaction, especially via the Net, could offer a vision of freedom and a shared humanity, the predominant assertion is that the Internet may become the means of global surveillance and personal alienation (Aycock 1995; Silver 2000; Fisher and Wright 2001). Additionally, cyberspace has been criticized as being the "perfect market place" where, alongside goods, information itself is commodified and saleable at a price (Stallabrass 1995, 10, 20) to those who can afford it.

Apart from socio-political, cultural and economic approaches to the medium's actual and/or potential function, impact and influence on society, the Internet has also been understood and interpreted through a number of religious and metaphysical lenses, some of which ascribe to it spiritual qualities.

These perceptions derive from particular understandings of religion and its communicative function. For example, Arthur (1993a, 1) highlights that every expression of human devoutness is, inevitably, a mediated expression which comes through a variety of means of communication, such as words, symbols, music, architecture and so on. Moreover, as Fore states (1993, 5), communication is the essential function which religious activities have in common. Also, in Lehikoinen's (2003, 16) view, there is an exceptional compatibility between religion and the media, in the sense that not only does religion possess a substantial number of communicative objectives, but it also has a message of great significance to convey. Taking into account that throughout their history, religions, especially the institutionalized ones, have proved quite able to extend continuously to new regions (Lehikoinen 2003, 15), one can appreciate that, as a rapidly evolving global communication technology, the Internet could be perceived by religious institutions, organizations and groups as a fascinating new medium for further developing existing methods of communicating their messages.

This can be seen quite clearly in, for example, the Catholic Church's view of and approach to the media, which are understood as "gifts"[13] that enable the Church to disseminate its message. The fundamental role of the media in the religious communicative process, is, on the one hand, acknowledged by the Vatican through the expression of the Church's gratitude to the world of communication for the opportunities it offers to religion in general and to the Church in particular (Pope John Paul II 1989),[14] and on the other hand, especially with regard to the role of ICTs, is clearly evident in the presence of the immeasurable amount of online activity related to religion. For example, the number of religion groups listed in Yahoo's directory is 101,703.[15] This number does not include the alt.[16] religion, or alt.spirituality, alt.philosophy, alt.atheism and so on—groups which are too numerous to be counted. Moreover, the Web is hosting the e-presences of almost all— if not all—religious expressions, understandings and interpretations. A small sample of such presences include: Hindu net; Sivananda yoga; Sufism; Wicca; Kali-Yuga; Catholic Church for Global Justice; Pagan Web; ADIDAM; Rastafarian; Raelian Movement; Theosophical Society, Jainism; Religious Science; Shamanic studies; Mazdaznan Temple; ECKANKAR, *Religion of the Light and Sound of God*; Church of Satan, Troth; Bon religion; Alpheus, Lion and Lamb Ministries, Dominican Vodou, Virtual Voodoo, Gaia Mind, Pantheism and the Irmandade da Boa Morte (Sisterhood of the Good Death).

Other utterances, within the Christian framework, equate the Web with the Word and/or God.[17] This kind of perception ascribes to the Web the quality of sacredness which bestows on to it a different dimension. Such discernment is also found in various theoretical analyses of cyberspace. For instance, examples of such approaches and/or definitions include contemplating cyberspace as the place where all humanity may meet in disembodied form, completely free from the boundaries of the body in a state of pure consciousness; as an "emerging satsang"; as the "new Jerusalem"; as a "multi-dimensional illuminated living web"; as "strengthening people's spiritual bond around the world" (Benedickt 1991; Davidson 1995; Wertheim 1999; Brown 1996; Cobb 1998).

Conceptual clarifications

Religion/religious

The title of this thesis incorporates three terms which may need to be defined in order to provide its conceptual platform. "Religion" is perhaps the only term in humanity's wealth of signifiers that does not correspond to a single signified and, in some cases, as noted by Smith (1998) and others (Herbrechtsmeier 1993; Fitzgerald 1995), the term has been applied, mostly by Western scholars, to non-Western cultures in which the concept of "religion" was totally absent.

Although the term is used innumerable times every day by vast numbers of people in a multitude of different contexts, no single use is in agreement with another; no one perception of "religion" corresponds to another. Despite scholars' efforts to provide a fixed etic notion of "religion", defining the term has been, and still is, a problematic endeavour, for there is as yet no consensus among scholars on exactly "what constitutes a religion" (Barker 1992, 145). However, as Fitzgerald (1995) points out:

> [w]e need working definitions as part of our methodology. Definitions are not final statements of absolute truth, but part of a working methodology which make explicit what is and is not included, what is the focus of our field, what distinguishes it from neighbouring fields, and so on.

Thus, in order to discuss or present a case as religious, it is necessary to have a conceptualization of religion which cannot but be based on existing denotations. A search for a definition of "religion" results in a plethora of definitions from scholars, individuals and religious authorities/organizations/leaders. Since there is no consensus on one definition, it could be assumed that each of these definitions, in essence, expresses the views, understandings and interpretations of the term, as these have been developed within their providers' particular socio-cultural, educational, economic and ideological matrix.[18]

The variety of definitions shows that there are no delineated boundaries circumscribing the term. In some cases the boundaries are exact while in other they are ambiguous; some attempted definitions are narrow, but others are broad; some are based on the understanding of religious participants, that is, from an insider's point of view, while others derive from an outsider's stand-point. For example, while narrow definitions, which focus on the belief and worship of a god/superhuman being, exclude Buddhism (Herbrechtsmeier 1993), broad definitions may be quite "all-encompassing [in] that they could include ideologies such as Marxism" (Barker 1992, 145).

The problem of defining and/or conceptualizing "religion" becomes more evident when "religion" is addressed within different theoretical or cultural contexts. As it appears, the term carries preconceived semantic and cultural interconnections which are reflected in the language, methodology and sample gathering of different studies about the subject. For example, Mahan (2005), points out that examinations of religion in American life are still "limited to the announcement of the activities of a few dominant or privileged religious groups". Herbrechtsmeier (1993), in his work on 'Buddhism and the Definition of Religion', underlines that people in "the West are predisposed to believe that religion has to do with the worship of superhuman beings". Fitzgerald (1995), examining the term "religion" within the Japanese context, suggests that

> [b]y and large "religion" scholars who are not doing straightforward theology, or the more covert variety called phenomenology, are in fact studying values and their institutionalisation in different cultures.

Definitions prove quite troublesome when a new "religious" expression (termed New Religious Movements, NRMs) appears and academics embark on its study. Depending on the definition, a NRM may be categorized as a religion, cult, sect, church and so on.[19] This would not be problematical if the categorization was solely used as an academic methodological tool. However, outside academia the result of the categorization process, not only of NRMs but of "religion" in general, may have considerable implications, especially in the legal and judicial areas which deal with issues related to "religious persecution", "refugee status", "conscientious objectors" and the "charitable status" of a religion.[20] Furthermore, the ways in which "religion" is understood and defined legally in a given state may vary from quite broad to very narrow, giving rise to further implications, especially within the areas of human rights and freedom of religion. For instance, a narrow legal definition may be seen as a judgement on certain beliefs and practices in terms of the extent to which these are acceptable to society or the legal system (Gunn 2003).

The ongoing debate among scholars involved in philosophy and the study of religions on whether and how the term "religion" can be defined has resulted in the formation of a typology of definitions. Gunn (2003) suggests that the process of defining "religion" has two components: the first is the "underlying metaphysical assumptions about the nature of religion (*what* is being defined)" and the second concerns the "type of definition that is to be used (*how* the term is defined)". The first component has produced an extensive range of theoretical approaches which Gunn (2003) divides into three categories: (a) "religion in its metaphysical or theological sense", as for example, the underlying truth of the existence of God and/or the *dharma*, etc.; (b) "religion as it is psychologically experienced by people", as for example, the feelings that the notions of divinity or ultimate concerns, the holy, etc., generate in the religious believer; and (c) "religion as a cultural or social force", that is, the particular symbolisms, ceremonial actions and performances that hold a community together and/or distinguish it from others.

Each of these approaches has generated an abundance of interpretations of the term "religion" which have been divided into various categories.[21] For Gunn (2003) the most important forms of definitions are the "essentialist" and the "polythetic". Beckford (1980) identifies as the most commonly used types of definitions the "functionalist" and the "substantive". An essentialist definition identifies the "elements that are *necessary* for something to be designated as a 'religion'" (Gunn 2003, original emphasis). Equally, the substantive, according to Beckford (1980), refers to phenomena that embody distinctive properties which do not materialize in other phenomena. Furthermore, Beckford notes that substantive definitions assume that religion has "an essence...which can be known for certain by intuition" and as an example of such an approach he uses Otto's (1950) idea of the "wholly other". The functionalist approach focuses, not on the content of a "religion", but on its contribution to the stability, survival and control of society. Perhaps the first functional definition of "religion" was formulated by Durkheim (1912), who emphasized the effects of the feelings of solidarity that participation in religious ceremonies evoke, thus supporting social cohesion and community unity.

While essentialist/substantive definitions imply one essential component (i.e. a belief in spiritual beings, a god, etc.) as being the fundamental element of a religion, shared internally by the participants, functionalist definitions ignore the one essential feature and offer an "outsider's" perspective by giving emphasis to what a religion does and what purpose it serves.[22] Some examples of substantive and functional definitions are: "a strong belief in a supernatural power or powers that control human destiny";[23] "a subjective relationship to certain metaphysical, extramundane factors. A kind of experience accorded the highest value, regardless of its contents. The essence is the person's relationship to God or salvation";[24] "belief in supernatural or divine power that invites expression in conduct and often involving ethics and a philosophy (or a specific system of such belief and conduct)";[25] "a set of attitudes, beliefs, and practices pertaining to supernatural power";[26] "[b]elief in and reverence for a supernatural power or powers regarded as creator and governor of the universe. A personal or institutionalized system grounded in such belief and worship. The life or condition of a person in a religious order. A set of beliefs, values, and practices based on the teachings of a spiritual leader. A cause, a principle, or an activity pursued with zeal or conscientious devotion;"[27] "[s]ystem of beliefs and practices concerned with sacred things and or symbols uniting individuals into a single moral community";[28] "relieves anxiety and enhances social integration".[29]

However, there is a middle way between these two strands which is found in the form of the polythetic definition. According to this type of definition not all "religions" necessarily have to have specific elements in common. Known as *"the family resemblance approach"*, credited to the philosopher Ludwig Wittgenstein (1963, 31), the polythetic approach to definitions generally implies that

> all members of [for example] the family called "game" *more or less* shared a series of traits or characteristics, just as no two members of a family are exactly alike but, instead, each *more or less* share a series of characteristics (name, color of eyes, blood type, etc.). (McCutcheon 2004, original emphasis)

Although it is not clear where to set the boundary between a game and a non-game, that does not render the definition of game to be useless, as exact boundaries are only necessary for exact purposes (Wittgenstein 1963, 33). Furthermore, for Wittgenstein (1963, 32), an inexact definition is the best way to describe something, for polythetic definitions are like a thread where "the strength of the thread does not reside in the fact that some one fibre runs through its whole length, but in the overlapping of many fibres".

In this study the term "religion/religious" is understood and used in a Wittgensteinian sense and employs Michael York's[30] definition in which religion is seen as

> a shared positing of the identity of and relationship between the world, humanity and the supernatural in terms of meaning assignment, value allocation and validation enactment. A religion need not accept or believe in the supernatural, but it takes a position on it. Likewise, some religions deny the reality or at least value of the world, but they still take a position.

Discourse

Throughout this study the term "discourse" is understood and used in the Foucauldian sense. For Foucault (1972), "discourse" is a corpus of thought and writing that is united by having a common object of study and a series of common terms and ideas expressed in a clear and/or definite phraseology. Perceived as such, discourse allows the examination, study and analysis of a wide variety of "texts", from different genres, different geographical settings, different cultural backgrounds and different historical periods. For instance, the discourse on religion could include scholarly works, works of art, novels with religious context, writings by clergy, monks etc., as well as writings about religion from other disciplines.

Foucault differentiates discourse from language by defining discourse as a body of statements that are clearly different from any other groups of statements, or as "practices that systematically form the objects of which they speak" (1989, 49). In *The Archaeology of Knowledge* Foucault focuses on the relationship between discourses and the real, and on understanding the fields of knowledge. For him, every era has a dominant set of discursive formations/structures that people accept and follow unconsciously. Consequently, Foucault interprets discourse as a system of representation; as a way of representing the knowledge about a particular subject matter at a particular moment in time. As such, discourse constructs the subject and at the same time it defines and produces the objects of our knowledge through/via its regulating statements.

In Foucault's view (1989, 44), discursive formations create a totality, outside of which people find it hard to think. Discursive structures are shaped by the internal mechanisms of a discourse (Mills 1997, 48–49) as well as by the external. As Foucault (1972, 45) points out, discursive structures exist "under the positive conditions of a complex group of relations" that are placed in social spaces, having their own objects, architectures, behaviours and norms and their class interests and biases. A discursive structure can be noticed in standardized ideas, opinions and ways of thinking and behaving that exist within a particular context, and in their effects. Thus, it is plausible to assume that there is a religious discourse, because religious bodies, as well as individuals, behave and "talk" within the parameters of a particular framework when they define themselves, or are defining others, as religious. These discursive frames distinguish the borderlines within which is placed what it means to be religious, in a particular sense. For instance, while for some Buddhists abstaining from certain foods is part of their discursive structure, for others it is not; and while for some, to be religious is closely associated with certain external practices, for others religiosity is simply a matter of "inner" development.

Discursive structures may determine the style of appearance, the types of practice and the overall universe of meaning of a religious establishment and/or an individual. Discourse, therefore, may also influence how ideas become practices and are used to prescribe the conduct of others. For Foucault (1972, 224), discourses compose objects and events that are accepted as real and authoritative. Thus, Mills (1997, 49) suggests, the study of a discourse, apart from examining the linguistic patterns, should also incorporate an analysis of the "support mechanisms" that produce and sustain it. Discursive structures can change when a new counter-discursive element is introduced and widely accepted.

The term "discourse" was chosen particularly for this study for a number of reasons. Firstly, many sites are representations, or extensions, of the offline discourses that the different religions proclaim. Secondly, the websites could be perceived as a new counter-discursive element which, on the one hand, add a new dimension to the existing "body of knowledge" presented by the different religions and, on the other hand, have the capacity to function as new forms of discursive structure. As such, they not only legitimize cyberspatial discourse but, by doing so, they also open the way for new cyberreligious utterances. Consequently, one may assume that since cyberreligious discourse is accepted by people as approved and authoritative, its discursive structures "legalize" and, in a way, promote the use of hardware and software for religious practices. Examples of such usage can be seen in the creation and development of virtual churches, mosques, temples and synagogues, among others, that provide a wide variety of services to their followers including online rituals.

The point made here is that the "subject", in this case the cyberreligious expression, is not only produced within the discourse, thus becoming the object through which power and knowledge are relayed as Foucault (1972) proposed, but is also subjected to the discursive formation of the particular period and culture, thus being itself constructed. As a result, cyberspatial religious discourse determines and manufactures the object of people's knowledge and governs the ways in which the subject can be understood, made meaningful and disseminated. As is the case with all different cyberspatial discourses, e-religious discourse represents its current ontological character, as this has been reconstructed by current socio-cultural, political, economic and educational circumstances, one of which is the creation and wide adaptation of ICTs by a number of institutional bodies and individuals. Religious discourse has always presented a particular "image" of its object, and today this "image", which is perceived as a given reality, is being reconstructed through new discursive formations influenced by ICTs.

Finally, the term "discourse" is used for its connotations especially within the area of "discourse analysis", which can be characterized as a way of approaching and thinking about a topic/subject. Discourse analyses do not provide "absolute answers to a specific problems, but enable us to understand the conditions behind a specific 'problem' and make us realize that the essence of that 'problem', and its resolution, lie in its assumptions; the very assumptions that enable the existence of that 'problem'".[31]

A History of Religious Discourse and Cyberspace

From 1993 to 2000

Religion is, without doubt, a dominant force in human culture. Religious manifestations on cyberspace raise important issues about the status of religion on computer mediated communication (CMC), and, more generally, about the evolution and development of religion in what some decide to call a "post-modern" age (O'Leary 1996, 782–83), that is characterized by the development of ICTs, and advancements in biotechnology which shape the foundation of what Escobar (1996, 57) calls the "regime of cyberculture".

First contact

My initial involvement with the Internet began as early as the beginning of the nineties when, as an undergraduate, I discovered the "wonders" of the online world. Soon enough after these early visits I realized that surfing the Net could provide me with additional information about the subject of my studies, which added a new kind of discourse to the one to which I was academically accustomed. However, this initial journey was more an explorative one, motivated by personal interest and, to some extent, fascination with the new medium, rather than a systematized academic investigation.

By the mid-nineties though, having acquired some experience of "being online", my casual surfing unfolded a plethora of diverse information about different religious utterances that were available on the Net in various forms. That led to the formation of some initial observations which, at that time, pinpointed specific questions regarding religion on the Internet. For example, what was the message of the religious discourse found on the Internet?

This observation prompted a number of questions, such as: Who participates in religious discourse in ICTs? Is cyberspatial religious discourse an essentially elitist discourse (articulated by religious leaders) or is it also formed at the grass roots? Although the answers to the questions were situated exclusively in the available online information, there were a number of problems, the main one being the issue of classification. For instance, would it be possible to create a classification system of the uploaded information which would retrieve only the relevant information found in the waves of the Internet ocean, and how would such a system facilitate the understanding of the phenomenon?

The first attempt to create a categorization which would provide at least a basic framework of religious utterances on the Internet resulted in the formation of my first typology consisting of five categories of religious expressions (Karaflogka 1998), which, at that time, seemed quite adequate. The categories as formed in 1998 were: objective, official, personal, subjective and "accidental discovery". The *objective* type comprised the Web pages of universities, of institutions, and of academic journals. The *official* type consisted of the official Web pages of different religious and spiritual beliefs. Almost all religions, grand and small, old and new, known and unknown, are present, and they occupy either a small or a large space on the Net: the Mormons, C of E, the Holy Mountain, Jehovah's Witnesses, the Vatican, the Atheists, the Christiadelphians, Shinto shrines and other Japanese religions to mention but a few. My third type, the *personal*, included the pages which had been uploaded by individuals who wanted to share their beliefs, to communicate with fellow believers and others, to exchange ideas and experiences and sometimes to debate the doctrinal dimension of either theirs or another religion.

The *subjective* type was the discourse produced by the perception that some people have about a religion other than their own or a critique of a religion or a religious situation. The *"accidental discovery"* type referred to the discovery of relevant sites as a result of following hyperlinks rather than searching specifically for their subject matter.

First changes 1999

As might be expected, my ignorance became evident after only a few months, through the discovery of new sites that added multiple new sub-categories[32] to my main types. An updated second typology was then formulated (Karaflogka 2000a), in which the main types were reduced to three. The term "objective" was changed to "academic" signifying that the scholarly voice does not necessarily imply objectivity. The "personal" type was subsumed under the heading "subjective", and I kept the "confessional" as a third type. My rationale was that, irrespective of the overabundance of diverse sites, the uploaded information derives from either a scholarly analysis, or a particular religion's perspective, or, finally, from a precise standpoint of an individual, group, or organization. A supplementary element that was added to the unfolding picture of e-religious appearances was the issue of ministry. With the development of online communication and the explosive growth of the Internet, the shape of priesthood in the future seemed certain to be transformed.

It could be suggested that changes were already occurring in ministry, because of changes in humanity's culture brought about by the new ways people connect, exchange information, and re-structure their views of reality (Pokorny 1997). These changes were seen in the concerns of church leaders and the activities that different churches initiate in order to address the emerging issues surrounding ICTs and their relation to society and religion. Examples of such activities are the increasing numbers of links devoted to online catechesis and guidance, and conferences devoted exclusively to the issues ministry faces due to the adoption of ICTs by the wider population. For instance, sites or links within sites such as, "Ask the Imam", "Virtual Fatwa", "Ask the Rabbi", or "Ask a Rabbi", "Ask a Priest", "Ask a Monk" (related to Buddhism), "Ask a Guru" (related to Hinduism), "Ask the Shaman" and "Ask the Oracle" are increasing in numbers. Furthermore, the Newtech 1998,[33] an international conference hosted and co-chaired by Denver's Archbishop Charles Chaput, on "The New Technologies and the Human Person: Communicating the Faith in the New Millennium", presented papers which referred to the impact of CMC on social and religious life; the position of the Church and the new justice issues, globalization and so on. In 1999, however, the European Christian Internet Conference (ECIC)[34] addressed different issues, such as: Being a church on the Internet, Supporting mourners on the Internet, and Pastoral care on the Net. The participants, mostly clergymen, expressed their enthusiasm about embracing the Net into their pastoral activities. Perhaps the most striking issue was the idea of cyberfuneral[35] (Karaflogka 2002, 284).

Religion *on*—religion *in* (late nineties–early twenty-first century)

With the continued progression of my surfing and the addition of new findings into my data, a different pattern started to emerge, which gave me a new insight into religious discourse and its relationship to cyberspace. The second typology was dismissed less than a year later, following a reappraisal and a reassessment of my findings based on different criteria that resulted from a key observation. In particular, although computers have been mediating different discourses for some time, the point at issue now, as Poster (1995a) emphasizes, is that the machines enable

> new forms of decentralized dialogue and create new combinations of human-machine assemblages, new individual and collective "voices", "specters", "interactivities" which are the new building blocks of political formations and groupings.

Poster's point drew attention to the possibility that the Internet, apart from being seen as a mere communicating tool, may also be perceived as a new environment in which things happen. This opened the way to realizing this duality in the nature of the Internet. Was there any empirical evidence to support the extent to which the Internet has been or is being used either as a tool and/or as an environment? Discoveries of novel religious narratives that presented original, imaginative, divergent and unconventional perceptions of and approaches to religious ideas and practices led to the delimitation of cyberreligious discourse into two main categories, namely *religion on* and *religion in* cyberspace, taking the two to refer to two different entities. What I called "religion *on* cyberspace" referred to the information uploaded by any religion (institutionalized or not), church, individual or organization which also exists and can be reached in the offline world. In this sense the Internet is used as a tool. "Religion *in* cyberspace", on the other hand, denoted a religious, spiritual or metaphysical expression, which is created and exists exclusively in cyberspace. The Internet in this case is used as an environment. This distinction is an important one, not only because the two phenomena are completely different from each other, but because (a) it facilitates the research process and the analysis of the e-religious discourse, (b) it provides the necessary tools for observation and monitoring the development of New Cyberreligious Movements (NCRMs) and their relationship with and utilization of cyberspatial technology, and (c) it provides a necessary tool for observing the probable shift of religions *on* into religions *in*, that is, the extent to which the religions, which use cyberspace as a tool, will accept and adopt cyberspace as an environment (Karaflogka 2000a; 2003). I created the term "New Cyberreligious Movements" in January 2000 to define novel religious expressions. An explanation of the term reads: New because they address issues using a new medium and introducing new possibilities; Cyberreligious because they mainly exist and function online; Movements because they can, potentially, mobilize and activate the entire human population (Karaflogka 2002, 286).

The third typology was graphically represented as shown in the diagram below to underline that religious discourse, or indeed any discourse, placed either *on* or *in* cyberspace, cannot be classified in terms of solid, polarized types, but as fluid arrangements which merge into a spectrum, for cyberspace itself is not inflexible and confined but is constantly moving, expanding and evolving (Karaflogka 2000a, 2002).

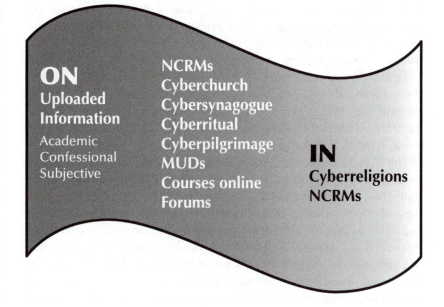

ON
Uploaded
Information
Academic
Confessional
Subjective

NCRMs
Cyberchurch
Cybersynagogue
Cyberritual
Cyberpilgrimage
MUDs
Courses online
Forums

IN
Cyberreligions
NCRMs

General observations and specific identifications

Although unsystematic, my exploration of religion on the Internet produced some observations which, in retrospect, provided a valuable
starting point for the development of this thesis' research body. These
observations could be summarized as follows: Firstly, the socio-political
aspect of ICTs. This was evident in the widespread promotion of ICTs
by the mass media. Every day, several times a day, all media (TV, radio,
and newspapers among others) highlighted (and still do) that the Net is
a global computing network that makes it possible for people to communicate with one another over great distances quickly and cheaply,
to inform and be informed about hundreds of thousands of specialized
areas. This became obvious in the amalgamation of the Internet by the
media into their communication matrix, by offering and to some extent
expecting their viewers/readers to communicate their opinions via ICTs.
This attitude of the mass media expressed an implicit perspective which
either assumed that access to the Internet was widespread, or addressed
a particular section of the audience, giving preference (that is giving the
opportunity to reply, comment etc., in other words to participate in the
debate) to those who did have access, ignoring those whose only means
of communication would be snail mail.[36]

Secondly, the semantic aspect of the information communicated via
ICTs highlighted the idiosyncratic language of cyberdiscourse. Whatever
the reason for communication, the communicating process is manifested, if not almost exclusively, at least to a great extent, as a textual construction. Communication via the Internet takes a wide variety of forms
that are all based either solely or partially on text. Language is essential
for many obvious reasons. It is the main tool through which our thinking
is expressed and our modes of reasoning become manifest. However,
discourse in cyberspace is enacted by a new language, which needs to
be explored. While sound, syntax and vocabulary form the discursivity of conventional language, words, colours, images, sound, movement, symbols and design form the discursivity of the invented language
of the Web. Despite the similarities that conventional and cyberspatial discourses might share, there are fundamental differences between
them, two of which are: (a) the freedom the NET offers, in both uploading and downloading information, which essentially transforms people's
capability to publish; (b) the morphology of the idiosyncratic language
employed in cyberspatial discourse. It would appear that the structure
of e-religious discourse is far richer than its linguistic content alone, for
a new activity—human computer interaction—is involved. This new
field of visualized information demands an imaginative approach and
an entirely new mentality from both creators and users. Furthermore, it

demands a dynamic relationship between a plethora of new signifiers and the signified. Thus, "language"—the term is used here in a broad sense and includes both textual and visual elements—was identified as a key component of the study matter.

The third observation relates to the distinctly diversified forms of religious and cultural discourses which existed in the equally distinctly diversified realms of the Internet, especially those of NCRMs, and the implications these utterances brought to both the research and analysis of the subject. Constituting a form of postmodern religiosity, cyberreligions demonstrate a wide range of human motivations and attitudes concerning religious thinking, emotions, beliefs, impulses, practices and responses to the religious reality as the creators of these sites perceive it to be. This immediately raised questions concerning the extent to which cyberspace was perceived and regarded as a sacred space, and the possibilities opened up by such perceptions to religious practices.

Furthermore, the information uploaded by the different religious bodies and individuals raised questions related to their attitudes towards, perceptions and utilizations of ICTs and the varying forms in which these perceptions and utilizations were manifested. All these indicated the need for a systematized data collection, examination and analysis of religious landscapes, as they appear on the cyberscenery, which, in turn, would enable the development of a wider understanding of cyber-religious discourses.

Contextualizing Religious Discourse in Cspace 2000–

Goals and perspectives

Introducing cyberculture

> Roberta enters the space for her upper-division computer engineering class at Virginia Tech and notices that no other students are here at the moment. She sifts through last week's lecture notes and this week's homework assignments and takes what she needs. Then she strolls over to the community center, checks which films are playing at the Lyric Theater, and notes their times. Finally, she makes her way to the Bamboo House, orders some beef and broccoli and half a dozen potstickers, and requests a delivery.
>
> Then she logs off.
>
> (Silver 2000)

Celebrations of the beginning of the twenty-first century by countries all over the world were characterized by a mixture of wild enthusiasm and a sense of relief. While the first welcomed the new millennium, the latter reflected the alleviation of the anxieties that Y2K had brought to all institutions, especially financial ones, globally.[37] In the dawn of the new millennium the first critical appraisals of the developing cyberculture were formed, which examined the literature on the subject and its various dispositions. Silver (2000, 19), in a historical presentation of the surfacing subject of cyberculture, divides the approaches to cyberculture into three phases, namely "popular cyberculture", "cyberculture studies" and "critical cyberculture studies".

The first, mainly descriptive in nature, originates from journalistic discussions and is characterized by its limited dualism,[38] and use of the Internet-as-frontier metaphor.[39] The focal point of the second phase is predominantly on virtual communities and online identities and is characterized by a stream of academic works. In the third phase, Silver (2000, 19) remarks, the notion of cyberculture is extended and it incorporates four areas of study such as "online interactions, digital discourses, access and denial to the Internet, and interface design of cyberspace". Silver's genealogy of cyberculture—an amazingly helpful tool—is of considerable importance, in that it provides a platform for critically evaluating existing literature and also for setting the parameters of future studies.

Different works investigating the effects and possible impacts of ICTs on several areas of human experience form a vast body of literature found in both popular and academic contexts. Examples include studies investigating issues such as Internet culture (Shields 1996; Jones 1997; Benedikt 1991; Horn 1998), identity (Bruckman 1992; Reid 1995; Turkle 1995), gender (Matheson 1992; Spender 1995), education (Salmon 2000), the human body (Featherstone and Burrows 1995a), Internet addiction (DeAngelis 2000), power and politics (Jordan 1999), community (Smith and Kollock 1999, Rheingold 1993, Wellman and Gulia 1999, De Vaney, *et al.* 2000), ethics of cyberspace (Hamelink 2000) and philosophy of technology (Ferre 1995; Ess 1996; Floridi 1999).

Studies on religion and the Internet

There is a wide range of research available on religion and the Internet from various perspectives,[40] but as yet, a critical and more synthetical approach is lacking. For instance, religion within the realm of ICTs began to be investigated in the last part of the nineties/beginning of 2000. Some works dealing with the subject include: presentation of the relationship between religion, spirituality and cyberspace (Zaleski 1997), understanding cyberspace as a sacred space (Wertheim 1999), the question of spiritual life in cyberspace (Cobb 1998), the mystical aspect of information technology (Davis 1998) and the metaphysical side of virtual reality (Heim 1993).

Other studies explore the impact cyberspace may have on religious issues, scriptures and on the human soul (Babin and Zukowski 2002; Groothuis 1999); also Beaudoin (1998) offers a theological interpretation of the implicit spirituality of pop culture; Brasher (2001) examines both the meaning of cyberfaith and the future of traditional religion; Bunt (2000) looks into Islam and its relation to the Internet and addresses a number of issues, including how information technology affects the way Islam is perceived, interpretations of the Qur'an and religio-political issues. A broader view of issues regarding religion and the Internet, which includes "issues and strategies", "religious ethnography", "surfing Islam", "cult controversies" and "anti-cult terrorism" to mention but a few, is offered in the edited collection of Hadden and Cowan (2000). It should be noted, though, that apart from manuscripts and collections, an additional number of academic works in the form of short articles and conference presentations offers a wide variety of approaches to the subject matter. Additionally, a vast amount of information about religion, religions, spirituality, esotericism, beliefs, practices, personal accounts, explorations and so forth, exists in the literature of popular culture found in both commercial (magazines, newspapers) and personal publications (websites, blogs).

Limitations of the existing literature

Despite the high quality and wealth of materials offered by those works, they prove problematic in their target areas, the issues they address and the socio-economic, political, cultural and religious biases they carry. The point made here is that the above-mentioned works are mainly North American, which by default denotes a particular view of technology, given the fact that North America is not only highly advanced technologically, but was also the pioneer in both promoting and endorsing ICTs.

These works deal with issues such as: sociological approaches regarding the concepts of identity and community, recruitment, authority, conflict; theological approaches regarding the place of the Church or of the gospel in ICTs and the potential destructive impact of cyberspace to the human soul, to the notions of truth, community and the Holy Scriptures; techno-spiritual approaches related to the sacredness of cyberspace, the computers' ability to transcend themselves and to perceiving the Internet as facilitating humans to experience and approach God.

Thus, while the literature of popular culture is dichotomized between harsh cyberutopianism and mild neo-Luddism, the academic literature lacks critical rigour related to structural and operational aspects of ICTs. Hence, an evaluation of the academic works, utilizing Silver's model, suggests that they fall into the categories of either "popular cyberculture" or "cyberculture studies", for they fail to address and/or to incorporate into their analysis any issues from the critical cyberculture studies category. More importantly, their focus—mainly on identity and community—excludes a wide range of other religious manifestations online.

However, religion is a multifaceted entity and, although what religion is all about remains indeterminate (Taylor 1998, 1), it is certain that within ICTs religion is manifested in a great number of diversified ways, which need to be considered if this specific area of the study of religions discipline is to be fully investigated. Yet, ICTs are themselves complex and multifaceted and they have introduced (and will continue to introduce) to their users a wide variety of loci, such as chat rooms, MOOs, blogs, websites, 3D virtual reality environments and 3D multi-users' virtual reality environments that offer a number of novel and unique opportunities for self-expression. Each locus, though, has a distinct character and purpose and operates in distinct ways; consequently it should be perceived and approached as a *sui generis* milieu, within which the users can be either creative and proactive components or just participant observers.

It could be suggested therefore that, despite the substantial body of academic research, a critical systematic study on the subject has not yet been available. Yet, empirical evidence[41] supports the view that cyberreligious activities will grow in both number and types, which in turn creates a great need to develop adequate mechanisms in order to advance and facilitate their investigation.

This work is intended to be such an inquiry.

Scope of the study

Every researcher has some prior knowledge of their topic, some form of association. It is not feasible, according to Charlotte Aull Davies (1999, 3), to research something with which there is no contact. Thus, due to my previous experience, it was becoming clear to me that there was indeed a new phenomenon in the making that, to some extent, could be characterized as being independent from its offline counterpart, needing therefore to be investigated and studied as such.

Any academic inquiry into a given subject requires a set of tools which would provide the necessary framework upon which the investigation will be based. Equally, regarding the exploration of the notion of religion and its relationship with ICTs, a specific collection of theoretical as well as methodological devices is requisite. This study has both the strengths and weaknesses of any typical interdisciplinary project of this kind. Since the goal of this study is an attempt to construct a new avenue for researching religious occurrences on the World Wide Web, it does not follow the perspective of any previous research, but complements existing works by adding another dimension to the debate.

The primary concern of the thesis is to contribute to the current research regarding the presence of traditional religions on cyberspace, the formation of novel ways of "talking" and practising religion, and the construction of New Cyberreligious Movements in cyberspace, indicating the necessity for a paradigm shift in scholarly approaches to cyberspatial religious discourse. One of the aims of this paradigm shift is to conceptualize Web theory as integral to the study of cyberreligion, in order to generate conceptual change and renewal.

As we look for new models of religious expression on the Internet, it is, as Bedell (1998) identifies, in an "environment where patterns of communication and community formation are undergoing transformations". These transformations occur within a multitude of different agents related to ICTs, such as technical, cultural, educational, economic, social and political, which are interconnected and interrelated and affect one another substantially. It is suggested, therefore, that ICTs as a new medium, advancing technologically and geographically (spreading worldwide every day), need a distinctive terminology that will distinguish them from any other media. Moreover, assuming that the polymorphic composition of ICTs creates different perceptions of and attitudes toward religion and cyberreligion, it seems appropriate to introduce a new subject area, that of e-religion, which will specifically study cyberspatial religious expressions using clearly defined apparatuses.

Hence, starting with the assumption that there is no adequate theory and methodology for studying religion within the realms of ICTs sufficiently, the central focus of the thesis is, therefore, the formation of a theoretical and methodological framework which will advance the practical, as well as the theoretical, understanding of e-religious utterances.

Identifying the field

Systematic research for the thesis began with a pre-existing body of information derived from my previous experience and interaction with the subject. This information, as noted earlier, constituted a basic understanding of the diverse constructions of the existing cyberreligious discourse, as well as its future possible development, and a framework which set the initial parameters of the study. It also indicated the limited availability of scholarly works on the subject, which in turn underlined, on the one hand, the necessity for such an endeavour and, on the other hand, the extent to which religion still remains a neglected area of academic study, especially within the areas of the emerging fields of ICTs. Detailed here are a number of themes and ideas that have formed the core of my research theories and structured the nature of the research. These central concerns have informed the direction of the research, in that they provide a conception of the subject matter that as yet has received little or no academically orientated attention, the result of which, to date, is an area of considerable size and of heterogeneous theoretical and practical utilizations, such as websites, and which remains unacknowledged. The aim of this study is to contribute to this area.

As noted earlier, ICTs are polymorphic and multidimensional, offering multiple settings for investigating the phenomena as they appear. Furthermore, this complexity is reinforced by the innumerable activities that take place in each and every realm of ICTs. These in turn resulted in a narrowing of the spectrum, and in the identification of the website as this study's "field". Websites, which have been interpreted as "cultural representations" (Wakeford 2000, 34) and as "visible artefacts" (Markham 2004), offer a dynamic field for study, for they embody a number of interrelated elements that must be taken into account and incorporated into the research design and analysis. As already mentioned at the beginning of this section, websites are found in many different forms; they provide an immense source of information about religious attitudes of institutions, individuals and groups.

Issues and considerations

A number of issues have been identified as fundamentally important to the study's development. The first matter in question relates to the field itself, in the sense that researching a new "field", such as the Web, requires at least a basic knowledge of the "field's" ontology. That being so, three fundamental areas, namely Web epistemology, theory and methodology, have been identified as forming the field's ontological nature, as well as this study's structural frame. Although this study focuses only on the Web, which excludes from the discussion any other Internet applications, it should be noted that some observations, especially epistemological and methodological, could be applicable to other Internet usages, as, for example, email and message boards. Moreover, the issue of accessibility cannot be ignored in any investigation of online activity.

A second issue to emerge was that of the terminology used. For instance, each website is an autonomous discourse, despite being a constituent of, and constituting, a structure (the Web) that is governed by its own directives and protocols. It is, in turn, also part of another structure (the Internet).

However, in all works on the subject there is an interchanging of the terms the "Internet", the "Web", "cyberspace" and "online" which implies homogeneity, that is, that each of these terms refers to one and the same entity. Consequently, definitional clarifications were seen as necessary.

The third issue is related to the temporal fluidity of the field. The peculiarity of the Web, in terms of its relation to time, became evident when I started creating my own websites database in the late nineties.

A couple of examples will clarify the problem. A website devoted to, say, a cyberchurch that had been discovered and added to the database in 1998, when visited again after few months was not available; it had "disappeared". In addition, a site of a religion, discovered and added to the database in 1999, whose main and distinguishing features had been noted, revealed, when visited in 2000, that some of contents previously recorded as its key features had been replaced by new ones. While the first parameter indubitably draws attention to "information lost", the second evidently underscores the notion of "information revised". Both parameters prove to be crucial methodological problems, in that they show that considerable changes may occur in the study area which must be taken into account. The outcome of such an observation was the invention of the synchronic vs. diachronic dichotomy as a methodological apparatus for addressing both "information lost" and "information revised" cases.

A further issue that was recognized as being integral to the research process and intertwined with methodological aspects was the diverse elements that constitute the wholeness of the field. Therefore, the research design and the investigational processes could not progress without clearly defining, in advance, the components of the field. Thus, multimedia and hypertext were characterized as additional methodological issues, in that their presence or absence can influence the overall presentation of a site's identity. The point regarding the medium's capability of being perceived in multiple ways (Markham 2004; Jones 1999b; Mann and Stewart 2000), specifically as a tool for communication or as an environment of socio-cultural constructions, is the final issue which is thought to be an important part of the research design.

All these points resulted in the formation of the body of this study which is divided into three main chapters: epistemology, theory, and methodology.

Defining the field

What does "being online" really mean?

To simplify concepts and their relation to one another, I have formulated an analysis that briefly outlines meanings and the boundaries that separate them. "Being online" could be considered as a condition which is characterized by four constituents:

The first, which is an undeniable necessity, is the combination of hardware/software tools that form that entity we call the Internet.[42] In essence, it is a planetary compilation of computer networks, collaborating with one other using common software.

The Internet consists of millions of computers connected to one another by modem, wires, fibre optic and microwave links, and lately by wireless (mobile) devices all over the world. It is also composed of a number of multiple data systems (developed independently), of which the most popular and important are: email, USENET groups, Gopher, Internet Relay Chat (IRC), and the World Wide Web. In view of the fact that the Internet is owned neither by any organization, government nor individual, an explicit definition becomes problematic, if not impossible. Consequently, there are a number of different definitions, such as "a network of networks based on the TCP/IP[43] protocols" and "a community of people who use and develop those networks", that have been employed to determine the Internet's identity and/or purpose. Krol and Hofman (1993) avoid a direct definition and propose that

> [t]he Internet can be thought about in relation to its common protocols, as a physical collection of routers and circuits, as a set of shared resources, or even as an attitude about interconnecting and intercommunication.

As a matter of fact, the Internet is maintained by a vast menagerie of telecommunications organizations, research centres, universities, commercial firms, IT corporations, political and religious groups, NGOs and private individuals who, through their mutual cooperation, ensure the exchange of data among their networks.

"Being online", which incorporates the quality of connectivity, also requires another feature, that of "something" to connect to. In this case, that "something" is the content and context of the uploaded information, or as we know it in one word, the Web.[44] This subsection of the Internet has two main advantages over the rest of the Net. First, it allows browser software (such as Netscape Navigator or Internet Explorer) to display multimedia-rich contents such as sounds, graphics, pictures and videos. The second and more important difference is its use of hypertext, which allows any part of the Web to be linked to any other part expeditiously and easily. In short, and apart from the software differences, their distinctness is that the Internet began as a text-based enterprise, whereas the Web began as a multimedia enterprise. One of the most interesting differences between the Internet and the Web is that while the first enables the interconnection of contacts, the latter enables the interconnection of content (Kerckhove 1998, 80).

Another aspect of "online" is the place where the act of connectivity and interactivity takes place, and that is cyberspace. Cyberspace, a further term that has been added to the vocabulary of both Internet users and researchers, in being equally, if not more, problematic and controversial than the Internet, presents us with difficulty in defining it. The reason for this is located in the complexity, not only of the concept itself, but also of the diverse contexts within which cyberspace is situated, perceived, comprehended and interpreted.

From the moment the Internet became widely available, the unlimited actual and potential opportunities for new expressions offered by the Web provided the framework for the development of a number of theoretical approaches and metaphysical assumptions about cyberspace's nature. These will be examined in more depth in the theoretical section. At this point, and in the context of introductory analysis, I present the two main perceptions of cyberspace.

The term "cyberspace" was invented in 1984 by William Gibson in his science-fiction novel *Neuromancer*. In this novel, where the narrative takes place in both the physical and the cyberspatial world, cyberspace is

> [a] consensual hallucination experienced daily by billions of legitimate operators, in every nation, by children being taught mathematical concepts... A graphic representation of data abstracted from the banks of every computer in the human system. Unthinkable complexity. Lines of light ranged in the nonspace of the mind, clusters and constellations of data. Like city lights, receding... (Gibson 1995, 67).

A less fictional and metaphysical definition is that of Barlow, who ascribes the term cyberspace to the present-day configurations of computer networks (Featherstone and Burrows 1995b, 5). One could argue that the *New Penguin English Dictionary*'s definition for cyberspace as "the notional environment in which communication over computer networks occurs" (2000, 346) is, in essence, the Barlovian interpretation of the concept, which describes cyberspace as the place where we are when on the phone (Jordan 1999, 55).[45] In either case, cyberspace should be understood as a space/place, which although part of the network, is nevertheless completely different from it.

Thus, the Internet, the Web and cyberspace, albeit entirely distinct from one other, are thought of as closely intertwined, so that often the terms overlap and people refer to the Internet as synonymous with either the Web or cyberspace. Although this intertwining of terms may be technically accurate, in the sense that neither the Web nor cyberspace[46] can exist outside the Internet, I prefer more explicit terms to indicate clearly the qualitative differences between the Internet, the Web and cyberspace. Distinguishing the terms, isolating therefore each one's technical and conceptual attributes, results in differentiating the actualities from the potentialities of the medium, and also in contextualizing the multifarious theoretical and metaphysical approaches to its parts. Furthermore, the distinction, especially between the Web and cyberspace, is significant, in that, as will be shown in the following chapters, it is an important theoretical and methodological issue. The last, but by no means the least, constituent of "being online" is the agent (in this case the user) who carries out the acts of connectivity and interactivity. The presence of users, also known as "surfers", "netizens", "viewers" and "visitors", to mention but a few, is an absolute prerequisite for the existence, sustainability, development and evolution of, not only of the Web, but of all ICTs.

Structure of the Thesis

The thesis comprises seven chapters: "Introduction", "Literature Review", "Web Epistemology", "Theory", "Research Process and Method", "Methodology" and "Conclusions".

Literature review

The aim of the literature review is twofold. On the one hand it presents the works that have been used in the development of the theoretical foundation of this thesis, and on the other hand it critiques contributions to the fields of cyberculture, Internet research, popular techno-religious rhetoric and academic studies on the subject. This will develop a framework showing how the process of investigating and analysing concepts including "online religion", "cyberreligion", "cyberspace as a sacred space" and "spiritual life online" is contributing to e-religious discourses.

This literature review will help to establish the theoretical framework and methodological focus needed for an original input into the question of religious manifestations in, and their relationship with, "technoscience".[47] This chapter therefore provides the theoretical underpinning of the thesis, by reviewing the relevant literature on technology, religion and technology, and cyberspace.

Web epistemology

This chapter, the first component of the "field's" ontology, is concerned with knowledge, with particular reference to the field's structural and operational properties which can have significant ramifications for the outcome of research. The chapter investigates the issue of accessibility which is divided into two main sections: access to the Web and access to the information. The first section examines themes such as information rich–information poor (classic example of cultural imperialism), affordability, class division (socio-economic imperialism) and also socio-cultural and political reasons that contribute to the inclusion/exclusion process. The second part investigates how the Web stores, processes and disseminates information and, in addition, presents issues such as: politics of search engines; manipulation of information; systematic inclusions and exclusions of sites and the politics and culture of software and retrieval systems.

Theory

There are a number of philosophical, spiritual and socio-political theories and approaches to digital technologies which derive primarily from an over-enthusiastic utopian perspective or from a dystopian neo-Luddite one. These approaches and perceptions comprise the conceptual body upon which the cybertheoretical foundation has been based. Consequently, in order to study adequately the diverse religious occurrences and the different emergent cyberreligious phenomena as they appear on the Web, it is necessary to take into account how these phenomena are using the Web. However, the utilization depends and builds upon the perception of the medium. Therefore the theoretical foundation that surrounds the relationship between contemporary socio-cultural tendencies, religion and information technologies, is essential for it sets the ideological premise upon which cyberspatial conceptualization is placed.

The chapter begins by providing a brief presentation of the theoretical framework within which the concept of communication is found. Proceeding to different theories of technology, such as instrumental, substantive and critical, the chapter introduces the main ways in which technology in general is understood. It then moves to the relationship of technology with religion through time, ending with the latest techno-spiritual approaches and cyberspace theories, completing thus the second part of the ontology of the field of this study.

Research process and method

The chapter is a detailed account of my thinking process upon which my research was based. It offers a step by step "guide" of my assump-

tions, preconceived ideas and the changes that took place in my thinking mode as my study was developed. Additionally, the chapter presents
the limitations and possible weaknesses of my study and it outlines the
method I selected for researching the Web and collecting my samples.

Methodology

The chapter presents, justifies and analyses a critically formulated set of
methodological issues, such as hypertext, hypertext links, interactivity,
multimedia and time and their repercussive effects on the autonomy,
independence, relationality, form of discourse, ideological affiliation and
aesthetic layout, of a website, to mention but a few. It proposes an iconoclastic methodology which consists of two main temporal divisions,
namely synchronic and diachronic. The novelty of the phenomenon,
its complexity and multitudinous plurality have led to the adoption of a
multi-semiotic ethnography (MSE), which is thought to be more appropriate for uncovering and explaining meaning, processes, contexts, and
unanticipated phenomena of a multidimensional field such as the Web.
Components of MSE include: observation ethnography (Bainbridge
2000, 57); hypertextual analysis, which refers to examining the main
text and the discourse of the links; visual analysis, which is related to
images, graphics, video and animations, and symbolic representation,
which is the analysis of the implementation of colours, sounds, symbols
and design. In addition, the chapter develops a typology of cyberreligious discourse employing Stephen Sharot's (2001) sociological framework and comprises both theoretical and empirical evidence. This
completes the third and final part of the ontology of the field.

Conclusions

This chapter begins by presenting the assumptions that are confirmed
and those that are disputed. It then continues to answer the questions
raised by the research and draws attention to the changes that the Web
has introduced in the religious normative framework.

2 Literature Review

Introduction

The aim of this literature review is twofold. On the one hand, it presents a critical appraisal of the existing works on the subject of religion and the Internet, and, on the other hand, it introduces the literature that facilitated the construction and development of the theoretical body of this study, namely, the works which have contributed to the formation of the study's epistemological, theoretical and methodological aspects.

To date, there are no specified examples of academic attempts to examine religion within the context of ICTs. The field is characterized mainly by essayistic efforts rather than systematic research bodies. This, however, is applicable solely to academic studies, for in popular or quasi-academic areas the question of religion and the Internet/cyberspace has been explored in a variety of different works which derive mainly from particular perspectives.

By evaluating the contributions to the fields of cyberculture, Internet research and techno-religious rhetoric found within electronic communication, the review develops a study of how the process of investigating and analysing concepts, including "religion and the Internet", "online religion", "cyberreligion", "cyberspace as a sacred space" and "spiritual life online", is contributing to cyberspatial religious discourse. This literature review will aid in establishing the theoretical framework and methodological focus needed for an original input into the question of religious manifestations in, and their relationship with, ICTs by presenting selected works that deal with issues related to: theories of technology, epistemology of the Web, and methodology. This chapter therefore provides the theoretical underpinning of the thesis, by reviewing the relevant literature on religion and computer mediated communication (CMC). This study integrates a variety of different resources that have been available in both printed and electronic forms. It should be noted that the study, apart from incorporating academic works that have examined the issue of religion and ICTs, also includes works from popular culture, for these works are substantially instrumental to the formation of cyberreligious rhetoric.

As noted earlier,[1] this study implements Silver's model for classifying the various writings. The reason for this lies in Silver's excellent account of the development of the field of cyberculture studies, along with concepts and ideas that have been included in the several accounts of the subject, as well as those which have been neglected.

Themes and subjects

The existing literature on the area of digital technologies, incorporating the themes of CMC, cyberspace, the Internet and the World Wide Web, derives from a wide range of disciplines such as philosophy, sociology, computer sciences, postmodern theory, media and cultural studies. These works (see above, p. 18), which should not be seen as exhaustive, but rather as indicative,[2] clearly underline that information technologies are considered as influential forces, evolving rapidly towards a "strategic" power in societies, which has the capacity, not only to reshape the currently existing socio-economic, political, educational, cultural and religious status quo, but also to create new ones.

Structure of the review

The chapter is divided into two parts. The first—existing explorations and examinations—is a presentation of works on religion and ICTs and of works that explore ICTs through particular techno-spiritual lenses. The second—cognitive/epistemological foundation—is devoted to selected works that have been used for establishing the theoretical, epistemological and methodological framework of this thesis.

The structure of the review is based on Silver's model,[3] that is, the writings are grouped according to the three categories: popular cyberculture, cyberculture studies and critical cyberculture studies. This categorization is quite valuable in that it provides, on the one hand, a historical interpretation of the existing literature, which in turn presents the evolution and development of the subject, and, on the other hand, it facilitates the identification of the strengths and weaknesses of each work within the field.

Existing Explorations and Examinations

Religion and the Internet

Both the actualities and potentialities of ICTs have generated a number of discourses which lately have began to include in their bodies the subject of religion. The issue of religion, and its presence in and relationship to ICTs, embodies a number of different features that need identification, exploration, investigation and analysis, for ICTs themselves include a wide variety of means through which religion can be expressed, manifested and questioned. Some features of the different expressions, manifestations and utterances have begun, at the end of the nineties and beginning of the twenty-first century, to be addressed in a number of different ways.

Issues and concepts

These writings can be classified as belonging to two major categories, namely "academic" and "popular". While the "academic" refers to works composed by scholars in various fields, such as Bunt's (2000) monograph and Hadden and Cowan's (2000) collection, the "popular" refers to works composed by journalists, computer scientists, evangelists and ministers, such as Zaleski's (1997), Wertheim's, (1999), Babin and Zukowski's (2002), to mention but a few.

The rationale for incorporating popular material in this study is based on two factors: First, the inadequacy/scarcity of academic literature on the subject of religion and ICTs and the lack of systematic research, especially in the area of the discourse of religious websites. Secondly, popular culture has formed, and will continue to form, the theoretical backbone of cyberreligious utterances and practices. Therefore, if we are to develop an understanding of the use of ICTs by the different religious traditions, including NRMs, and also of the theoretical and/or ideological framework behind the formation of cyberreligious phenomena, it is appropriate to draw data from popular material.

As computers, the Internet, and artificial intelligence systems become more sophisticated and more widely available, the question of whether people can find spiritual life in cyberspace begins to be asked. Depending upon one's perspective, the Internet can be seen either as an instrument of communication and/or transmission of religious information, or as a setting where a number of different religious activities can take place. Regarding religiosity online, as a distinct occurrence, it is the sacralization of cyberspace that motivates the formation of certain religious phenomena. Questions, such as whether cyberspace is a sacred space, or whether it has a soul, or whether it is evolving alongside people towards a unifying global consciousness—all parts of the sacralization process— are examined and, to a greater or lesser extent, answered in the literature of popular cyberculture.

The "popular" category provides the opportunity for a further categorization, in that some works derive from a particular confessional perspective, while others do not appear to express an explicit confessional point of view. This, however, does not mean that they are bias free. On the contrary, both academic and popular writings, with

only a couple of exceptions,[4] originate from North America, implying a particular bias which derives from the subjectivity of the place
itself, as shaped by its social, economic, cultural, political and religious
constituents. Furthermore, one also needs to be aware of the idiosyncratic biases of each author which may derive from their personal,
academic and/or religious universe of meaning, which in turn may
have an effect on their choices of research topics, as well as on their
processes of analysis, synthesis and presentation of the interesting and
innovative ideas set forth in their works.

Popular cyberculture (C-culture)

Non-confessional

In this category, the works of Zaleski (1997), Wertheim (1999), Davis
(1998) and Brasher (2001) are located, for they all clearly demonstrate
the key characteristics of popular C-culture. For instance, they are
mainly descriptive, they use the Internet-as-frontier metaphor and they
propound a computopian approach to ICTs.

Wertheim[5] (1999), in *The Pearly Gates of Cyberspace*, adopts a historical approach, a genealogy of space from Dante to cyberspace, in which
she uses the works of philosophers, scientists, artists and theologians to
illustrate the progressive development of the different qualities that the
notion of space has acquired through time. Perhaps one intriguing equa-
tion is that of cyberspace as the "heavenly city of the new Jerusalem", a
concept also found in Benedikt's work *Cyberspace First Steps*.

Wertheim explores the space beyond the physical world, the "ultimate map of Christian soul-space" (43) as Dante describes it, and
she perceives the Divine Comedy and the elegance of perspective
in Renaissance painting as the virtual realities of their time, which
communicate culturally meaningful encodings of earthly and heavenly
space.

Mentioned initially in fictional literature, the fourth dimension—hyperspace—became the focal point for philosophers and mystics, giving rise
to idealistic and mystical philosophical systems known as "hyperspace
philosophy" (Wertheim 1999, 192). The "higher-than-three-dimen-
sional space"—hyperspace—discourse, according to Wertheim, which
inspired notions such as "higher intellect" and "mystical wisdom" (194),
was also enriched by artists and scientists, the former providing artistic
interpretations while the latter offers scientific explanations of hyperspa-
tial reality. Wertheim argues quite logically that cyberspace has displaced
the concept of hyperspace to become a kind of "metaphysical gateway",
a threshold into an entirely new dimension.

For Wertheim (1999, 227), cyberspace is "an emergent phenomena [*sic*], something that is more than the sum of its parts". As a space, which exists "somewhere" but is immaterial, cyberspace incorporates the dualistic view of reality that separates the physical from the intangible. Her analysis of MOOs and MUDs and the role they can play in "psychosocial experimentation" (240) and psychoanalytical therapeutic processes (239) supports her idea that cyberspace reflects a desire for a "collective mental arena" (230) in which people can explore different aspects of themselves. The essence of cyberspace is its role as a network of relationships.

Proceeding to cyber-soul space, Wertheim examines the religious language of cyberspatial rhetoric, most notably the idea of uploading one's "soul-data" on a network where "immortality, transcendence, [and] omniscience [are] dreams beginning to awaken" (263). Apart from charting through time how technological advances and new philosophical thought about space influence our contemporary understanding of cyberspace, Wertheim also traces the roots of virtual reality (VR) and conceptions of spiritual space back to mediaeval times and the artwork of Giotto, where virtual and physical spaces were united. In other words, her account of cyberspace brings back the "Christian soul space" and the immaterial world lost in modern science. It should be noted that her approach, deriving from Christian Western European culture, excludes any other tradition and/or cultural perspective and her use of existing scholarship on cyberculture is to some extent dated. Despite its weaknesses the book introduces some of the historical background and contemporary ideas held by the creators of the emerging technology of digital networks, upon which the theory of the spirituality of cyberspace is based.

Zaleski[6] (1997), in *The Soul of Cyberspace*, embarks on ethnographic qualitative research (interviews), in which he considers how technology is changing people's spiritual lives. His broad exploration includes the views of Muslim, Jewish, Buddhist, Christian and Hindu Web representatives, as well as those of pioneer scientists in the fields of artificial intelligence, virtual reality (VR) and virtual reality modelling language (VRML). As his introduction Zaleski uses the case of Partenia, the virtual Catholic diocese, which demonstrates that the Web allows "a worldwide hearing of every voice" (4), even those who are marginalized by the dominant religious traditions.

Zaleski raises a number of questions such as: Is the Internet the new frontier of spirituality? Will the PC displace the church, the mosque, the temple and the synagogue? Will the World Wide Web evolve into God? His answers derive from the views that the different religious "leaders" hold about the nature of cyberspace. It is not surprising that all of them agree in that they use the Internet to offer information about their tradition; to offer guidance to their devotees and to provide some online tools for meditation, and/or prayer. However, although they believe that the real spiritual contact is within the physical world, acknowledging therefore the limitations of the medium, they quite enthusiastically accept not only the spiritual potentiality of cyberspace, but also its capacity to function as a global unifying apparatus.

Zaleski's encounter with the different religions remains within the boundaries of selected representative traditions or branches of each of the four major religions. This by itself presents a restricted view of how the Net is perceived and understood by the wider religious community. Although it is understandable that there are limits to what or how much one can investigate, it would have been more informative if he had included other belief systems, or if he had justified his selection. CMC, VR and VRML experts interviewed by Zaleski express some intriguing ideas, such as information as energy (1997, 32) and the notion of memes (36). The common thread between these interviewees appears to be that when we are all wired to one another, the circulation of energy, as information, will be transformative. An emerging consciousness (an idea created by Teilhard de Chardin in 1925) will free us from the enslavement of our separate and alienated selves, thus generating/releasing rapid change that would be unthinkable and impossible without the presence of the medium.

All these, as well as viewing the Internet as "a new ecosystem where those creatures [memes] will be able to grow" (37), imply an underlying religio-spiritual framework surrounding emergent technological advances. The overall tone of the book is descriptive and to some extent exploratory, but it fails to answer the primary question: Does cyberspace have a soul, as the title of the book suggests?

Davis'[7] "Techgnosis" is a narrative of how people's use of technology has generated an entirely new paradigm of myths and mysticism, which captures people's imagination, giving rise to techno-spiritual perceptions and attitudes, even within an assumed secular, rationalistic era. For Davis this paradox was the driving force behind the composition of TechGnosis, which, as he states, is a "secret history of the mystical impulses that continue to spark and sustain the Western world's obsession with technology, and especially with its technologies of communication" (1998, 2). Davis, by tracing the histories of technology, knowledge, and spirituality, seeks to reveal the techno-mystical impulses of humanity, by binding technological advancements to spiritual yearnings. He presents the historical roots of spiritual imagination and yearning in hermeticism, shamanism and alchemy and suggests that the ancient spiritualities function even better in cyberspace, where consensual realities are more easily constructed (17–23; 172–73).

Consequently, he moves through a diverse collection of sources from equally diverse time periods, thus, from Plato, to Hermes the Trismegistous (who is the ruling spirit of the Internet), to neo-Platonists, to the inventors of the seventeenth century, to Ong and McLuhan, and from Homeric moments to Classical Greek, to Roman, to the twentieth century and so on. A large part of the book is devoted to science-fiction writers and UFOs, and he draws connections between science-fiction script-lines and Heaven's Gate members' fascination with outer space. VR, in Davis' work, is another high-tech creation that enables metaphysical ambiguities of the simulated to enter into today's world. Cyberspace is analysed both as a term and as a system, and an intriguing point of TechGnosis is the perception of shamans as the first spiritual cyborgs (1998, 132). Davis examines a number of spiritual groups such as the Extropians, the Gurdjiefean Work and the Church of Scientology, and suggests that these spiritual techniques have strong cybernetic elements (129–39).

His work is well referenced and filled with different philosophical, religious and spiritual theoretical frameworks. In his view, technology has played an influential role on both the environment and on the ways that people understand and perceive the world. He suggests that, more than any other human invention, ICTs have the capacity to transcend their status as a thing, simply because they allow "for the incorporeal encoding and transmission of mind and meaning" (5). ICTs have proved new interfaces between the self, the other and the world beyond; they are therefore becoming themselves parts of the self, the other and the world beyond (4). Davis is well aware that the Internet as it exists today is no more than a tiny slice of the new frontier he envisages, which being a cyber-technology, that is, a self-regulating system, like any other cybernetic system eventually develops unanticipated properties of its own. This could be seen as the contemporary myth that surrounds ICTs. However, as Davis states, magic is a myth and myths shape machines into meanings; this metamorphosis is evident here and now, but there is another myth that computers have yet to conjure: the myth that they can act as portals to another world, another dimension of space itself (189).

It should be noted that all the above books remain within the confines of a theoretical approach and none of them explores any cyber-spatial religious phenomena.

Brasher (2001) attempted to fill this gap with her work *Give Me that Online Religion*. Although Brasher's book is more a personal account of what she perceives religion online to be, rather than an academic investigation, it nevertheless presents some interesting ideas, as for example her four groups of Internet users: Techno-Idealists; Virtual Anarchists; Virtual Tourists; and the Virtually Oblivious (101–15). Each of these groups of users, according to Brasher, is developing its own rules to play by when living online. Brasher predicts that "[o]nline religion is the most portentous development for the future of religion to come out of the twentieth century" (17). She asserts that "wisdom Web pages and holy hyperlinks that are the stuff of online religion possess the potential to make a unique contribution to global fellowship in the frequently volatile area of interreligious understanding" (6). Additionally, and because cyberspace undermines "xenophobia", minimizing thus "interreligious hate", Brasher declares that

> just as "real" religions are acknowledged and supported in the form of tax abatements, one political argument this book makes is that online religion should receive comparable public acknowledgment and support. Its successful development harbors important hope for the future of civil society (7).

What Brasher does not explain is what form the acknowledgement and support would or should have: What does she mean by "online religion" and what does it refer to? Is it one entity? Who should get the support; who should not and why? Who should decide to grant acknowledgement and support and by whose authority? These questions remain unanswered. Brasher makes bold unsubstantiated statements in her work, such as, "[o]nline religion is a consequential spiritual practice for a sizable portion of the cyberspace population, a group whose size increases exponentially month by month" (69) which to some extent undervalues the academic authority of the book. Additionally, it is too early yet to make such assertions, for any real change regarding online religion and/or cyberspirituality will become apparent in the future, when a historical outlook on the WWW and its different applications and utilizations will have been developed.

Confessional

Another example of popular cyberculture literature is the works which could be classified as "confessional". This category includes the works of Hammerman (2000), Groothuis (1999), Cobb (1998) and Babin and Zukowski (2002). The common denominator of these writings is that the authors examine ICTs and their relationship, impact and/or influence on religion, society and people as individuals, from their own particular religious perspective. Consequently, these theological interpretations examine issues related to the status of the human soul and the developing idolatry toward a human product (ICTs), which nevertheless is perceived by some users as means of liberation and to some extent salvation (Groothuis 1999); finding God in cyberspace and God's digital nature (Hammerman 2000); cyberspace's capacity to expand

and develop humans' spiritual evolution (Cobb 1998) and the Catholic Church's role in and relationship with ICTs (Babin and Zukowski 2000). These themes, along with those of community, immortality, identity and disembodiment, are manifested in the body of the narrative gradually, as the personal journey of each author in cyberspace develops. Each work reflects the author's perception of and attitude toward ICTs, which in turn determine the overall character of each work.

For instance, Hammerman[8] (2000), in a retrospective presentation of his experience of cyberspace which included pilgrimages to the Western Wall, Mecca, the Meenakshi temple in Madurai, the Vatican and Kosovo, asserts that God exists all over the Internet. Hammerman's conclusion is the result of, on the one hand, his pilgrimages to different sacred sites, and on the other hand, by referencing passages from the Old and New Testament to the cyberexperience. For example, he analyses the extent to which the passage "in the beginning there was the Word, and the Word was with God, and the Word was God" (John 1:1) reflects the suggestion/proposition that the experience of God online begins with the Word. Since all communication, interaction and activity within ICTs is performed primarily via texts then, as Hammerman states (2000, 130), God is found in ICTs through the redemptive power of the written word.

His exploration moves toward revealing the "hidden things" of cyberspace, as he is well aware of the medium's capacity to incorporate both "good and evil" (139) by visiting a site[9] that, in his view, presents adequate examples of the "good vs. evil" debate.[10] Hammerman concludes that both the presence of a good vs. evil website and people's responses to the site's poll, reveal the "inherent need for balance" (143). Furthermore, to challenge his own assertion about God's presence online, Hammerman explores sites devoted to Nietzsche and the sixties' "God is dead" movement. Hammerman interprets the very existence of these sites as a reaffirmation of his belief that cyberspace is the world of the evolving inner God (143–44). Although Hammerman's computopian perspective is clear throughout his work, it is different from that of Davis and Wertheim, in the sense that his observations, analyses and conclusions derive almost entirely from his own interaction with ICTs. Despite the fact that he is a rabbi, which could allow for a stronger Jewish bias, Hammerman shows openness and respect to the medium's multicultural character.

Groothuis[11] (1999, 53–54) states that he avoids a definite position by asserting that ICTs may have profoundly damaging effects on sentience if they are accepted uncritically. In his work, he juxtaposes cyberspace experiences with that of "real life", arguing that cyberspace has the capacity to imperil the human soul because machines are not mere tools, but shape their users by equipping their imagination, language, thinking and acting processes with powerful new images and new ways of communicating and behaving. This may occur, as he affirms, because the Internet has the ability to eliminate both the user's body and the user's individual identity. This, which clearly advocates the immortality of the soul and its superiority to the physical body, according to Groothuis, is based on Gnostic, Hindu, Buddhist and New Age ideas (37). However, as he explains, these ideas, especially the Gnostic approach to matter, guide the perception of the physical in a way that opposes the Christian doctrine of creation, humanity and God himself (45).

Another aspect of the physical body that is ignored in cyberspace existence is the incarnation of God in Christ, which reveals that the material should not be denied, especially because Christ's embodiment served humans' spiritual liberation (46). Therefore, in Groothuis' view, Christians should not seek liberation from matter in cyberspace, as this is neither in the Hebrew Scriptures nor in the New Testament. Rather, they (Christians) should expect to rise, as Christ did, to an everlasting, embodied life fully vindicated from sins (46). Within the framework of the physicality of the body and its importance in people's spiritual wellbeing, Groothuis examines cybersex and its repercussions on the human soul. In his view, cybersex embodies two aspects of pagan spirituality, namely the craving to overcome the material world through mystical experience and the veneration of sexual energies (101). Taking into account cyberspace's capacity for simulation and anonymity, Groothuis underlines the consequences of cyber-intimacy by pointing out the numerous possible variations[12] of such an intimacy in cyberspace and their power in eliminating and devaluing people's sexual identity (101), which results in promiscuity and immorality (102). Employing passages from the New Testament, Groothuis lists the "Yes" and "No" of sexuality and alerts people that cybersex is more "akin to hell" (104).

Groothuis' Christian[13] theological analysis of cyberspace also covers issues such as virtual community, hypertext, techno-shamanism, cyber-evangelism and "faulty worldviews" (156) that are examined, analysed and presented in juxtaposition to the Gospel, revealing thus their inadequacy to offer a "correct" comprehension of cyberspace (157). Although he claims that he intends his work to be balanced between the utopian and dystopian views, in reality, as he himself recognizes, his book tends to include more "rant than rave" (155). However, this work certainly will be highly appreciated by Christians who may feel uncertain about having an active participation in cyberspace, as it provides clear guidelines/explanations of what is acceptable and/or what is not, and what is in accordance and what is not, with the doctrinal dimension of Christianity.

These books target a particular audience and they are advertised and recommended as essential reading in various confessional oriented sites.[14]

Another example of confessional approach is the work of Jennifer Cobb[15] (1998). Cobb, like the other authors, is keen to find the cross-over between cyberspace and religious thinking. Motivated entirely by her personal theological background, Cobb embarks on a journey in which she involves de Chardin, Wilber and Whitehead as her philosophical sources in support of her claims. Cobb considers Deep Blue's chess victory over Gary Kasparov as a testimony of computers' current ability to transcend their mathematical foundation of zeros and ones. For her, IBM's Deep Blue computer move that Kasparov called a "Hand of God", demonstrates that the computer unveiled "style and personality" (6). Additionally, she suggests that, while people accept computers and their advanced capabilities in relation to humans, they feel that "creativity and intelligence" (7) are exclusively human characteristics. However, as Deep Blue illustrated, "computers are beginning to display flashes of creative problem solving" (7).

Cobb explores the infinite, available probability of "divine presence" in this new digital medium by utilizing Jesuit palaeontologist Teilhard de Chardin's combined lifelong passions of God and science. Starting with Teilhard's theories, Cobb asserts that, as technical systems become more complex, something graceful, inspired and entirely unforeseeable "emerges" (49, 58–59). Leaving out all the negative aspects of digital technology, she accentuates the positive, reaching conclusions such as,

> [c]yberspace will organize social and cultural configurations on the planet, ones that will carry with them myriad opportunities for change and growth. These opportunities are fundamentally expressions of spirit in action, the movement of spirit in form through the universe. If we work consciously with these movements of spirit and incorporate them into our spiritual awareness, the potential is there for cyberspace to journey with us on the divine path of evolution. (125)

rendering thus divine a communications medium. One could argue that Cobb's need to reconcile technology and spirituality is the driving force behind her amalgamation of theories such as process theology (Whitehead), synthetic evolution, artificial intelligence and virtual reality, which are presented quite obscurely.[16] This lack of clarity in the writing makes the book a difficult read, resulting in some points that may be of importance being missed or incomprehensible. Thus, although Cobb has endeavoured to produce an innovative analysis of cyberspace and the divine experience that manifests in cyberspace (99), which she compares with the divine force that permeates the entire universe, she fails to articulate clearly her argument and the theories she employs to support it. To avoid being criticized as favouring Judeo-Christian theology, Cobb utilizes some examples from Eastern traditions. For instance, she uses the Hindu god Indra as a metaphor for cyberspace and the Chinese notion of yin and yang (50, 106–107) as reflecting the idea of positive and negative elements of contemporary physics. Despite that, however, her account is strongly influenced by her Christian theological background.

From a different angle but within the Christian—in this case Catholic—tradition, the work of Babin and Zukowski (2002) addresses the issue of employing ICTs to promoting the Catholic Church's message. Acknowledging the importance of the Internet as a new arena for evangelizing, Babin and Zukowski pinpoint that the Catholic Church has not yet fully grasped the opportunity that is offered to her, and state that for the Church not to be in the Internet would result in cutting herself off from a historical moment (64). Furthermore, according to the authors, the Church must be "in" not only in order to present her doctrine, but more importantly, in order to implant the "life-giving presence of Christ" (64). In a way, by passively participating in the Net activity, the Church would show that—contrary to Christ—she denies the world its body.

Babin and Zukowski take a rather radical approach by suggesting that, nowadays, communicating the faith has to be in accordance with contemporary models of communication, which in their view are predominantly those of commerce (used by the whole world) and the Internet (which directs to the future) (70–71). While aware of the controversy that the use of the term "commerce" may create, the authors assert that it expresses the most influential way of life of contemporary societies. Recognizing that market economy has become increasingly dependent on ICTs, the authors indicate that the Church should integrate the values of commerce and marketing, if she is to get involved with and utilize the "new culture" provided by the systems of relationships brought about by ICTs (71–72).

This integration would not be something new for the Church. On the contrary, as in the past the Church has "baptized" other strategies of teaching, guiding, proclamation and action, Babin and Zukowski suggest that a similar action can be employed for commerce and ICTs, in the sense that they can become the Church's way of communicating the Gospel. Thus, they conclude, it is not so much endorsing commerce but Christianizing it (72). As already mentioned, the authors view ICTs as an excellent arena for evangelization, which they define as a "conversation on the world's marketplace to exchange spiritual goods" (81) incorporating, thus, the key characteristics of the "new culture". ICTs, in the authors' understanding, force the Church to follow Paul's example and become a traveller, going everywhere, daring everything and discussing with everyone (101). That means that within the global village, the Church meets and interacts with all kinds of different ways of thinking and believing, thus providing her with the opportunity to practise the motto "the Church proposes never imposes", which is more imperative today than ever before (106). The interaction of the Church with the people via ICTs implies, according to the authors, acceptance of pluralism, which leads to a dialogue that should be characterized by "equality of partnership in communication and freedom to form one's own conclusions" (107).

Babin and Zukowski perceive ICTs in a positive way, avoiding over-stated computopianism. They clearly understand ICTs being more than a mere tool, and are keen to embrace all existing and future ICTs' applications, accepting them as opportunities for the Church to enter the twenty-first century. Their work provides a different angle on Christian perception and utilization of ICTs. The way in which the views of Babin and Zukowski differ from that of Groothuis is very interesting, in the sense that the former appreciate, accept and admire the very same aspects and issues that the latter understands as dangerous and damaging. Perhaps the contrasting perceptions derive from the differences found between Christian denominations. Extended research on how denominational differences are expressed in ICTs would be interesting and illuminating.

Despite their weaknesses and biases, the value of all these works is found in their techno-spiritual and/or techno-religious and theological analyses and explanations of ICTs, which, to either greater or lesser extent, may have been responsible for the formation of the theoretical and ideological framework upon which the whole techno-spiritual ideology that prevails in cyberculture is based. This framework may, in turn, explain on the one hand the enthusiastic adaptation of ICTs by both organizational bodies and individuals, and, on the other hand, the emergence of new techno-religious formations which use ICTs, especially the Web, as their "temple". The diverse approaches of the presented works, either in their totality or just parts of them, are identifiable in various religious websites. As will be shown in the empirical section of the methodology, Websites' design, operation and structure reflect the institutions', organizations' and individuals' perceptions of ICTs.

Cyberculture studies

As mentioned earlier, the "cyberculture studies" category is characterized by works that focus primarily on the issues of virtual community and virtual identity. However, some new issues related to the sociology of ICTs also began to be examined, and ICTs started to be perceived as online spaces where creativity, imagination, construction and community could flourish (Silver 2000, 23).

In this category, the works of Bunt (2000) and Hadden and Cowan (2000) are placed. Although these works are different in their subject— the first focuses explicitly on Islam, while the second is a collection of essays on various themes—they share some similarities, which will be discussed later. Additionally, they are placed in this category for two reasons: Firstly, they present neither an overenthusiastic nor an over pessimistic perception of ICTs. Secondly, although they do address the issues of community and identity, they also incorporate other aspects such as politics, authority, and conflict to mention but a few.

Bunt's (2000) work on Islam and its relation to the Internet is the first academic exploration of a particular religion within ICTs. As his choices of themes for examination in the area of Islam, Bunt includes forms of Islamic expression online; Muslim diversity online; politics, Islam and the Internet; Islamic obligations and authority and cyber Islamic futures. As the author himself states, the intention of the book is to assess the impact of cyber Islamic websites and explore not only the way in which the sites represent Islam and Muslims, but also the possible influence on both Muslim and non-Muslim understanding of Islam and Islamic issues (1–2). His work shows his mastery of the area of his academic expertise and targets the specific audience of students of Islamic studies.

However, Bunt's work also shows a lack of deeper theoretical knowledge of ICTs. For instance, references such as "the Internet landscape or 'cyberspace'" and "thousands of Internet sites on offer in cyberspace" (2, 3), demonstrate that he equates the Internet with cyberspace, ignoring (or not knowing) the fact that the first defines the physical entities that constitute the whole network, while the latter refers to a metaphorical entity. In addition, the statement "whilst reference is made to e-mail, chat rooms and other forms of electronic communication, the central focus of this book is the Internet" (7), clearly demonstrates that Bunt has not grasped the technical side of his field, leaving thus a number of issues related to ICTs' epistemology unexamined. Furthermore, Bunt, by stating that the websites on offer are "accessible with few restrictions, to an international audience of hundreds of millions" (3), shows that he considers the question of accessibility to be neither crucial nor a widely spread one. Moreover, in the presentation of his method, Bunt lists "surveying the 'information superhighway'", and "e-mail interviews" (6). However, although he offers some methodological insights regarding the interviews process, he offers no account of the surveying one.

Therefore, issues related to search engines' and directories' operationality have not been included. Yet such an analysis would have provided valuable information about a number of issues that may surround the investigation of Islam in ICTs.

Bunt is not alone in presenting lack of awareness related to theoretical, epistemological and methodological questions. This is a common practice among the authors of almost all works that have been presented and demonstrates the necessity for an "all inclusive" approach when researching religion, or indeed any other subject, in the realm of ICTs.

A broader view of issues regarding religion and the Internet, which includes "issues and strategies", "religious ethnography", "surfing Islam", "cult controversies" and "anti-cult terrorism" to mention but a few, is offered in the edited collection of Hadden and Cowan (2000). The collection, which is the first systematic inquiry into the subject, attempts to explore the intersection of religion and the Internet, by offering essays based on both conceptual and empirical approaches.

Incorporating diverse outlooks, the volume is divided into four parts. The first part examines the topics of how the Internet can be employed to conduct research. The second part is devoted to essays that explore the different ways in which organizations, groups and individuals represent themselves and interact with others via the Internet. The third part is formed by two essays that focus on NRMs and anti-cult "Internet terrorism" (Introvigne 2000, 277). The final part of the collection describes how the Internet can be incorporated as a tool for teaching religion within the parameters of contemporary society. Although different essays are presented in more detail in different parts of this work, some general remarks are necessary.

For instance, with the exception of Bedell, who gives a detailed account of the method of his research, other authors neither provide nor consider methodological questions. So, while there is discussion about topics of researching religion online, there is no discussion of how the supposedly important topics could be investigated, what issues arise from such an undertaking and how they could be unpicked.

In particular, the authors of the works on empirical accounts have totally failed to include how they found the information they are presenting, difficulties they face in finding the information and so on, and how future research could become more efficient. Consequently, the works in this category lack evaluation and critique, not only of elements of their field, which are important to the construction of the research, but also of the concepts and issues that derive from the technical, structural and operational character of the field, that must be considered when researching religion and ICTs in general and the presented cases in particular.

Notwithstanding their methodological weaknesses, these works prove valuable in that, on the one hand, they provide foundational steps in the direction of religion and its multiple interaction with ICTs and, on the other hand, they open new avenues for extended research on the subjects and issues they put forward.

Cognitive/Epistemological Foundation

As has been stated earlier, in this study it is argued that in order to develop a methodological apparatus which would facilitate the research, investigation and analysis of religious discourses on the Web, it is imperative to have developed an initial in-depth understanding of the field's ontology. This part of the literature review presents the works that have been used in the process of acquiring adequate knowledge of the areas identified as constituting the ontological nature of the study's field.

These works are placed under the heading of "critical cyberculture studies", for they:

- move beyond the polarized approaches of utopian vs. dystopian
- provide in-depth analyses of vital information related to the field's structure
- provide the ways in which the field operates, stores and disseminates information
- provide valuable historical and critical accounts of the different:
  - theories of technology in general and ICTs in particular
  - theories of technology and religion
  - communication theories.

Critical cyberculture studies

On methodology

There are several different methodological approaches employed in the different studies/works on the subject. *Doing Internet Research* (Jones 1999a) and *Internet Communication and Qualitative Research* (Mann and Stewart 2000), both focusing on methodology, examine solely issues and methods for studying the Net and/or using the Net as a research tool.

Mann and Stewart focus on providing a data-gathering tool for qualitative research online. Setting the agenda, the authors introduce the concepts incorporated in the "researching the Internet" body of work and elucidate specific terms. Their presentation covers issues such as advantages and disadvantages of using the Net as a means of research; Internet accessibility and usage (especially related to gender and ethnicity); ethical questions associated with obtaining data via the Internet, such as confidentiality and consent, and, although they refer to Rinaldi's[17] ten commandments (2000, 59) for computer ethics as the beginning of an ethical frame, unfortunately they do not cite them. Netiquette of online communication is quite valuable, especially when different forms of communication, for example, email, chat rooms and so on, are used. The authors introduce methods of interviewing online and observational techniques and the examples used are appropriate and illuminating. Fully aware of the possibilities offered by the Net, Mann and Stewart present a detailed guide for conducting online qualitative research by providing very practical advice on how to handle participant dynamics, group conflict, and participant "confession" issues. Additionally they offer diagrams of different types of online surveys (email text-based and a web-page-based survey), a comprehensive glossary and an online consent form.

Within the same parameters is Jones' (1999a) *Doing Internet Research*, an edited collection of essays on methods and issues for examining the Net. The chapters put across primary questions and applications of methods that compose the underlying basis of research efforts. As Jones states, *Doing Internet Research* "is not a book that will (at least in any direct way) help people to use the Internet as a research tool. Rather, its goal is to assist in the search for, and critique of, methods with which we can study the Internet..." (p. x). Despite this statement there is little reference to the Net itself (few chapters have included any URLs) and to Internet topics such as sociological analysis of who uses the Net; studies of avatars; hypertextual discourse and content analysis of websites, to mention but a few. Half of the chapters deal with interpersonal communication and community, incorporating ethical issues such as, for example, privacy, confidentiality and consent. However, it is worth mentioning that Denzin (Jones 1999a, 107–25) in his essay "Cybertalk and the Method of Instances" which refers to control issues and cultural understanding reflected in "conversations" on the "alt.recovery.codependency" Usenet group between 1994–1995, was a passive observer collecting material without permission.

Although the approaches that the book covers vary, so does their evaluation. For example, the established method of participant observation, according to Kendall, offers "a better understanding of participants [sic] ranges of identity performances" and, also, it can "highlight the politics of identity" (1999, 71). In other case studies the authors recognize that traditional research methods are not applicable to the Internet, acknowledging therefore the need for "specific and carefully designed instruments that not only accommodate but exploit [its] features" (Witmer, Colman and Katzman 1999, 158). The collection is characterized by a number of methodological weaknesses. For example, in the chapters on quantitative research, instead of putting forward a wide perspective of the methodology they employ, the authors do not review the user logs, search engines, cookies, online surveys and electronic feedback possible on any page, all of which are possibilities offered by Internet technology. Nevertheless, some specific Internet features, such as intertextuality, nonlinearity and textual ephemerality are outlined, suggesting that there is ground for a methodological debate. However, the value of the book lies in the fact that it puts into perspective the question of Internet research methodology, opening thus not only a dialogue about the appropriateness of existing methods, but also the quest for new methods and/or new applications.

One key issue in Internet research is that of ethics. There are controversial views about the extent to which the Internet could/should be perceived as a public place. Alison Cavanagh (1999) addresses the question of ethics in online research in her article "Behaviour in Public? Ethics in Online Ethnography", by examining the public vs. private dichotomy. As she states, her intention is to "consider Internet research through the lens of established paradigms in social research".

Cavanagh employs a "Goffmanian framework" of analysis which primarily examines the function of language in social relationships, in order to differentiate between the public and the private sphere of human interaction. The key question thus, is whether online interactions, in the form of BBSs, mailing lists, forums and chat rooms, can be characterized as "public status" or as "private conversations".

Clearly, the focus of Cavanagh's concern is researching those areas of online social activity. As she points out, the answer depends entirely on how online textual interaction is perceived. If they are seen as texts per se, then according to her, "our only responsibilities...lie in issues of intellectual property". However, in Cavanagh's view, "textual production online [taken] as a form of self representation and production... [divorces] the text from the subjectivity of the 'author', aligning it instead as an interactive ritual". In this case the researcher does not investigate the personal expressions of an individual but the "strategic means and forms of interaction within the media". Since sociological research has accepted public behaviour as a legitimate research object as long as the research focuses upon the different ways of interaction and not upon the acts of specific individuals, Cavanagh concludes that online textual interactions are public status, available therefore for research. Cavanagh's analysis contributes substantially to the public vs. private debate and unquestionably her work is beneficial to those who research textual interaction. Furthermore it offers helpful insights into general research of online environments for the rest of us who are interested in different aspects of cyberspatial discourse.

Researching religious phenomena, as they appear in advanced information technologies, offers the possibility of adopting multiple methodological approaches, such as, for example, anthropological and ethnographical. Arturo Escobar (1996, 121), in his anthropological account and critique of cyberculture, poses some questions, for example: "How do people relate to their technoworlds? Would it be possible to produce ethnographic accounts of the multiplicity of practices linked to the new technologies in various social, regional and ethnic settings?"

The answer to the latter question is found in the work of Mason and Dicks (1998). In their article, taking into consideration the nature of hypermedia, they introduce the "multi-semiotic ethnography".[18] It should be stressed at this point that Mason and Dicks' analysis refers to the use of hypermedia as a device which offers distinct ethnographic "authoring innovations, such as the linking together of data, analysis and interpretation in the same medium, and the juxtapositioning of materials in written, visual and aural forms". Within this framework of functionality, the authors present the benefits of what they call the "ethnographic hypermedia environment (EHE)", which, apart from text, combines a number of different media such as video, sound, graphics and so on. In their view, EHE not only opens the path for original elucidation, but also invites the readers to perceive the EHE as a "shifting matrix of connections rather than a fixed grid of self-contained narratives", because of its capacity to integrate other media, resulting thus in what Kress (1998) calls a "multi-semiotic code of representation". This code allows images, sound and graphics, for example, to have a more active role than as merely complementary to the text. Images and other integrated media infused with meaning become part of the communication act. Mason and Dicks analyse EHE in detail, but the predominant concern of their exploration is the functionality of hypermedia in ethnographic narrative. One, however, could see a double role to EHE. On the one hand it is the tool for multi-semiotic ethnographic literature, but, on the other hand, it could be the platform for a multi-semiotic research method of religious cyberspatial discourse.

In "Welcome to Cyberia" Escobar identifies five "ethnographic domains", which unwrap the field for research of cyberculture. The important point in Escobar's and others' studies is the absence of any reference to the necessity of researching religious encounters in the digital worlds. While new technological innovations, cyber communities, popular compu-culture and the "political economy of cyberculture" (124) are presented as research areas, which could provide us with some insights about the production, application and utilization of advanced technologies, the issue of religious construction of reality in CMC remains unquestioned. To these, one could put forward questions of a theoretical and methodological nature. For example, to what extent is it legitimate to refer to our society as an information society? Do we have enough scientific evidence to support the claims that "we are going through a technological revolution"? What are the implications and ramifications of such claims in religious thinking and religious meaning-making? How is religion responding to the challenge—if we accept that this is the case—of advanced information technologies? According to technophiles, the use of computers and technology in general would appear to affect all facets of life. However, Escobar (1996) expresses reservations about the extent to which the transformations envisioned by technology designers are indeed in the process of becoming reality (115). But even if this is a valid claim, whose lives are affected and why, and whose lives remain outside the technological revolution and why?

The difference between the above works is that while some, for example Mann and Stewart, are explicit in their focus and analysis of the Net as a research tool and the implications and impacts of such a tool, others are either ambiguous in their objective, as in Jones' work, or multifunctional, as in Mason's and Dicks'. Neither study, however, provides a distinct methodology for investigating cyberspatial phenomena other than interpersonal communication and online communities. Yet the Internet and its by-products, the Web and cyberspace respectively, have the capacity to generate a plethora of occurrences, "happenings", events, experiences and situations, each one and/or all of them situated in different contexts. If, in these parameters, the time and space variables are added, then a *sui generis* methodological scheme is necessary. This study will focus on the development of a theory, a methodology and actual methods for examining the religious cyberspatial landscapes.

Apart from the studies presented, a number of works have offered analytical exegesis on issues such as hypertext, hypertext links and cyber-time, to mention but a few, which substantially shape the research, the findings and their interpretation; thus they are included in this study.

On epistemology

In order to develop both a theory and a methodology for investigating religious manifestations online, at least a basic understanding of the ICTs' functionality is required. That is: How is the uploaded information distributed? What is the role of search engines, portals and default settings in the search process? Do ICTs have a democratic nature, offering equal opportunities to all voices? These are some of the questions that

Rogers' (2000a) edited collection of essays attempts to answer, providing us with what Rogers (17) calls "Web epistemology".

This book, quite complex and more for a specialized audience, is an overview of technical considerations, as for example, how one can come up with new ways of determining which websites offer good quality and relevant material (113). Examining issues of "site's authority" (151), the politics of hyperlinks (153), "discourse map[s]" (154) and their consequences in the overall image of a site, Rogers and Morris, the authors of "Operating the Internet with Socio-Epistemological Logics", provide a well-informed perspective of the construction of a website. "The Public Good Vision of the Internet and the Politics of Search Engines", by Lucas Introna and Helen Nissenbaum, identifies the hidden problem of inclusion/exclusion that seems to be operating within the functional structure of the search engines. Although quite difficult to read in places, it is a valuable publication, not only because it is the first to address issues of epistemological nature, but also because it includes detailed and informative illustrations of websites. Rogers' collection has provided a wealth of insights on the subject of Web epistemology. Yet, a number of other sources have also contributed to the advancement of knowledge of the Web's retrieval systems' operationality. For instance, valuable and up-to-date information has been provided by a number of both academic and corporate sources, including "search-engine-watch", "invisible web.com", University of Berkeley and Microsoft.

On theory

The different applications of the Internet create a new field in which distinct social, cultural and religious occurrences take place. In order to study these occurrences we need to develop at least a basic understanding of particular theories of technology which will possibly elucidate why these occurrences materialize in the way they do. Furthermore, they might explain the origins of sacralization, spiritualization and divinization of cyberspace, and also illuminate the doctrinal dimension of the emergent cyberreligious phenomena. There are two branches of theoretical and/or philosophical analyses which are related to the subject of this work, the first being the different theories of technology in general, and the second, the critical approaches to the theories that surround the Internet, the Web and cyberspace.

A number of works address the different theoretical and philosophical approaches to technology. Feenberg has investigated the concept of technology in several works, such as *Critical Theory of Technology* (1991), *Questioning Technology* (1999), and (with A. Hannay) *Technology and the Politics of Knowledge* (1995). Ferre (1995) works on philosophy of technology, Ess (1996) reflects on philosophical perspectives on CMC,

Dreyfus (2001) focuses on the Internet, Floridi (1999) explores the ideas of AI, the Internet, and the digital revolution among others, and Kellner (1999, 2001) addresses a number of issues related to theory and philosophy of technology.

From the moment ICTs entered into the arena of everyday living, their social, economic and cultural impact moved beyond exploratory inquiries to reach a level of more theoretical debates and investigations. A number of works have dealt with digital narratives and their ideological and philosophical underpinnings, such as Coyne (1999), Herman and Swiss (2000) and Jordan (1999). These works, looking either from a political or philosophical perspective, critically analyse the theoretical frameworks which, according to the authors, shape our understanding of newly introduced concepts, including information technology (IT), digital culture, computer mediated communication, virtual reality, cyberspace and so on.

Coyne's book, *Technoromanticism*, dealing with both romanticism and rationalism, examines the notions of unity, transcendence and wholeness, as well as those of division, multiplicity and fragmentation. According to Coyne, revealing what digital narratives conceal is fundamental because they are "influential in the kinds of products and systems we demand" (15). Coyne, examining the notion of unity, connects technoromanticism to the Enlightenment movement—a response to the rationalism of that period (29)—and he draws parallels between contemporary technoromantic culture and the romantic intellectuality of the eighteenth and nineteenth centuries. Moving to the themes of multiplicity and fragmentation, Coyne turns to empiricism and rationalism to explore the notion of reality through the concepts of space and symbolic representation. Coyne's seminal analysis offers some grounds for recognizing the source of the over-excited, over-positive portrayal of the changes, benefits and overall elevation of society found in great numbers within the utopian narrative about IT and CMC, AI (artificial intelligence), VR and AL (artificial life).

Herman and Swiss' collection of essays published in 2000, "explore the Web as a complex nexus of economic, political, social, and aesthetic forces" (1). In other words, the essays cover such subjects as the physical production of Web material, the nature and distribution of its content and how it is utilized. Confronting digital technologies as dialectical phenomena possessing the potential to either become Panopticon or vehicles of resistance and counter-hegemony, the book, embodying both theoretical insights and empirical considerations, investigates utopian/dystopian views of the Web. Additionally, being more socio-political in its approach, this work investigates the commercial side of IT; its connection to capitalism; and the even wider division between the rich north and the poor south that is inevitable as the Web becomes more dominated by e-commerce (McChesney 2000, 33). Apart from the economic, social, cultural and political arenas, Mosco (2000) identifies further areas that are affected by information technology. Examining the changes that IT brings to our comprehension of geography and space, Mosco argues that, inescapably, the concept of citizenship has to be re-addressed, as it is found and developed within the new settings of cyberspace and "technopoles" (Mosco, 44). The association between information technology and progress—"techno-evolutionary discourse" is examined by Berland (2000, 238) as being itself a "cultural technology" which influences the ways we think about and experience our bodies. Berland concentrates her attention on the idea of the posthuman and conducts an analytical inquiry into the very fashionable notion of evolution found in the computopian discourse of the digeratis. In the course of discussing all these, as well as other issues, such as Web governmentality, neoliberal cybercapitalism, commercialization of the Web and the ethics of hypertext links and power, the book's contributors investigate how the Web is put together, how it is used/misused as a medium, and how the either hyperbolically enthusiastic or pessimistic discourse surrounding it define public consciousness about digital technologies. Overall, the authors of the Herman and Swiss collection question and deconstruct the hype of the Web, challenging thus the "utopianism of Negroponte and others" (7) who, believing in the enchanting nature of technology and in capitalism as "a fair, rational and democratic mechanism" (7), embrace and promote cyberlibertarian ideologies.

Tim Jordan's (1999) book, *Cyberpower: The Culture and Politics of Cyberspace and the Internet*, falls within the same framework. As the title implies the book analyses politics, technology and culture as elements of cyberspace, locating the character of power in the "virtual lands" (7). Jordan employs Webber's, Barnes' and Foucault's descriptions of power to construct his own theory of cyberpower, in which he discusses which individuals and groups determine how cyberspace is ruled now and in the future. Distinguishing cyberspace from the Internet and considering it as a virtual reality that exists parallel to the physical one, Jordan analyses it as a separate and autonomous entity having its own culture, societies, politics and economics. Jordan, clearly concerned with the concept of power, introduces the term "technopower" (100) which refers to the "constant oscillation between technological tools that appear to individuals as neutral things and social values found in the design and construction of tools" (103).

This book, "a cartography of powers" (3), as Jordan himself states, sets the historical roots of cyberspace. Criticizing science-fictional presentations of cyberspace in the second chapter, the author underlines the focus of the book. Moving from individual users to the "superpanopticon" (180) of Bill Gates, Jordan investigates the concept of power at three levels: the individual, the social and the imaginary. As assistants in his examination Jordan employs nine myths of the electronic frontier. While quite dense at times, this work provides a provocative exposition of the culture and technology of cyberspace. Furthermore, perhaps the book's most important point is the analysis of the concept of power and of what Jordan calls "technopower elite" (129).

All the above-mentioned studies are important for they provide a critical appraisal of the origins, development and maintenance of particular social, economic and political narratives about the Internet and cyberspace, which promote a libertarian culture of high tech. This, according to Barbrook and Cameron, forms what they call "the Californian Ideology" (1995). A highly political critical essay published online in 1995, the Californian Ideology (CI) is a strong criticism of the extreme techno-utopianism which endorses laissez-faire economics, social Darwinism, and "born-again" eschatology. Overall, it could be said that these studies form a counter-discourse, which, in challenging the technophilic celebratory narrative, lays the foundations for a theorizing and juxtapositional critique of technocapitalism (Kellner 1999), technoromanticism, technological mysticism (Stahl 1999) and so on.

Religion and technology

Exploring concepts such as religion, culture, technology and their relationship can become very problematic because each term bears a number of different meanings. Newman (1997) attempts to eliminate the problem of definitions in his work on *Religion and Technology: A Study in the Philosophy of Culture*. Although he stresses the difficulty of defining such complex terms, he implicitly interprets them through his examination. Newman divides his book into five chapters. In chapter one, "Religion and Antitechnology", he assesses the writings of scholars, such as Gilkey and Ellul, who, holding the view that technology is antireligious or, what Newman calls "religious antitechnology" (4), develop a distinct criticism targeting technology in general because of technology's hypothetical role in threatening religious doctrines, practices and spirituality. Newman in the chapter "Technology and Techne" undertakes the demanding task of defining technology; of presenting technological paradigms and historical accounts of the usage of technology, ending with the relation of technology to techne as this has been scrutinized by Aristotle and Plato.

As might be expected in a book about technology, culture and religion, it examines the question of whether technology increases or decreases freedom. In the section "Technology and Progress",

Newman enquires into the extent to which different antitechnologists have diminished technology. In so doing, Newman focuses specifically on technology's contribution to social, cultural and personal progress. A thought-provoking idea that Newman puts across is that of "technology as a religious endeavour" (109). He points out that much of religion is made by humans, therefore, in a sense, religion may be considered as technology. Focusing on technology's agreement with certain impressions, positions, principles and moral imperatives of the Western monotheistic faiths, Newman examines the role of those faiths in having promoted technology (112, 132). In his final chapter Newman summarizes all his previous ideas and attempts to pull together technology, religion and culture as "aspects of the same fundamental human endeavour" (6). While slightly weak in its conclusions, Newman's work approaches excellence in that it offers a systematic evaluation and a critical interpretation of the relationship of technology to religion and vice versa. Perhaps the most valuable input of this book, particularly as regards this study, is its citations of the Bible and the Torah, in which the author traces the references that have been used by both supporters and opponents of technology.

There are two main themes regarding the question of religion and its relationship with technology. Firstly, why has the Western Judeo-Christian culture developed such an extraordinary obsession with technology? Secondly, is modern technology a purely secular phenomenon? Noble (1997) answers both questions in his work *The Religion of Technology: The Divinity of Man and the Spirit of Invention*. Noble, focusing exclusively on North American society and its obsession with technological gadgets and religion, traces the different forms in which religious beliefs have acted as a driving force behind the development of science and technology. Through his historical account he covers a thousand years of preoccupation with technology from the ninth century to atomic science and the space programme of the sixties, concluding with today's advancements of AI, AL and genetic engineering. Highlighting religious remarks made by scientists, their religious convictions, church membership and all imaginable uses of the word "God", Noble's thesis is that the apparent divergence of the paths of religion and science/technology is in fact illusion, and that the two have followed common paths for thousands of years. Back in the ninth century, Noble states that Erigena introduced the idea that the mechanical arts are "man's links with the Divine" (15). By the sixteenth century religious and/or spiritual implicit language regarding the "useful arts" (39) became more apparent. The second half of Noble's account examines the religion of technology in four major projects of contemporary techno-science: nuclear weapons, space exploration, artificial intelligence, and genetic engineering.

None of those projects can be understood purely in terms of being useful to the improvement of the human condition; rather, they are also "technologies of transcendence" (9, 114, 174), promising to leave the disdained limitations of the body behind and to open a new, brighter chapter in the history of humanity.

Investigating the explicit religious ideology of those projects, Noble exposes the utopian technological discourse in a very powerful and critical manner. Although his work is crucial because it provides an extensive and explanatory narration of the religion of technology, it has some weaknesses which do not diminish its value, but put into perspective his overall examination. To illustrate, he highlights only one aspect of the religion of technology: religious millenarianism. Even within this one aspect, Noble has a tendency to generalize. It seems that, for him, all strands of Christianity are equal. He does not differentiate, for example, between different dogmas of Protestantism, or even between Protestantism and Catholicism. Additionally, it can be said that Noble is so keen to present not so much an argument but more a forceful critique of the religious character of technological advancements.

It appears that in the last few years scholars from across disciplines realized that a demythologization of the hype about technology is needed if one wants to put into perspective the notion of technology. Stahl (1999) does exactly this in his book *God and the Chip*. His study argues that much of the talk about technology is magical and implicitly religious. Responding to these utopian claims of "technological mysticism" (7) Stahl proposes a shift towards "redemptive technology" (8) that is based on implementation and interest for society. Stahl demythologizes technology by indicating its implicit religious character. He explains how popular accounts of technology are based on a set of foundational myths, such as the notions that knowledge is power, that technology is gendered, that technology is infallible, and that technology equals progress. Using a variety of sources of futurist writings, *Time* magazine and a selection of computer magazines, the author, through content analysis of the use of religious and magical language in articles on computing, aims to disprove these myths. Borrowing a term from metallurgist Ursula Franklin, the author suggests a shift towards a "redemptive technology" practice which could be the alternative to the present dominance of "technobabble" (8). Stahl combines the theoretical with the empirical, drawing material from both academic and popular literature. This combination of sources, which this study intends to follow, is quite important in that it presents the views, perceptions and attitudes of the sources that are more likely to influence the general public's opinion.

Final Remarks

The author of this study has reached the conclusion that it is appropriate and to some extent necessary to examine the discourse of non-academic sources, as these form the majority of information about the socio-political and cultural transformations which do or do not take place in people's interaction with ICTs. Additionally, the corporations closely intertwined with the Internet (especially software monopolists like Microsoft) play a crucial role in guiding the market not only towards specific products, but also towards a particular ideology. As Deck (1998) points out, the relationship between "what people want" and the "enormous propaganda industry whose task is to direct desire" is so close that the two should be perceived as one and the same. Therefore in certain areas of the study, such as epistemology, corporations' sites as well as information provided by corporations related to ICTs have been used.

Regarding the works related to religion and ICTs that have been presented in both "popular" and "cyberculture studies" categories, it seems that they possess some common denominators. For example, one commonality is that none of these works takes into consideration that cyberspace does not exist outside the domain of ICTs. This means that it is bound to the epistemological issues that surround ICTs in general. For instance, in their effort to argue either for or against the divine character of cyberspace, the authors fail to consider that even if the "universe's divine force" exists indeed in cyberspace it is only accessible to a small minority worldwide. Furthermore, the substantive element of ICTs, namely the information, activities and interactivities flow, is directly intertwined with their infrastructure and the hidden economies that govern that infrastructure. In addition, the diverse theoretical approaches offered in these works do not exist in isolation, but are the result of general theories of technology that have been developed as a response to, and as ways of, understanding technological advancements and their impact on human society and culture. In a way, they could be characterized as microcosmic views which are nevertheless parts of the macrocosmic framework that defines and analyses technology in general. Interestingly enough, these works also express, to either greater or lesser degree, the two opposing views that surround ICT, namely its perception and use either as a tool or as an environment, which, it should be noted, has not received any thorough attention.

This study aims to fill this gap in the scholarly literature on the subject.

3 Web Epistemology[1]

Introduction

Epistemology, as a branch of philosophy, examines the procedure by which information is processed, analysed and classified. Borrowing this idea from philosophy, the term is used here to underline the importance of "know-how" in the investigation of the Web as a socio-political, cultural, economic, educational, commercial and, in particular, religious arena.

Having identified the Web as the field and the parts of the field's ontology as theory, epistemology and methodology, this chapter addresses the question of knowledge, arguing that operational and structural aspects have significant repercussions on individuals and institutions participating in Web activity. Web epistemology is fundamental to this study because it provides the understanding of the field's properties, and this can determine and/or decisively influence the outcome of research. For example, any attempt to discover cyberreligious utterances is primarily determined by the researcher's knowledge of three factors: (1) the field's structural architecture and geography; (2) how to use existing search systems (directories and search engines); and (3) the implications of the way these systems operate and collaborate. Several scholars (Rogers 2000a; Shields 2000; Tate and Alexander 1999; Miller 2000) have identified the need to investigate the Web through a critical perspective, employing a pragmatic approach by focusing on the sociopolitical aspects of the Internet debate.

In this chapter, theoretical assumptions will be juxtaposed with empirical evidence from researched samples, in order to evaluate the system's performance and identify possible bias. The objectives can be summarized as: exploration and evaluation of the field's foundational constituents (such as accessibility), analysis of its operationality (the ways by which information is processed and disseminated), and investigation and critique of its structural characteristics (deep and surface Web, browsers, portals, and search engines).

Accessibility

The Web's[2] simple functioning has allowed millions to use it to access the Internet and its different applications (Jordan 1999, 123). Despite its user-friendly interface, Web utilization is contingent upon a number of determinants, the most prominent being access. Although this study is not concerned with the "identity" (age, gender, race, education etc.)[3] of the Internet user, nor with the impact of the Internet on society or vice versa, accessibility is addressed because it is a consequential component of the field's nature. It is only access and the continuous presence of many users that establishes the Web as an actuality, rather than an empty "nothing", as the imaginative site *Gray day* reveals.

Worldwide accessibility and a multiplicity of users also implies the enhancement of the Web's content/context in terms of cultural, intellectual, political, religious and socio-economic diversity.[4] Finally, translocal and transnational diversity of users implies aggrandisement of the notion of subjectivity[5] of cyberreligious phenomena and broader agglomeration of users suggests a wider discursive production of subjectivity. Therefore, the production and dissemination of e-religious discourses, and interaction with them, is directly related to access to the medium. Limited access to the Web, and to the Internet in general, implies restricted access to e-religious developments and exchanges. Furthermore, while the voices of the higher socio-economic groups that have privileged access to the Web inevitably dominate e-religious discourses (which then influence developments in the world at large), the religious concerns of those excluded from the Web are not represented in cyberspace and have no such impact.

Accessibility involves accessing the environment—the Web, and accessing content/context—information. While Web access depends on several factors independent of the Web (technical infrastructure, literacy, cost, equipment etc.), accessing information relies on factors dependent entirely on the Web, such as its structure, retrieval systems and general operationality. Both aspects raise epistemological and methodological issues relevant to researching religious or other phenomena on the Web.

Access to the Web

While the early Internet was accessible only to computer professionals, its proliferation has transformed it from specialized tool to evocative domain, with many possibilities for activities and interactions. "The Internet" is still widely perceived as an instrument able to overcome the limitations of other forms of mass media, offering the conditions for broader involvement as producers, not just consumers, of ICTs, and resulting in increased participation, choice and balanced relations between senders and receivers (Anderson 2000). Yet these benefits depend on what I call the "transitory/adaptive process", that is, the passage from mere observer to active user. Any such reconstruction of relationships with ICTs is conditioned by several factors, principally access. The variable level of access—from 69.8 per cent of the population in Iceland to virtually 0 per cent in Afghanistan[6]—has been termed "digital divide";[7] a division between the "have-nets" and the "have-nots". A systematic investigation of access must differentiate between a region's access to the Internet (requiring electricity and telecommunications), namely "global access" and Internet access by individuals within a region, or "local access". Digital divide exists at both global and local levels.

Local access

Access and its product—digital divide—refers not only to how many citizens are connected, but also their location, financial and educational status, and levels of availability of ICTs in their country, educational institutions, workplaces and households. All these parameters affect inclusion/exclusion, and hence maximize or minimize the disparities between the information rich and information poor.

Exclusion factors

Exclusion from the Web is particularly evident in respect of women, the elderly and the disabled. Regarding the disabled, according to Tim Berners-Lee, inventor of the WWW, "the power of the Web is in its universality. Access by everyone regardless of disability is an essential aspect".[8] Until the mid nineties, people with certain disabilities were excluded from the Web, but in 1997 the Web Accessibility Initiative (WAI) became part of the World Wide Web Consortium's (W3C) commitment to lead the "Web to its full potential include[ing] promoting a high degree of usability for people with disabilities". The National Centre for the Dissemination of Disability Research (NCDDR) encouraged developers to design accessibility into ICT hardware and software.[9]

Specialized software accessibility packages such as pwWebSpeak[10] and IBM's talking Web browser Home Page Reader[11] and email package are designed for blind or partially sighted users, people with dyslexia or learning difficulties, or users learning new languages. In 1998, Bill Gates announced a plan, to "dramatically increase" Microsoft's accessibility initiatives[12] (see e.g. Microsoft's "Accessibility Technology for Everyone" site featuring "assistive technology").[13] Despite the industry's willingness to answer these needs, the cost of the answers raises the issue of affordability, another significant factor in nations' and individuals' capability to get connected. As Katz and Aspden (1998) indicate, lower income groups are more likely to be excluded.

Women and seniors

Recent reports[14] proclaim that the UK has the second highest percentage of women online (42 per cent) and the highest percentage (83 per cent) of senior users who get connected on "a regular basis",[15] apparently making Web surfing the primary hobby of the British senior population, though qualitative research might qualify these statistical findings.

Comparing UK results to international ones, one can speculate on the leading determinants of access. For example,[16] reports referring to different continents and/or countries provide the following:

> The use of online communication tools by Asian women is increasing, according to NetValue (NUA, 18 February 2002). The latest figures indicate 25.1 million women using the Internet in France, Germany, Italy, Spain, Sweden, Switzerland and the UK, compared to 40.1 million men. The largest female Internet audience is in Sweden (46 per cent of women online). Germany and France both have 39 per cent, while Italy has 31 per cent and Spain 29 per cent (NUA, March 2002). Webchek research indicates that 49 per cent of South African Internet users are women (NUA, 30 January 2002).

Summaries or headlines can be misleading. Because they "announce" percentages or employ catchphrases they may suggest a general increase, yet when the full statistics are in view the real socio-economic implications become noticeable. The headline "The number of Hungarian women going online has almost tripled over the past three years" heralds a report showing that Hungarian female users tend to have higher levels of income than non-users; 79 per cent own a mobile phone, 64 per cent a credit card and 43 per cent have some form of savings.

Reports on connected seniors in the US show that:

> In 2000 half of the adult population in America did not have Internet access. Other demographic findings showed that only 13 per cent of those aged 65 and over have access to the Internet, while 59 per cent of those between the ages of 50 and 64 do not go online (NUA, 26 September 2000). In 2001 15 per cent of US senior citizens are reported to have Internet access, and 69 per cent of those go online every day (NUA, 10 September 2001).

The report found that online US seniors are more likely than others to be married, well educated, and have high retirement incomes.

Access and income

From the above samples one could conclude that the leading determinants for Internet access, apart from race, gender and age,[17] are educational and economic levels. The Nielsen survey substantiates this, showing that in the US the number of online individuals with household incomes between $100,000 and $150,000 rose by 20 per cent in a year to nearly 15 million. Individuals in this income bracket accounted for 12 per cent of the total US online population. By comparison, individuals in households earning less than $25,000 and between $25,000 and $50,000 grew 2 per cent and 5 per cent respectively over the same year (Nielsen, Net Ratings, 2002). Similarly, the UK's Office of National Statistics[18] revealed that levels of access depend very strongly on income, with around 82 per cent of online households in the highest income group, compared to just 10 per cent in the lowest. The UK ONS survey on "Reason for not using the Internet" indicated that 38 per cent of UK adults had never accessed the Internet. Of these, 42 per cent expressed no interest, while 30 per cent declared they had no means of access and 26 per cent claimed lack of confidence and skills as the reason.[19]

Educational and cultural factors

A couple of locational studies present us with an indicative framework within which the above statistical data could be explained. Katz and Aspden's (1998) empirical research was conducted in the USA and offers valuable insights into the Internet's impact specifically on American society and who is online, who is not, and why. Katz and Aspden (1998) identified two digital divides, one relating to "awareness", the other to "usage". Less educated, economically disadvantaged, old, and black/Hispanic[20] people were unlikely to "be aware" of the Internet. Those less educated, economically disadvantaged, old and female were unlikely to "be Internet users".[21] Thus, "cost, access and complexity" are key obstacles for Internet use.

These results show that for some (e.g. less educated) people, "awareness" does not signify "usage". Even if the hurdle of cost were somehow removed, access would still be problematic. An ethnographic survey in San Diego demonstrated that there are also psychosocial barriers that dissuade socio-economically disadvantaged individuals from becoming involved with computers, let alone the Internet (Stanley 2001).[22] Responses demonstrate that reluctant attitudes towards ICTs are closely intertwined with (a) judgements about ICT's usefulness in advancing socio-economic status; (b) fear and perceived inability to comprehend computerized technologies and thus use them effectively; and (c) beliefs that being "computer users" collides/does not correspond with culturally influenced gender issues and roles (Stanley 2001). An equivalent survey in the UK might disclose some of the reasons for the 38 per cent of the British population who had never accessed the Internet.

Thus the question of native/local digital divide is a multilayered one, bringing the digital divide debate of a country into the ambit of socio-economic imperialism because, as the US Organization for Economic Cooperation and Development (OECD) Information Technology Outlook for 2002 suggests, differences in spread and utilization of ICTs may create new kinds of social divides and emphasize existing ones relating to income, education, race, gender, age, family type and sub-national regions.[23]

The digital divide is not one entity but a complicated patchwork of varying levels of ICT access, basic competence in ICT usage, and ICT applications among peoples and, as shown below, among countries as well.

Global Access

> "Half of humanity has never made a telephone call"
> (Thabo Mbeki, 1995, G7 Summit)[24]

Exclusivity becomes more evident if access is analysed on a global scale. In developing countries IT infrastructure (phone lines, computers, even electricity) is in its infancy or totally absent.[25] For example, 76.24 per cent of computers-in-use globally are in fifteen countries, with 30 per cent of all computers-in-use worldwide in the USA. International Telecommunication Union (ITU) figures show nearly 30 PCs per 100 people in the UK, but in countries such as Malawi one PC for every 10,000 people,[26] and more Internet hosts in Manhattan than in the whole of Africa.

Although an accurate count of the online global population is not yet feasible, several surveys[27] provide us with estimates about the numbers of the world's netizens and useful data about the penetration of ICTs worldwide.

Global statistics

In 2000, the connected world in numbers was:

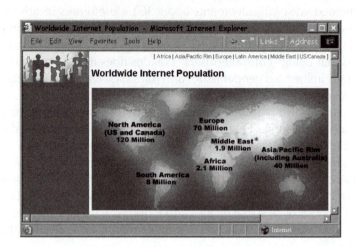

Of the 2.1 million netizens of Africa, 1,622,000 were in South Africa, which leaves 478,000 for the rest of the continent.[28] While more than half the USA's population use the Internet, in Latin America and the Caribbean only 3.2 per cent do so. Finland has more Internet users than the Caribbean states and Latin America put together. Sub-Saharan Africa and South Asia are almost completely offline, with a share of 0.4 per cent (Zanker 2001). Since in Africa there are only 14 million phone lines, 80 per cent of which are in six countries, it is understandable that "industrialized countries, with only 15 per cent of the world's population, are home to 88 per cent of all Internet users".[29]

Moving to 2002, the numbers of connected populations change to:[30]

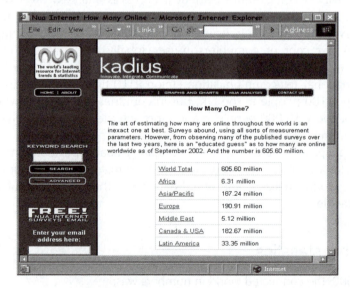

In Africa, the UN Information and Communication Technologies (UNICT) Task Force[31] reports that the number of dial-up Internet subscribers rose by 20 per cent between 2001 and 2002. However, excluding the more developed South Africa and northern Africa, only 1 in 250 Africans uses the Internet, compared to 1 in 2 of the population of North America and Europe.[32]

Inadequate or absent infrastructure results in enormously high Internet connection costs, but the development of wireless communication technologies offers a solution. In countries such as South Africa, far more people are connected to a cellular network than a landline. This, according to SAVANT, makes South Africa an "emerging country with the highest penetration of wireless technologies in the world".[33] Wireless communications are more favourable in regions with infrastructural underdevelopment. As the International Telecommunication Union (ITU) reports,

> at the beginning of 1991 there were fewer than 22,000 mobile cellular subscribers in the whole of Africa, but by the beginning of 2001 there were more than 11 million. Pre-paid subscriptions also secure payments from customers in advance of the service being provided which greatly facilitates the collection of charges. As a result they make cellular telephony accessible to a much wider audience, and are potentially one of the best opportunities in the world today for achieving universal access.[34]

Because ICT facilities are increasingly viewed as central for socio-economic development,[35] a number of initiatives from the private sector supported by the UNICT Task Force are attempting to provide "wireless opportunities for underserved populations"[36] with the scope to expand "digital inclusion" to the countries of the south for better inclusion in the global economy and participation in "E-velopment" and "E-volution" (Zanker 2001).

A number of cases may illustrate the socio-economic advantages to rural, underdeveloped communities when the infrastructural barriers are removed.[37, 38]

Obstacles

Technological infrastructure and economic development are not the only obstacles to global access, since both may be overcome. Moreover, as Warschauer (2003a) points out, the term "access" is better understood as having two parameters—a narrow and a wider perception of the term. The narrow view perceives access only in physical terms, meaning having a computer and Internet connection, which does not ensure access to the information society. The wider refers to the ability to employ ICTs effectively, ensuring access to broader social engagement and inclusion.

Obtaining access to computers and the Internet depends to a greater degree upon the cultivation of "social capital",[39] which proves to be a significant aspect, as surveys show,[40] and to a lesser degree upon mere physical engagement with computers (Warschauer 2003a). Unequal levels of literacy and illiteracy in the world's population seem to be additional key factors for preventing the reduction of the digital divide.[41] For instance, in China, for the population above the age of 25, the rates of illiteracy in 1990 were 17.2 for men and 42 per cent for women. In Saudi Arabia 6 per cent of men and 18.9 per cent of women are illiterate. The difference in percentages accelerates in age groups above 25 in Saudi Arabia, where 24.9 per cent of men are illiterate as opposed to 55.3 per cent of women.[42] These numbers, although indicative, highlight the fact that language may be seen either as a deterrent, or as an exclusion factor for both access and usage, especially if in the issue of illiteracy the English language is included.

Language. The predominant language of the cyber-environment is English. As a tool of communication, using one's mother tongue, the English language is applicable only to a minority of the world's population, yet as the following chart[43] shows, the use of English in the Web is overwhelming.

Chart of Web content, by language in 2002

English	68.4 per cent
Japanese	5.9 per cent
German	5.8 per cent
Chinese	3.9 per cent
French	3.0 per cent
Spanish	2.4 per cent
Russian	1.9 per cent
Italian	1.6 per cent
Portuguese	1.4 per cent
Korean	1.3 per cent
Other	4.6 per cent
Total Web pages:	313 bn

This excessive percentage of English usage is attributable to a number of reasons. The first, as Pandia[44] proposes, is the fact that the most Internet concentrated countries such as the US, Canada, the UK, Ireland, Australia and New Zealand have English as their native language. Additionally, in some countries, such as India, Jamaica and

Egypt, for example, English is widely used in education and business. The second reason is related to search engines' functionality, in the sense that a website, for example in Portuguese, will not achieve high positioning in the search results of the main search engines.[45] Hence, most sites, those being commercial, educational and/or of general interest, are either in English or they include an English version.[46] It has to be noted that although the non-English-speaking online population increases steadily,[47] the language of business sites and e-commerce is almost exclusively English.[48] Furthermore, it appears that, as "leapfrogging" advances and the development of M-commerce[49] on an international scale increases along with the need, especially of developing countries, to access as wide a market as possible, proficiency in English would become paramount.

Other evidence challenges the notion that English dominates the Internet, for several reasons. Firstly, as projections estimate, the non-English-speaking online population will continue to increase[50] and the non-English websites will overtake the English ones (Crystal 2001, cited in Warschauer 2002). Secondly, studies[51] verify that ICTs can, potentially, benefit minority languages and dialects (Kraidy 2001, Warschauer 1997, cited in Warschauer 2002) which have been marginalized and are almost impossible to use in other media. Thirdly, there is the development of direct machine translation (Kraidy 2001, 38) and finally, as Kraidy suggests, there is the possibility that a global language might emerge that could outshine English.

However, the above arguments do not take into consideration that: there are new, and to some extent uncommon, linguistic forms of diglossia[52] (a form of linguistic amalgamation of two languages or dialects) that evolve within the matrix of online communication, which favour English, especially in the contexts of business, formal communication and education (Warschauer 2002; Paolillo 1999); machine translation software is still underdeveloped and its translating capability is quite deficient for wide utilization.[53] English dominance is not so much of an issue regarding computer and Internet applications, as it is regarding operating systems and software creation and development. Thus, despite the decrease of "language divide", it appears that English is—and will continue to be—the lingua franca of certain areas of the Internet such as e-commerce and business sites (Warschauer 2002; Carvin 2000b; Tong 2001, 71; Bridges.org[54]). Language is not just a communication tool but also a content carrier, in the sense that most Internet information is still in text format. In consequence, the literacy/illiteracy dichotomy should not be understood only in terms of basic educational efficiency, which is indeed crucial, but also in terms of possessing the necessary equipment and skills to navigate the Web, to discover the relevant information and to make use of it (Warschauer 2002; Carvin 2000b; Yu 2002). Furthermore, the literacy/illiteracy dichotomy becomes a further obstacle if it is perceived as an instrument of producing and publishing Web content.

Digital divide. All the above referenced reports and statistical data on "global access" demonstrate that digital divide, internationally, is extensive and, as a number of studies (Rodriguez and Wilson 2000; Bridges. org 2001) reveal, there are no signs that it will narrow down in the near future. The reasons for this continuing inequality lie in the fact that when the information-poor just manage to get access to basic ICTs, the information-rich have already leapt ahead to broadband, wireless fidelity, telematics and so on, thus widening the chasm which appeared to be narrowing. They also show that while "global access" is thought to be intertwined only with the technological infrastructure of a country and that "local access" is thought only to be subject to the social, economic and educational conditions of individuals, as well as, in some cases, to personal preferences and/or state of affairs, in reality this is not the case. They demonstrate that digital divide is a complex, multilayered and multi-contextual issue that should not be perceived as being confined only within the limits of infrastructural and physical paraphernalia, but as expanding into far wider realms related to cyberimperialism (Ebo 2001a; Rusciano 2001), cybercolonialism (Tong 2001), economic development, education and community (Carvin 2000b; Warschauer 2002, 2003b; Yu 2002). Over and above that, the concept of digital divide is fluid and changeable, for it is also determined by two more factors. On the one hand it is the different socio-economic and political ideologies of the policy makers,[55] which may have serious repercussions on the efforts to decrease the disparity between the "haves" and "haves not" at both national and international levels; and on the other hand, it is the different degrees of access that exist between individuals and countries.[56] Nevertheless, people all over the world do "connect" to the Internet and explore and make use of its applications.

Notwithstanding the connected 605 million people of the planet, netizens still represent a small percentage of the global population. If we consider that the planet's population is six billion, 38 per cent of which resides in India and China (Population Reference Bureau[57]), and that Africa has 842 million inhabitants (GeoHive 2002), then it becomes evident that the percentage of the "connected" is only 10 per cent of the planet, with Africa having less than 1 per cent of its population online. It is therefore plausible to suggest that there is no sufficient number of people connected and no sufficient volume of Web activity to support and/or justify claims that "being online" is a global phenomenon, unless the terms "global", "globalization", used in the discourses of the digerati, really refer to an exceedingly "localized", but nevertheless perceived as global, environment. Consequently, statistical numbers place Berners-Lee's vision of the Web's universality in a different perspective by revealing that universality is far from achievable. They also attach to this study a number of question marks, as well as to any other study about both the Internet's and the Web's social, cultural, political, educational and economic impact. As, for example, in this study's subject matter, the emerging questions could be: Who has a voice and whose voice is silent? Whose religion? Whose beliefs and practices are expressed? Who participates in virtual religious practices? Who ascribes to cyberspace the qualities of the "sacred" and "transcending space" and so on?[58]

Political aspects of access. Although there are studies that draw attention to possible links between the Internet—a western developed technology carrying all western cultural and ideological "artefacts"—and cultural imperialism (Ebo 2001a), cyberimperialism (Rusciano 2001) and cybercolonialism (Tong 2001) brought about by the cultivation of notions such as globalization, transnational corporations and global capital, Kraidy (2001, 28) argues that these notions do not encompass all elements of the Internet. Instead, he offers a re-conceptualization of the Internet and suggests that "glocalization" is a more accurate term to signify the multifaceted duality of the Internet, that is, its capability for fragmentation and cohesiveness, as well as for restriction and emancipation (2001, 28). Therefore a critical assessment of the Internet has to include its propensity to become either a liberating medium (at least to those who have access to it today and potentially to the entire human population), or an instrument of dominance and control. This aspect of the Internet attaches to access an additional dimension. Postulating the key obstacles for Internet use and taking into consideration the issues discussed earlier, it is suggested here that access, in certain locations and contexts, is also determined by political factors that transform it from being an issue associated with socio-economics, education, race and gender, to an issue associated with governmental-constitutional policies.

Access as political/religious weapon. There is a twofold manifestation of the political dimension of access and its repercussions. On the one hand, access to the Web denotes the availability of a reactive and responsive tool. As such, access can become an empowering political instrument with unprecedented consequences.[59] There are a great number of cases of "hacktivism",[60] and, within the domain of religious activity, there are a number of religious coalitions, partnerships and collaborations that are using the cyber-environment to express their opposition or support for a number of socio-political and economic issues.[61] In addition, the most well-known examples demonstrating the emancipatory attribute of access are the cases of Partenia and Falun Gong.[62] Through the website of Partenia[63] Bishop Gailot can move horizontally, communicating, in a wholly new way, religious as well as social and political issues he believes to be important. In other words, and despite the fact that Partenia is a Catholic diocese, its Web pages reflect the particular understanding that Jacques Gailot holds for his work (Zaleski 1997, 4). Furthermore, Partenia's congregation is offered a place where it can express its views about both religious and socio-political issues. Partenia is a response to the monolithic character of the Catholic Church, and proves, as Cobb indicates, that cyberspace provides opportunities for "evolutionary social function, enabling spiritual and political work to unfold in new ways" (1998, 76).

The other example, which qualifies as representative of the "force for the breakdown of authoritarian political control" (Rodan 1997), is Falun Gong.[64] On April 25, 1999, ten thousand followers of Falun Gong gathered in Tiananmen Square, in an astonishing demonstration—coordinated and organized mainly by email—which stunned the Chinese government and the rest of the world. They were protesting against the decision of the Chinese regime to outlaw the Falun Dafa meditation movement. Since then, several demonstrations have taken place (the latest in December 2000)[65] with the same demands: freedom of speech, expression and association. Yet, perhaps one consequence of the 1999 demonstration is that while there were 8.9 million Chinese Internet users at the end of 1999, the number leapt to 16.9 million in the first half of 2000, as the survey by the China National Network Information Center (CNNIC) showed.[66] It could be argued that this sharp increase of users underlines the Internet's capacity to uncover new avenues not only for individual political expression (Rodan 1997), but for collective action as well.

Political control of access. The second manifestation of the political dimension of access is found in the ways in which access to ICTs is appraised, that is, the ways by which the power of access to undermine authoritarian systems and institutions is assessed and evaluated by different governments worldwide, for as several scholars have indicated, the arrival of information technology (IT) has predominantly been regarded as a force for the breakdown of authoritarian political control (Rodan 1997; Rusciano 2001; Warschauer 2000; Taubman 2002; Altintas et al. 2002). Therefore, despite the extent to which a country is technologically advanced, access can still be restricted and/or controlled by oppressive governmental mechanisms for a number of reasons. For instance, leaders of dictatorial regimes firmly believe that they, only, know the requirements and conditions of the country. Hence, in their effort to diminish potential political and social change, they keep any sources of foreign influence under strict control (Taubman 2002). Moreover, the Internet's capacity to function as both a receiver and a transmitter implies that citizens can not only access ideational data but they can also publicize regional information to both a native and a global audience (Taubman 2002). This results in the distribution of ideas "antagonistic" to those of the regime (Altintas et al. 2002) which may provoke domestic political disturbance, as well as the exposure of the local political situation to the international arena.[67]

Examples of such governmental restrictions are the cases of Saudi Arabia, China, Singapore, North Korea, Iran and Myanmar.[68] While the growth of the Internet creates economic opportunities for these countries, it also creates a political threat, since as previously noted, it opens up doors to a variety of political and social views which are not in accordance with those allowed by the countries' firmly controlled media. As a result, in Singapore for example, the government launched severe regulations to bring the Internet under control, demanding all organizations and individuals with Web pages discussing religion or politics to register with the Singapore broadcasting authority and forcing all Internet service providers (ISPs) to prevent the availability of "objectionable content" (including content which can "excite disaffection against the Government" or "undermine the public confidence in the administration of justice") (Warschauer 2000). Similarly, Myanmar's (formerly known as Burma) military junta only opened access to the Internet in 2002. With only one ISP and high costs, the regime makes certain that access is available only to a small number of people. Reuters reports that currently Myanmar has around 20,000 users, but estimates suggest that the number will increase to 200,000 within the next couple of years.

In the widely-circulated "Declaration of Independence of Cyberspace" (1996) Barlow of the Electronic Frontier Foundation[69] declares: "Governments of the Industrial World… I declare the global social space we are building to be naturally independent of the tyrannies you seek to impose on us". Barlow goes on to suggest that the world of cyberspace is one where all people may enter without "privilege or prejudice accorded by race, economic power, military force, or station of birth. Anyone, anywhere may express his or her beliefs, no matter how singular, without fear of being coerced into silence or conformity".

Additionally, the conviction that, since there are not any policemen on the Net, therefore everybody has total freedom to go wherever they want (Henderson 2000), demands an examination of whether the Web surfer is indeed free from any other restrictions or biases apart from those (infrastructural, economic, educational and political) discussed earlier.

Access to Information

Introduction

The empowered content interconnection, implied by Barlow, is observable as people, being consumers, scientists, activists or ordinary netizens, are increasingly using the Web to find material that interests them. From buying goods, holidays or medical treatments, to scientific interests, academic resources and courses; the list is literally endless. Similarly, individuals and groups are using the Web to publish their views, to contest, to protest, to agree, to support, to promote, to advertise, trade and sell. Organizations, both governmental and non-governmental, are also increasingly using the Web to disseminate, communicate, broadcast, advertise and circulate, ideas, policies, ideologies, issues and concepts. All these activities, including the electronic catalogues of national and local libraries, museums, banks, educational institutions, books online and e-department-stores, to mention but a few, which underline the infinite size of the Web, as well as its infinite possible utilizations, constitute the content and the context of the Web.

While accessing the Web depends entirely on factors that are unrelated to the Web itself, accessing its content depends entirely on the structural and operational properties by which the Web is governed. As Introna and Nissenbaum (2000, 39, 42, 43) suggest, the advantages of the billions of terabytes of information and the active involvement of millions of users around the world "depend on a number of contingencies", indicating as the most prominent one the operational structure of search engines. Furthermore, Patelis (2000, 50) points out that the surfing experience of users is no longer free and according to their choices, but has become a customized one, like the act of communication itself, conveyed and organized in a specific manner. Additionally, extending their observations, it is suggested here that online activity, as both casual surfing and searching, as well as successful retrieval of requested information, depend on the one hand on the functionality of both hardware and software technical developments and design, and on the other hand on the structural organization of the Web content. Consequently, isolating the content of the Web, as the existing academic works on the subject do, from the technical foundation that supports it, results in a misleading and distorted presentation of the topic of the study, for, as Patelis (2000, 51) explains, it does not acknowledge the intertwining of the different industries and their role in shaping and structuring the online activity.

Hence, any critical analysis of religious utterances, either discursive or practical in nature, has to take into consideration the contribution of the technical infrastructure to the research process. It is important to note that all technical infrastructural components[70] of the Web are amended, adjusted and reconfigured as the Web is enlarging. Therefore a differentiation between what the author calls "pre-expansion" and "post-expansion" periods of the Web would elucidate the changes[71] that occurred in the Web's structure, in its search systems' operation, and their consequences. Additionally, the terms, especially the "post-expansion" one, would be useful when addressing the newest developments of the Web, such as for example the Semantic Web,[72] as they appear to be the results of the ever-increasing demand for and usage of the Web. While "pre-expansion" refers to the period that starts from the Web's conception in 1989 up to its full public availability in 1996, "post-expansion" refers to the period from 1996 onwards when the number of uploaded sites began to accelerate rapidly.

Structure of the Web

The versatility of contents clearly demonstrates the enthusiastic adaptation of the Web by different users and its anarchic structure. According to Rogers (2000b, 12), the Web, perceived as anarchic, prospers only when the user is thought to be in power. This perception was widespread in the "pre-expansion period" of the Web's history, during which access to information, at least to those who were connected, was free and straightforward, in the sense that all online material was available to netizens without any restrictions, whether technical or financial.

As the size of the indexed Web[73] increases, for example from 320 million pages in 1997 and 800 million pages in 1999 (Lawrence and Giles 1999) to 2.1 billion in 2000[74] (Cyveillance 2000), so does the need, faced by the Web designers, Webmasters, Web keepers and software engineers, to create mechanisms which would classify the uploaded information into separate categories, implementing thus a taxonomy of Web content. Furthermore, augmentation of the Web material results in intensified dependency of the users on devices such as directories, portals, search engines and Web rings that facilitate and materialize the search and surf activity.

Taking into account the basic principle upon which the Web was created, that is, universal and unrestricted access and connectivity of uploaded information, it could be suggested that the underlying elements of the "pre-expansion" period are interconnection and free access to Web content. The "post-expansion" period, however, is characterized by newly added elements, such as technological and ideological developments derived from the utilization of the Web by a continuously increasing number of agents, which transform the Web from a free, global, public communication and information resource, to a commodity accessible at a price.

Deep Web

For Introna and Nissenbaum (2000, 25), the technical aspects of the retrieval systems, as well as their design and their overall functionality, become political issues for the reason that "what people (the 'seekers') are able to find on the Web determines what the Web consists of for them". Additionally, it would be added that apart from the search systems' operationality, the Web's content construction, which also defines its subjectivity, becomes a political and a cultural issue.

For example, as stated earlier, the Web works under a hypertext metaphor that means that it operates via a series of nodes and links. A user can search or browse a piece of information—a node—and, when they see a link, they can activate it, reaching thus some other node of information—this being internal e.g. a document, an image, a graphic and so on, or external, that is another website. However, there are a substantial number of nodes which are irretrievable because, although they exist on the Web, they are neither detectable by its search mechanisms (search engines), nor indexable by its structural composition (links, directories and so on). The reason behind this invisibility of data can be found in a confluence of events that occurred at the beginning of the "post-expansion" period, which significantly altered the previously celebrated universal character of the Web. These events, as Bergman (2001) points out, started with new software developments and the commercialization of the Web by the directories and search engines and later, with the establishment of e-commerce.

Regarding the new developments in the software arena, the introduction of online database technology and the consequential modification of Web servers to permit serving the new database-build Web pages generated a shift in the Web's direction, from static Web pages to dynamic (Bergman 2001). That shift, reinforced on the one hand by the increase in the number of users and on the other hand by commercialization[75] of the Web, resulted in the division of the Web into two categories: one, being public, open and free, named "surface" Web, and the other being private, closed and hidden, known as "deep"[76] Web. Briefly, standard content of invisible Web pages include archived material, digital exhibits, statistical sources, museums, e-shops and a whole variety of full-text databases such as dictionaries, encyclopaedias, online books, newspapers and both academic and popular journals and e-zines. Information that is new and dynamically changing in content is also included in the deep Web, as for example, news, job postings, available airline flights, weather forecast, hotel rooms, stock and bond prices, market averages, discussion databases and so on[77] (Cohen 2002). Another important section of the deep Web is the increasing number of sites that require a log in and some registration process. In these, newspapers, commercial publishers (e.g. CUP, Routledge etc.) and libraries (e.g. Questia) set up sites that feature full-text versions of hard-copy publications.

This division of content, and the fact that searchable databases are neither indexable nor retrievable by today's search engines, appearing therefore invisible to the average seekers as they search the Internet, has several implications for both users and researchers. Moreover, the prediction by computer scientists that the size of the deep Web will continue to grow exponentially (Bergman 2001; Lyman and Varian 2000) clearly underlines the importance of mastering the deep-Web search process. Information stored in databases is accessible *only by query*, that is, by first accessing the database and then finding the information needed. This is distinct from the static, fixed Web pages of the surface Web, which are documents that can be accessed directly (Cohen 2002). That implies that, for the casual user, who perhaps due to inadequate knowledge regarding surface and deep Web, depends on the operationality of the standard search engines, a substantial amount of information which may be useful or important remains hidden.

For the researcher, the division of the Web's content implies a number of issues. Firstly, she needs to be aware of the diverse important and valid resources available in the deep Web, those being the millions of documents of various, free or by subscription libraries of the world, national and international statistics, art galleries, census information, to mention but a few. Secondly, she needs to be aware of the limitations of existing search systems regarding their capability to retrieve information accumulated in the deep Web. Thirdly, she needs to know about the specialized tools which are capable of extracting information from the perpetually expanding[78] deep Web. Finally, she needs to be aware of the tools' operationality, that is, the way in which they find the requested information. For instance, because the technical structure of databases does not allow search engines' robots to enter their stored information, only specially developed mechanisms[79] have access to databases.

Surface Web

The information of the surface Web appears to be scattered, uncontrolled and unclassified. Although this was totally true in the pre-expansion period, in the post-expansion period it is only partially true, for in reality, information has been, is and will be continuously organized, classified and to some extent controlled. The reason for the systemization of information on the Web is grounded in the formation and development of presentational, navigational, and retrieval tools, such as browsers, portals and search engines.

The epistemological analysis of these structural instruments is necessary, for they incorporate significant and highly important repercussions for both users and researchers, mainly because they dictate online activity. It should be noted, however, that the analysis of these Web tools is solely focused on and restricted to their implicit or explicit political repercussions on Web activity and not on the technical aspects, which are beyond the comprehension and knowledge of the author.

Browsers

A browser is software which interprets[80] the programming language (HTML) of the Web into words, graphics, images and sounds that appear on the screen when a site is viewed. The number of existing browsers today is quite substantial.[81] However, the most common and widely used is Microsoft's Explorer which controls 80 per cent[82] of the market with Netscape a distant second.[83]

Although it seems that the browser is directly related to technical developments produced by the software industry to facilitate the relationship between users and the new medium, its "by default"[84] presence in every computer's operating system transforms it from a mere technical application to an epistemological issue, carrying a number of hidden aspects that need to be revealed. For instance, there is the question of the browser's functionality. The browser is the means by which users access the Web, view Web documents and travel through websites. Therefore its importance and power in shaping and to some extent controlling the surfing experience becomes evident (O'Dochartaigh 2002, 14; Altena 1999). In other words the importance of browsers lies in their technical capabilities. Consequently, depending on the architecture of their software,[85] browsers have the capability of presenting the same Web page in different ways. Altena (1999) defines this as "technological relativism", namely, being equipped with a different browser, the user observes a different Web reality. For example, since the browser is in essence a lens through which the coded information of a Web page appears as meaningful to the user, this Web page may appear more "bluish" through one browser or more "reddish" through another.[86]

Similarly, as the browser also facilitates travel through the sites, it becomes a means of transportation which determines the experience of space. At the same time though, it also becomes a time machine, in that it determines the speed at which the experience of travelling occurs. The experiencing of both space and time, as Altena (1999) succinctly expresses it, could be crucially altered by the mode of transportation used. Thus, for instance, a "fast" browser may present the Web as a manageable space ready to be explored easily and quickly, while on the other hand, a "slow" browser may present quite the opposite. Furthermore, an outdated browser would not be able to interpret a page which is designed by the latest software. In both cases the users perceive the Web in a particular way, which, unknowingly to them, is dictated to them by their browser.

Yet there is one point here that needs to be addressed. Browsers not only exist by default, they also provide users with the facilities of customizing the settings of the browser in a personalized way.[87] This reflects the great effort (and money) that has been made (and spent) by ICTs industries to persuade the users to "build" their personal computing environment according to their own preferences, aesthetics and lifestyle (Rogers 2000b, 11). This "self-made-layout", however, is superficial and illusory, giving on the one hand to the users the false impression that they are in control of their surfing activity, and, on the other hand, as Rogers (12) underlines, diverting the focus of the analysis from the default settings. The point made here is that while the user may feel she is partially the "author" of the browser—by redesigning it—in fact, she just follows predetermined steps allowed by the browser's corporation. An additional point is that the majority of users (both casual surfers and researchers) have neither the technical expertise to evaluate, assess and/or compare the browser that they given, nor to upgrade it and/or install a different one. This, according to Tetzlaff (2000, 124), means that transnational software corporations, such as Microsoft, compromise and, to some extent, eliminate any possibilities for alternative visions of cyberspace.

Portals

Another feature of the Web, a key characteristic of the "post-expansion" period, is the "portal". A key word search "what is a portal" in Google produced 51,300,000 hits, the first of which was "Web definitions for portal". The page offers twenty-eight definitions provided by diverse sources, such as universities, governmental and commercial sites. Although the definitions overlap, some examples are valuable in that they demonstrate the ideological character of portals:

a grand and imposing entrance (often extended metaphorically); "the portals of the cathedral"; "the portals of heaven"; "the portals of success".[88]

A website that becomes a user's primary starting point for access to the Internet. AOL and Yahoo! are examples of portal sites.[89]

A high-traffic website with a wide range of content, services and vendor links. It acts as a value-added middleman by selecting the content sources and assembling them in a simple-to-navigate and customize interface for presentation to the end user. Portals typically offer such services as Web searching, news, reference tools, access to online shopping venues, and communications capabilities including e-mail and chat rooms.[90]

Usually used as a marketing term to describe a Website that is or is intended to be the first place people see when using the Web.[91]

A Web "supersite" that provides a variety of services including Web searching, news, white and yellow pages directories, free e-mail, discussion groups, online shopping, and links to other sites.[92]

Therefore the principal points of portals, as they surface in the definitions, could be summarized as:

- a grand entrance
- the user's primary starting point
- high-traffic
- a wide range of content, services and vendor links
- a marketing term
- a Web "supersite".

These points indicate that, on the one hand, the primary function of portals is to generate financial gains, and, on the other hand, to create a comprehensive entry point for a huge array of resources and services. Hence an important function of portals is to offer a "familiar" point of departure for cyber-surfers (Elmer 2000, 164). Patelis (2000, 50–52), in her study of AOL, argues that separating the Web's infrastructure from its content presents both scholars and users with a misconception of the online experience, in that they tend to consider it materialized when they access a website. Yet Patelis highlights that the two are closely intertwined because it is the partnership of infrastructure and content that constructs and shapes the online activity. For instance, while in the pre-expansion period the choice of visiting a site was solely at each user's discretion, in the post-expansion period this very same choice becomes, as Patelis (2000, 50) underlines, "customized" by corporations such as AOL and Yahoo. Online interaction, for Patelis (2000, 51), should not be seen as consisting of different parts, but as an interconnected and consistent process of "structuration".[93] Patelis (51) calls the hidden political economies of portals and other navigational tools, "signposting". This "signposting" dictates the content users are able to find and also creates a sense of "territory, safety, property—a path through e-chaos".

Search systems

Advocates of the utopian vision of ICTs emphasize the revolutionary nature of the Web regarding its capacity to equalize, democratize and decentralize not only information itself, but also its accessibility. However, the first signs of unequal access to information on the Web were detected immediately after the Web's expansion. These signs appeared in changes of search activity. Search, in Net lingo, is the process of locating information on the Internet (either on a website, a newsgroup or on an archive), that is effected by employing search systems. These are divided into two main categories: search directories and search engines.

The paramount importance and power of the search systems for Web search activity can only be understood if one takes into account two parameters. The first is found in the discourse of the commercial Web industry, through which one can establish an understanding of how the systems operate and manage issues, such as placing a site in a directory, search engine results optimization, site promotion, site placement, popularity and so on; in other words, dealing with the search systems' engine submission and optimization services. The development of this industry is illustrated by the number of results the phrase "search engine optimization" has produced over the years, as the table[94] below shows.

January 1996 – January 1998	0 results
January 1998 – January 1999	524
January 1999 – January 2000	1,821
January 2000 – January 2001	9,001
January 2001 – January 2002	71,669
January 2002 – January 2003	170,682

The gradual loss of free and unrestricted access to information is presented both in the above numbers, and in the advertising discourse of companies dealing with search engine submission and optimization services, such as:[95]

> A major part of our success is that we analyze each website before it is scheduled for submission to the search engines. This analysis is the reason that the vast majority of our clients enjoy top search engine ranking.

Similar to this is the discourse about services that guarantee the acceptance of a site in the "leading" directories.[96] All these sites, mainly Web
development companies, emphasize the indispensable importance of
having "your site" placed in a major directory and explain the process
and the benefits of such an inclusion. At the same time as promoting
their products and/or services they also provide a valuable insight into
the politics of directories.

Both the above numbers and the advertising rhetoric highlight, on
the one hand, the accelerated rates in which Web information is com-
mercialized, and, on the other hand, as will be discussed later, the contribution of search engines to the "manipulation" of search results. The
second parameter, which is discussed in the following section, is placed
in the results of a survey about users' attitudes towards searching the
Internet for information.

Directories

The idea of a Web directory goes back to 1994 when Yahoo,[97] the first
directory, was created. The need for a comprehensive "table of contents" of the Web became evident when, just a few months after its creation, Yahoo celebrated its first million-hit day. A simple arrangement of
sites of personal interests by two students in 1994 turned out to become
in less than ten years

> a leading global Internet communications, commerce and media
> company that offers a comprehensive branded network of services
> to more than 237 million individuals each month worldwide. As
> the first online navigational guide to the Web, www.yahoo.com
> is the leading guide in terms of traffic, advertising, household and
> business user reach. Yahoo! is the No. 1 Internet brand globally and
> reaches the largest audience worldwide (Yahoo history 2001).

Since Yahoo's success, a number of directories[98] have been created, all
offering an impressive amount of sites divided in main subject-categories
and each category has been bisected into subcategories. It should be
noticed that directories are edited by humans and not by software
programs, as is the case for search engines. Consequently, each subject
directory has its own character, its own perspective, and that being so, its
own strengths and weaknesses. Although several factors including title,
description, keyword saturation, URL etc., play a determinant role in the
inclusion process, useful and informative content is also a leading component in determining whether or not a website gets listed. All human
edited directories usually include specific guidelines for submission in
their sites, which illustrate to potential "clients" the key elements that their
"under-consideration-site" has to have in order to be included. There

are some epistemological issues here that need to be addressed, in order to explain the inclusion process.

For example, depending on which directory it is submitted to, the reviewing time for a site varies from hours to years as in the case of Yahoo.[99] Yahoo is not the only Web directory; however, being acknowledged as the most popular multiple Web services provider, similar to AOL and getting prominence by all Web development companies in their statements, makes it the perfect example for investigating the pragmatics of directories. Taking into account that Yahoo was, until recently, the biggest directory accounting for over 53 per cent of all Web traffic[100] and that it is the biggest Web portal in terms of popularity and influence, it is plausible to assume that all agents—commercial, governmental, NGOs, religious, political, social and so on—would wish to be listed in its directory. Yet the editor of "Search Engine Watch" estimates that only about a quarter of all sites that apply to Yahoo get listed. This is perhaps attributable to two reasons. Firstly, the editors of Yahoo are overloaded, having hundreds of thousands of sites to review, and secondly, the guiding principles for the design of the submitted sites are extremely detailed.

Despite the fact that non-commercial sites may submit to Yahoo for free, Web development companies' advice is that paying the required fee will speed the review process and may increase the chances of inclusion. Yahoo's "guidelines for submission" section, however, clearly states that the fee simply gurantees consideration of and reply to a request, not necessarily a listing of the site. For example, in order for Yahoo to consider "your" site for inclusion in the directory,

> you must submit a valid credit card number as part of the registration form. You agree that your credit card will be charged the then-current, applicable **NON-REFUNDABLE** fee for expedited review and response. If your site is included, you agree that each year your site will be subject to an additional review for minimum site criteria and your credit card will be charged the **then-current** Annual Fee. Yahoo! reserves the right to remove your site from the Directory for any reason, in our sole discretion, including but not limited to failure to meet the minimum criteria in section 3.0 below.
>
> The current fee for Yahoo! Express for initial consideration in the Directory is a **NON-REFUNDABLE** fee of U.S. $299.00 applicable for each website submitted that does not include adult content and/or services. **If you are submitting a site offering adult content and/or services, the applicable fee for initial consideration in the Directory is a NON-REFUNDABLE FEE of U.S. $600.00.** All adult sites must be submitted to the most appropriate category under Business and Economy/Shopping and Services/Sex. You acknowledge that the payment of this fee is for consideration of your site

AND DOES NOT IN ANY WAY GUARANTEE THAT YOUR SITE WILL BE INCLUDED IN THE DIRECTORY. Your payment only guarantees that Yahoo! will consider and respond to your request within seven business days, by either accepting or not accepting your site. You expressly agree to pay to Yahoo! such fee whether or not your site is accepted or denied inclusion in the Directory.[101]

Apart from the financial demands, Yahoo also expects the site-under-consideration to meet a number of technical and functional criteria, which, as Yahoo states,

ARE MINIMUM REQUIREMENTS ONLY, AND YAHOO!, IN ITS SOLE DISCRETION, MAY CONSIDER OTHER CRITERIA BEFORE ACCEPTING, REJECTING, OR REMOVING A SITE.[102]

Among the different criteria the most striking one is perhaps the compulsory use of the English language. Notwithstanding that Yahoo offers its main site in a number of different languages, its directory sites are exclusively in English, or they must have an English version. What becomes indisputable after a careful analysis of Yahoo's guidelines is that the criteria for inclusion in the directory are ambiguous, leaving, therefore, room for subjective interpretation. This, in conjunction with the statement "Yahoo! reserves the right to decide whether, where, and how a site is listed in the Directory", indicates that Yahoo, alongside AOL and all other directories for that matter, "creates a sense of territory in the electronic frontier, …becomes a separate 'place', a destination for users, which offers a very particular service, an authored online environment" (Patelis 2000, 52). To Patelis' observation it could be added that, placed in this context, and taking into consideration its compulsory use of the English language which indicates cultural imperialism, Yahoo is transformed from a neutral Web portal to a distinct socio-political and cultural online presence that dominates quite a large part of CMC.

While the "big three", AOL.com, Yahoo.com and MSN.com, charge for expediting a submission, this is not the case for the Open Directory Project (OPD[103]), which still reigns as the largest human-edited directory that has not yet changed to paid submissions. ODP, which is hosted and administered by Netscape Communication Corporation, and owned by AOL/Time Warner, relies on a global network of volunteers who examine the sites proposed for submission and decide whether to include them. If one considers that, as of April 2002, the ODP had 3,261,127 sites within the directory, with 47,263 editors managing 46,932 categories,[104] then a number of issues become apparent. First, it is the issue of time (an estimate of five months) lapsing from the moment of submission to the moment of inclusion. However, although time is important (Dodge 2000, 83), in the sense that, by the time the site has been included, its information would probably be outdated, a more significant issue, which applies to all human-edited directories, is the editors' capability for objectivity, or the editors' capability to follow and apply the directory's guidelines consistently (Introna and Nissenbaum 2000, 27). In other words, one has to consider the extent to which the biases, personal preferences and cultural and socio-political frameworks of the editors, determine their decision process—to either include or exclude a site.

Search engines

An estimated 85 per cent of Web users employ search engines to discover the information relevant to their enquiry (Lawrence and Giles 1999). This observation demonstrates the influential power of search engines in the process of locating and retrieving information that "floats" within the chaotic environment of the Web.

Up to 1999 references/resources on the search tools of the Web were focused on the functionality of the search engines and tips on how to perform an effective Web search (Mitchell 1996; Peterson 1996); other works, employing comparative studies, examined the accurateness of specific search engines (Leighton and Srivastava 1997; Chu and Rosenthal 1996; Schlichting and Nilsen 1996). To these academic studies one should add a large number of sites compiled by computer scientists (Marks 1997; Search Engine Watch 1996), which provided similar information remaining within the same parameters of academic presentations, that is, those of functionality, effective retrieval, troubleshooting and guidelines for a successful use of search tools.

The issues for consideration in these works were the technical differences between various search engines, such as: some search engines probe on just directory and file names (the URLs); others also search on titles and headers of HTML pages; and others allow searching on the fulltext of documents. Despite the fact that most of the above-mentioned studies are, in places, highly technical in their subject matter and analysis, their overall conclusion after scrutinizing search engines' meticulousness was that their performance was far from ideal. In fact, Lawrence and Giles' (1999, 108) empirical research shows that "search engines are increasingly falling behind in their efforts to index the Web" and according to their findings, metasearch engines, such as MetaCrawler, substantially improve Web indexing because they combine the results of multiple engines (Lawrence and Giles 1999, 108). Schlichting and Nilsen (1996) reached similar conclusions in their evaluation of the performance of search engines and they indicated the need for a follow-up study which would observe, among other things, how many sites users actually look at when presented with the results of a search query (1996).

Such a survey, conducted in 2002 by iProspect,[105] presented the following results: three-quarters of Internet users use search engines. However, 16 per cent of those only look at the first few search results, while 32 per cent will read through to the bottom of the first page. Only 23 per cent of searchers go beyond the second page, and the numbers drop for every page thereafter. For instance, only 10.3 per cent of Internet users will look through the first three pages of results, while just 8.7 per cent will look through more than three pages. The study also indicates that 52.1 per cent of Internet users choose the same search engine or directory when searching for information, while 35 per cent use different ones. Furthermore, just 13 per cent of users reported that they use different search engines for different types of searches.

If the functionality of retrieval systems, that is, finding sites (indexing) and, placing results on the results pages (ranking), is taken into account, then this survey clearly indicates a number of points: Firstly, it reveals how influential is the role of search engines in retrieving and presenting relevant information. Secondly, as Introna and Nissenbaum (2000, 26) note, if a website is not found by search engines, then its presence can only be found through its URL. However, since the logic behind the formation of URLs (assuming that such a logic exists) is not known, then apparently the website will remain invisible. Finally, it highlights the proficient ability of search engines to guide the users towards particular results (i.e. those on the first results page). In 2000 there was a shift in search engine literature. Studies on the performance of search engines are now including new concepts and the overall approach is leaning more towards political and cultural issues rather than technical, as in the past. This adjustment of exploration was the result of an acknowledgement of the changes that were gradually occurring in the nature of the Web itself. For instance, Goggin (2000, 108) emphasizes that, to date, the infrastructural character of ICTs consists of commercially owned networks that cultivate a market-based approach to both telecommunications worldwide and to computer software.

Indexing. The exponential growth of the Web[106] demanded the design and development of innovatory software, which uses specified algorithms[107] also known as "spiders", "crawlers" and "robots",[108] which would manage the unmanageable undertaking of information discovery. The robots automatically visit and index pages so that they can return good matches for their users' queries. The way that this indexing is done, though, varies from engine to engine, and the details of the algorithms are usually secret, although the strategy is sometimes made public in general terms (Pringle *et al.* 1998). Another necessity, resulting from the proliferation of the Web, was that the functionality of search engines, being overpowered by the number of sites/pages, needed a form of reasoning for locating a site. It should be noted at this point that robot-based search engines' operationality, a complex subject embodying a number of different technical aspects and mathematical calculations, is beyond the scope of this chapter.[109] Rather, a simple and basic presentation of the main features of search engines' indexing provides here an understanding about the political economies of indexing and ranking and consequently their methodological repercussions.

"Crawlers" employ two dominant methods for locating. The first is searching for keywords. For example, Selbach (2002), in his article on search engine optimization, emphasizes the importance of incorporating in the design of a website "many sentences that contain many keywords" relevant to the subject of the website. The validity of this is supported by Pringle *et al.* (1998), who found that some, or all, of the search engines use attributes such as: number of times the keyword occurs in the URL; number of times the keyword occurs in the document title; number of times the keyword occurs in meta fields— typically keyword list and description and so on, when they index a website. Yet, studies on indexing (Lawrence and Giles 1999; Introna and Nissenbaum 2000, and Rogers and Morris 2000) show that search engines also follow links to find new sites. That implies a bias in indexing, because, since the engines follow links to obtain new pages, they are more likely to discover and index pages that have more links to them. The "link economy", Rogers and Morris (2000, 150) and others (Lawrence and Giles 1999; Introna and Nissenbaum 2000) suggest, results, on the one hand, in deeming as "authoritative" sites that have more incoming links than others, and, on the other hand, in biasing the ranking process.

Ranking. The method whereby the ranking process proceeds is of great significance in that, as Introna and Nissenbaum (2000, 30) underline, it intertwines the location of a site in the results' page with its importance (i.e. the sites that are presented in the first result page are more important than those placed in the second, third and so on pages). This, which has been explicated by Cho *et al.* (1998) in a highly technical paper, is based on four parameters and simply points out the following:

The relation of page P to query Q refers to the textual similarity between the page and the query (in keywords). "Backlink count" relates to the "importance" of a page, which is determined by the number of links to that page that appear over the Web. The more sites that are linked to a page, the more "important" it becomes. "Page rank" refers to the variable value of individual links. For example, the backlink metric should treat all links equally. However, since Yahoo's page, for example, has millions of backlinks that page is considered more important, so a link to it is also considered more valuable. In other words, a page is "important" to the extent that other pages, already seen as "important", link to it (Introna and Nissenbaum 2000, 30). "Location metric" refers to a page's location—URL—functionality. For example, depending on the parameters of the robot, URLs ending with .com may be perceived as more "important" than other endings, such as org, or ac. In addition, URLs having less slashes may be either included or excluded and so forth.

Both indexing and ranking are further biasing the accessibility of information on the Web. For example, Lawrence and Giles (1999) point out that the search engines DirectHit and Google make extensive use of "popularity" to rank the relevance of pages (Google uses the number and source of incoming links while DirectHit uses the number of times links have been selected in previous searches). Consequently, this indexing and ranking philosophy pressures Web page design to adopt a particular blueprint, which will be in agreement with the searching parameters of the engines. For instance, search engine optimization companies[110] offer a number of ways to efficiently increase the number of keywords within a website. The issue of "popularity" links was responsible for the creation of "link farms".[111] This practice, however, also referred to as "link stuffing", has been condemned lately by all search engines and they have amended their algorithms in order to recognize "artificial linkage". The fierce competition for high ranking has also generated the availability to websites to buy their way into the search results pages. Companies, such as Search Engine Optimization Centre,[112] offer "Preferred Placement" services and promise that they

> can place your website in top 3-5 results on Google search engine. Statistics show that an average rating for such positioning is 3000-5000 visitors to your website a month,… All you will have to do is to provide us with 5 key-words combinations under which you want your website to be found in the search engine. The cost for a positioning like that starts from $250 a month subject to the popularity of the different key-words combinations.

This "preferred placement", as Rogers and Morris (2000, 150) note, moves "above and beyond" the traditional methods of ranking by granting a larger traffic to those who can afford it. Hence, it becomes an additional issue that has to be taken into account when one researches the Web, especially when it is not clear that the first results are paid placements. Another important point, for both users and researchers, is the issue of affiliations. Most netizens and researchers are not perhaps aware of the fact that although there appears to be a wide selection of directories and search engines, in reality there are only very few because they collaborate with each other, often sharing the same sites.[113]

Final remarks

If "knowledge is power", then, according to Rusciano (2001, 21), "*accurate* knowledge is the only true source of such power". All the previously referenced reports and statistical data on "global and local access", and all the studies, analyses and investigation of the structural and operational features of the Web, indicate that the image of ICTs as an open, free and wholly accessible forum of information exchange is far from reality. Rather, as Rusciano (2001, 21) emphasizes, it has become the manifestation of an emerging form of economic cyberimperialism, governed by a technically literate elite who have mastered the art of selling access, information and advice on how to use ICTs, especially the Web. A traditional website attempts to organize related information about a particular topic, organization and/or service in a logical way that makes it easy for visitors to find what they are looking for.

The technological aspects of search engines and their functional limitations are not so much of a concern as the designers' and developers' decisions on how to tackle these limitations, and where to direct search engines' future development. For Introna and Nissenbaum (2000, 25), the decisions are political issues, for they can determine either the systematic prominence of some sites or the systematic exclusion of others. Consequently, knowing how search systems operate offers a significant understanding of what one is able to find. Since search engines and directories also sell prominence, websites can bypass the various time-consuming and uncertain inclusion processes by buying their way inwards and upwards, then, clearly, the diversity of the Web content is seriously questionable.

4 Theory

Introduction

Since its development and rapid expansion, the Internet and its by-products (WWW and cyberspace) have generated a considerable number of discourses which derive from its capacity to initiate new forms, not only of communication but also of socio-economic, cultural and political interactions.

Although sometimes exaggerated,[1] Internet rhetoric presents a number of approaches to, and perceptions of, the medium's actual and potential functionalities, which address their socio-economic and political ideas, as well as their religious, cultural and metaphysical concepts. Statements such as the "unprecedented impact of technology on society and culture"; the "magnitude of the Internet"; the "new social, economic and political transformations"; and the "globalization of resources and commerce" are, although to a lesser degree[2] than before, still in the agenda of policy makers,[3] academic institutions[4] and society in general. These approaches and perceptions comprise the conceptual body upon which different agents have based their cybertheoretical foundation. In order to develop an understanding of why the different religions, individuals, New Religious Movements (NRMs) and so forth are using the Web in the way they do, it is necessary to examine the diverse theories and perceptions of communication, technology and cyberspace.

The main purpose of this part of the study is, therefore, to provide a succinct account of the theoretical framework found in both academic and popular discourses, and also to examine the extent to which the socio-political and religious theories that circumscribe digital technologies may explain:

1. The embracement of ICTs, especially the Web, by institutionalized religions, non-institutionalized religions and NRMs, and the form of this embracement.
2. The creation of new religious/spiritual/philosophical cyber-utterances which, completely distinct from the familiar established forms of the world's religions, open new windows for the development of imaginative religious convictions, beliefs, practices and interactions.

In order to examine the above issues it is necessary to look at two main areas. The first is how technology in general is perceived and comprehended, which leads to an understanding of socio-political, economic and cultural responses. The second is the relationship of technology with religion, which leads to an understanding of religious, spiritual and metaphysical responses. For example, the exponential growth of the Internet has led to the genesis of: (a) a number of conceptions expressed in the techno-political discourses of technological mysticism (Stahl 1999), technoromanticism (Coyne 1999), cyberimperialism (Ebo 2001) and mythinformation (Winner 1986), and (b) a number of myths expressed in the techno-cultural discourses, which instigate a particular techno-religious/spiritual rhetoric ascribing to the Internet and cyberspace the qualities of sacred, holy, spiritual (Cobb 1998), Heavenly city (Benedikt 1991) and New Jerusalem (Wertheim 1999).

It is evident that Internet operation exists, to a greater or lesser degree, in all latitudes and longitudes of the world. However, it was conceived, materialized and began its expansion as a popular means of accessing information and communication in the USA. Today, despite the fact that parts of the world are well "wired", it is still the case that the vast majority of Internet users are citizens of the USA; it is therefore legitimate to concentrate on the theories and attitudes actually developed in North America, and characterize them as foundational to the theoretical cyberspatial discourse, even though the past may not turn out to be a reliable guide to the future.

Structure of the chapter

The chapter is divided into five sections, each of which addresses theoretical issues, perceptions and analyses of each of the areas that have been identified as important, for they are integral parts of the subject matter of this study. Consequently, theories of communication; technology in general; religion and technology; ICTs and cyberspace; and religion and cyberspace are explored.

Communication

The term "communication technologies" (CT), which incorporates all means and mediums of communication, including computer mediated communication, needs deconstructive unpicking in order to reveal all of its elements, its characteristics, its possibilities and its consequences.

The important role of communication technologies in influencing and shaping the development of society has been recognized by a number of communication theorists. For example, Craig (1999, 125) states that communication is a principal constitutive social process that explains psychological, sociological, cultural and economic factors. Moreover, Carey (1989, 86) understands communication to be a conglomeration of social practices, which is at once "a structure of human action—activity, process, practice—an ensemble of expressive forms, and a structured and structuring set of social relations". Innis (1951, 3) goes even further by suggesting that "...Western civilization has been influenced by communication" and that "marked changes in communications have had important implications". Communication, as a signifier, corresponds to a number of different signifieds. For example, communication is "the exchange of information"; the "use of common system of symbols"; a "verbal or written message"; a "system for communicating" (e.g. the telephones); a "system of routes for moving troops"; "techniques for the effective transmission of information, ideas, etc". (*Penguin Dictionary* 2000). Carey (1989, 15) explains that in the nineteenth century the transportation of commodities or people and the transmission of information were seen as identical processes, so both were defined by the term communication.

Fore asserts that all definitions found in a dictionary deal with communication as something that takes place between two or more people or things, leaving thus "communication as a relationship" between people and things totally unexamined. In his proposed definition, Fore perceives communication as "the process in which relationships are established, maintained, modified or terminated through the increase or reduction of meaning" (Fore 1987). In other words, Fore's definition provides the tools with which the process of communication can be scrutinized in such a way that all participating agents are included, the ways they affect and are affected, as well as the alterations and modifications of messages which can get either charged or emptied of meaning as the process, and all contenders involved in it, ceaselessly change. Heath and Bryant also perceive communication as a process which is in a constant state of change because of the divergent ways people use it (Heath and Bryant 2000, vii).

These conceptualizations of communication correspond to the complexity of the concept. Instead of a linear and one-dimensional representation of communication they demonstrate the multifaceted, complicated and multi-sensory character of the act, as well as that of the different means and mediums of communication. The complexity of communication is conveyed in the great number of theories that have been developed on the subject;[5] however, here is offered a brief and a concise account of the diverse perceptions of and approaches to communication, with the scope to provide a basic understanding of the concept and its applications.

Communication theories

Harold Innis, who examined the social history of communication by studying communication media of the last 4000 years, maintained that a key to social change is found in the development of communication media. In his study, Innis differentiates communication media as "time-biased" and "space-biased" (1951, 33). Time-biased media are resilient and weighty; they therefore have an extended life, which consequently means that their message remains intact over time. In contrast to those are the space-biased media which, being insubstantial and moveable, can therefore be transported over great distances. This suggests that the bias of media is in fact related to the propensity of the message to survive transmission and to have an impact over and beyond time and space.

Taking as an example stone, Soules (1996) explains that it is not so much the weight of stone that makes it a time-biased medium, but rather its capacity to resist the elements so that it may communicate its message through time. Correspondingly, space-biased media, such as paper, are capable of communicating their message through space. Innis connects his theory of communication media with the "monopolies of knowledge" that are prone to divide societies into those who are knowledgeable and those who are ignorant (1951, 4). Moreover, monopolies of knowledge support centralization of power and control, as for example the case of the educated priesthood and the illiterate population in the Middle Ages. Innis' time and space-biased media have been analysed in terms of what type of social structure they encourage and support. For example, time-biased media, such as orality and manuscript, were related to small, closed communities, democracy, dialectic and transcendental theorization (Innis, 9–10; Carey 1989, 134). In contrast, space-biased media such as print and electricity are connected to religious establishments, aristocracy, creation of empires and/or states, commercialism and technocracy (Innis, 49–50, 129; Carey, 134). For Innis, learning about other civilizations depends to a great extent on the nature of the media espoused by these civilizations, which in turn determines the "character of knowledge" they disseminate, not only in the initial sending but in our consequent reception as well (Innis, 34). Soules (1996) points out that McLuhan's famous "the medium is the message" derives from this idea.

One of the most commonly adopted theories of communication is the "transmission" theory, in which communication is simply defined as a process of sending and receiving messages or transferring information from one mind to another (Craig 1999, 124). In recent years scholars have tended to favour the "constitutive" model, which understands communication to be a constitutive process that produces and reproduces shared meaning (Craig 1999, 125). Interpreting communication as "ritual", which according to Craig is another definition for the constitutive approach (1999, 124), associates the concept with expressions such as sharing, fellowship, participation and "the possession of common faith". In this view communication not only concentrates on the preservation of society in time, but is also seen as an act which denotes shared beliefs (Carey 1989, 18). The difference, therefore, between the "transmission" and the "constitutive/ritual" models is that while the former focuses on the spreading of messages over space with the intention of control, the latter focuses on the ceremonial act which brings people together in fraternization and commonality (Carey 1989, 18). As a result, the reading and writing of messages is viewed as a dramatic ceremonial act which is not only a simple piece of information, but, in Carey's own words, a "portrayal of the contending forces of the world" (1989, 20).

A socio-cultural viewpoint on communication theory perceives communication as a process/activity which constructs and reconstructs social order (Carey 1989, 23), while a semiotic outlook appreciates communication as a symbol mediation process which explains and promotes the use of language as well as other sign systems to arbitrate between different perspectives (Craig 1999, 144, 136). In the phenomenological tradition communication is apprehended as the "experience of otherness". In this way, when subjected to a theoretical approach, communication elucidates the interaction of identity and difference in genuine human relationships and develops particular communication practices that facilitate and nourish authentic relationships (Craig 1999, 138).

The socio-psychological model views communication as the process by which individuals interact, express themselves and influence one another. This is achieved by the mediation of social and psychological tendencies such as emotional states, social and political attitudes, unwitting conflicts, biases and prejudices as these are adjusted by the social interaction (Craig 1999, 141–43). The cybernetic theory of communication interprets communication as information processing. For cybernetics, according to Craig, the "distinction between mind and matter is only a functional distinction like that between software and hardware" (1999, 141). Consequently, thought is nothing more than information processing; it makes sense therefore to suggest that individual thought is "intrapersonal" communication. Furthermore, it is also plausible to suggest that "groups think, whole societies think, robots and artificial organizations will eventually think" (Craig 1999, 141). Although the cybernetic approach reduces communication to mere function by stripping off all elements ascribed to it by the other views of communication, it does not imply simplicity. On the contrary, cybernetic theory challenges most assumptions about human and non-human information processes, contests simplistic views of communication and clearly indicates that communicational activities are far more complicated than they appear to be.

Craig (1999, 151) maintains that communication is open to any theoretical approach such as: feminist, where communication could be seen as connectedness; aesthetic, in which communication could be theorized as "embodied performance"; economic, in which communication could be interpreted as "exchange"; and spiritual, where communication could be understood as "communion on a non-material plane of existence". Similarly, Fore, believing that communication is the common denominator of all religious activities (Fore 1993, 55), offers a theological approach which attempts to articulate what communication "is all about", in the context of "what the world is all about" (Fore 1987). In his theology of communication, Fore suggests that communication is a fundamental part of human beings, their experiences and their relationships. Communication, therefore, according to Fore, is the "mechanism that connects the past, present and future" (Fore 1987). Focusing on the nature and content of Christian communication, Fore pinpoints that for the average Christian, communication is about testimony, evangelism, talking about how each perceives society, faith, practice and God. Yet, it could be suggested that this theological approach to communication could be easily applicable to any other system of beliefs, whether they are theistic or not.

The overall theoretical framework within which the concept of communication is placed has raised a number of issues. As regards contemporary communication technologies, it is as yet too early to suggest or predict how they will shape the "character of knowledge" of civilization. CMC can be defined as both a time and a space-biased medium because it has not only diminished spatial boundaries, but it has also the ability to preserve information through time.[6] Undoubtedly, CMC has altered our conception of time and space by virtue of its ability to make both appear either irrelevant or non-existent within its realm. However, it is important to remember that this irrelevancy exists only as long as we are "online", as long as we are "connected". Despite this, people (especially those who are older and computer illiterate) refer to CMC with the same amazement shown by people who are ignorant of writing, when they first become aware of the ability of individuals separated by space to communicate with one another via "talking leaves" (Harbameier, cited in Couch 1996, 171).

Equally astonishing was "disembodied speech" which, until the invention of the telephone, was considered a supernatural phenomenon, an ability possessed only by God, the dead and devils (Couch 1996, 171). The notion of disembodiment is a powerful component of religious e-discourse and, as will be shown later on, the belief that cyberspace has the capacity to offer eternal life is widely spread among computopian netizens. The idea of "disembodied speech", a key element of CMC, has altered the basic way of communicating. With only a few exceptions,[7] which are currently available to a small number of specialized users, until now and for the majority of Internet users, CMC mostly occurs as textual interaction which removes any personal information, such as gender, race, socio-economic status, physical features, tone of voice, body language and facial expression. This results in the "rehierar-chisation of communication based on criteria that were previously irrel-evant" (Poster, as quoted in Aoki 1994).[8] People, for example, in their personal communications, tend to focus on the message more than the messenger, and the availability of an archived transcript of the proceed-ings facilitates review of previous comments and discussion, focusing on important ideas and concepts (Aoki 1994). This is possible because interpersonal CMC is mostly anonymous, especially within the environ-ments of network places, such as chat rooms, MSN, MOOs, MUDs, BBSs and email lists.

One could suggest that the irrelevancy of the messenger is culturally determined, in the sense that while in the West the text may become depersonalized, separated thus from its sender, this is not the case for a traditional "Oriental" understanding where the text is entirely tied to its originator. The latter, however, is feasible only when the true identity of the sender is known. Because of the nature of communication via the Internet, which removes physical co-presence, participants are able to reinvent themselves. McKenna and Bargh state that when interacting with undisclosed others on the Internet, people tend either to conceal their non-mainstream inclinations (1999, 257), or to present qualities of their ideal self (1999, 259), or to create an imaginary new self alto-gether.

The Internet as a communication medium, apart from challenging centres of centralized power and control by offering equal opportuni-ties to its users to have their input (Warschauer 2002; De Vaney et al. 2000), has also introduced new aspects to all forms of communication, such as informality and new linguistic formations. For example, "con-nected" people, with the help of CMC, generate new subjectivities for a new type of citizenship based not on a common socio-cultural back-ground but on shared values, interests, ideologies and belief systems. Theorizing communication is an open-ended process for, as has been shown, the concept constantly changes as the technologies that facili-tate its manifestation change.

Communication is an essential process of existence. CT and CMC have brought changes to almost all areas of communicating. Contemporary communication technologies have shattered the traditional relationship between medium and audience. The "silent" audience which passively received the transmitted messages of long-established forms of mass mediated communication is progressively becoming active through the ability to participate, feedback and interact. This is possible because today's mass communication media (TV and radio) are shifting towards an interactive model which Heath and Bryant (2000, 377) call "transactional mediated communication" because it implies "an interpersonal communication relationship in which parties alternate in their roles as sender, receiver, and information processor and thereby exchange information". What seems to be the case is that, being in a constant flux of technological advancements, we need constantly to revise existing communication theories, to re-evaluate models of communication and to redefine terms and concepts.

The different theories of communication presented offer a valuable blueprint for identifying the views and tendencies of different religions towards communication via their website. Analysing a particular religion's website, focusing on its communicational aspects, one can discover that religion's standpoint regarding communicating with its followers, with other religions and/or with other socio-political bodies.[9]

Theories of Technology

What emerges from all academic and/or popular narratives on CMC, digital technologies, the Internet, the Web and cyberspace, is a series of concepts, impressions, interpretations and perspectives of ICTs which express and/or represent a political, social, economic and cultural *Weltanschauung*. Any attempt, therefore, to map the various religious landscapes and the emergent religious phenomena as they appear online, requires an examination of the theoretical structures of that particular *Weltanschauung*, if the roots of the relationship between religion and ICTs are to be contextualized.

Established theories of technology are developed within two main genres: the instrumental and the substantive. Authors such as Feenberg (1991), McOmber (1999) and Kellner (1999),[10] among others, have explored these views of technology, each adopting a different approach. While Feenberg employs a philosophical investigation, McOmber and Kellner embark on an analysis of conceptions and/or definitions of technology from a politico-economical perspective.

In instrumental theory, which according to Feenberg (1991, 5) reflects the prevailing view of modern governments and the "policy science on which they rely", technology is seen as a tool existing primarily for the service of its users. Instrumental theory, which is the most widely accepted, perceives technology as "neutral", that is, without evaluative content of its own, which implies that something becomes technology purely because of its position as a tool (McOmber 1999, 141). For the advocates of the instrumental theory of technology, as Pacey (1992, 2) indicates, when technology fails them or when it has negative consequences, it is not technology that is at fault, but the improper use of it by "politicians, the military, big business, and others".

Technology—as a mere tool—having no concern with the different objectives that it can be used to obtain, becomes amoral. This, according to Feenberg (1991, 6), means that technological tools are only by chance "related to the substantive values they serve". Additionally, within the frame of instrumentality, technology stands indifferent to politics, promoting thus the notion that any devices are functional in any socio-political context. Feenberg (1991, 6) explains that the socio-political neutrality of technology is the result of its "rational" and "universal character", which explains why a particular technology is expected to operate equally well in one society as in another. In this respect technology is independent from culture and can continue to be efficient in distinct eras, countries and cultures. McOmber (1999, 140), however, points out that the intention served by any given technology is, to a greater extent, imposed by the blueprint—that is, the overall design—of this technology and, to a lesser extent, decided by its users.

Another interesting and important element of instrumental theory, according to McOmber (1999, 141), is that its narratives emphasize the principal interconnectedness that steers technological advancements. Examples of such narratives can be found in the advertising discourse of Lockheed, where each new technology is linked with a technological achievement of the distant past, including "Stonehenge and the Space Telescope", "The Tower of Babel and Systems Integration", and "Ming Dynasty and the Space Station" (Hearit, as quoted in McOmber 1999, 140). Each example implies continuity in the process of technological development and, although the space telescope is far more complicated than Stonehenge, that the driving force for constructing the two implementations was nevertheless much the same, or to use McOmber's own words "[t]he more things change, the titles suggested, the more they stay the same" (McOmber 1999, 142).

In contrast to instrumental theory is substantive theory, mainly expressed in the perspectives of Ellul and Heidegger. The substantive theory, rejecting technology's neutrality, perceives it not as a tool, but as an environment, as a "new type of cultural system" (Feenberg 1991, 5) and a way of life, having therefore a substantive impact on society. While instrumental theory sees technology as obedient to established social, political and cultural values, substantive theory ascribes a self-ruling cultural power to technology that overrules all traditional or competing values. Substantive theory maintains, in Feenberg's (1991, 5) opinion, that "what the very employment of technology does to humanity and nature is more consequential than its ostensible goals". While, as mentioned earlier, in instrumental theory technology is regarded as "neutral", substantive considers it as an original variety of a cultural system that completely reorganizes the social world as an "object of control" (7). In this respect technology overtakes culture, politics and society and reconfigures the social milieu. The resulting "instrumentalization of society" (7) becomes thus a destiny from which the only escape is withdrawal.

This theoretical perspective depicts a pessimistic or technophobic view of technology, and is often defined as technological determinism. Proponents of technological determinism, such as Ellul and Heidegger, interpret technology as the foundation of society. Ellul (1964, 14) goes even further, suggesting that the "technical phenomenon" has turned out to be the describing attribute of all modern societies irrespective of political ideologies. According to Ellul's (1964, 6) understanding, technology "has become autonomous" from the socio-cultural environment in which it finds itself. This clearly points to a number of issues, as Feenberg (2000) notes, such as, that the technological devices people use determine their way of life; that means and ends cannot be separated; and that the manner in which people undertake their affairs determine who and what they are, or to employ Feenberg's own words "technological development transforms what it is to be human" (2000).

McOmber (1999, 142) addresses the issue of technological determinism in his analysis of the different approaches to technology, but he characterizes the substantive view as a "definition of technology", calling it "technology as industrialization". Indicating that for a number of scholars the "technology age" came into being in the eighteenth, and the beginning of the nineteenth century, thus placing technology alongside the industrialization of the West, McOmber (142) not only justifies his definition but also adds a Marxist dimension to the debate. Technology, in this sense, is the outcome of a process that took place at a particular historical moment and in a particular locale. Consequently, McOmber (1999, 143) notes that by referring to non-technological cultures as "preindustrial", it is implied that in due course those cultures will become industrialized. Such an account, in his reckoning, indicates "discontinuity", making technology therefore "as much an event as a set of practices or objects" (143). This outlook reinforces the standpoint of the polemics of technology that connect the rise of the technological age to technology becoming the influential power behind social change.

The difference between the two theories lies in the actual perspective from which each views technology. While instrumental theory disregards any socio-cultural implications of technology and focuses on its efficiency, which in other words means a progression from tradition to modernity, substantive theory underlines technology's cultural character, by stressing that in deciding to employ technological tools, we perform an unconscious cultural choice (Feenberg 1991, 7).

Information communication technologies

While instrumental and substantive theories have been analysed in terms of their applicability to technology in general, they are recruited also in discourses about contemporary technological advancements, especially with reference to computer technology and the Internet. Feenberg, in his *Critical Theory of Technology* (1991), posing the question whether technology is able to better attend to the needs of its creators, opens the way for a discussion of the extent to which technology can be characterized either as neutral or as deterministic. Kellner (1999), on the other hand, paying attention to "new technologies", pilots his concern on how the changes that technological advancements bring about in all aspects of life can be theorized without descending either into technological determinism or into a technophilic or technophobic mode.

Feenberg (1991, 14) succeeds in avoiding either a utopian or dystopian vision of technological development by employing what he calls "technological indeterminism", a frame of reference whereby technology becomes a setting of social contention. Even so, Feenberg's "indeterminism" refers to an alternative theory of technology—Critical Theory of Technology (CTT), which argues that the actual question is not technology or development *per se*, but the diversity of probable technologies and directions of development among which we must choose (1991, 14). However, especially regarding computer technologies, he is well aware of the fact that there is a tension between the design option process and the restraints placed on this process by the larger socio-political and economic milieu. Thus, in the critical theory he proposes, Feenberg (1991, 14) defines this tension as an "ambivalent" action of progress suspended between various possibilities. This perception differentiates technology from neutrality because it applies features of social values more to the design than to the application. Technology in this sense is not a destiny any more, but becomes what Feenberg (14) calls a "parliament of things on which civilizational alternatives are debated and decided". He summarizes this "ambivalence" in two principles that describe the social consequences of technological development: the "principle of the conservation of hierarchy" and the "principle of subversive rationalization" (92). The first principle explains how social hierarchy can, by and large, be sustained and reproduced as new technologies are launched, while the latter shows that new technologies can also be used to subvert the existing social hierarchy, by giving voice to those who are marginalized.

As has been shown, critical narratives about digital technology, as for any technology for that matter, fall into two well-known categories: the technophilic vs. technophobic, also known as computopian vs. computropian discourses (Hakken 1999, 17). Few, however, express a purely neutral view as for example Carey and Quirk (1989, 139), who in the *Mythos of the Electronic Revolution*, writes, "[e]lectronics is neither the arrival of apocalypse nor the dispensation of grace. Technology is technology; it is a means for communication and transportation over space, and nothing more". Quirk does not ascribe any evaluative character to technology and he believes that a demythologization of the "electronic sublime" is necessary. Yet as McOmber (1999), Birdsall (1996) and Kellner (1999) demonstrate, Internet technologies are closely interwoven with political and economic interests which, they argue, are responsible for the hyperbolic and overenthusiastic promotion of digital technologies.

Kellner (1999), along with Feenberg, holds the view that technology is socially constructed and that particular societal prejudices and interests are embedded in technological structures. Agreeing with Feenberg's position, Kellner underlines the necessity for a critical theory of technology. Presenting both computopian and computropian discourses, he points out their narrow view of ICTs and puts forward his version of a critical theory of technology. According to Kellner (1999), the best way of circumventing technophobic or technophilic approaches to ICTs is to investigate the so-called "information or knowledge revolution" as being a component of a new form of techno-capitalism which is the product of the union between the information and entertainment industries that produces what Kellner calls "infotainment society" (1999). In his analysis, Kellner connects the utopian narratives about IT, which promote and promise radical changes in all levels of life, with a global restructuring of capitalism and concludes that these narratives give rise to a particular ideology. Furthermore, Birdsall (1996) argues that the statements of the advocates of ICTs, those being governmental agencies, futurists, popular culturists, academics, or computer specialists, derive from a consistent political ideology which he calls "the Ideology of Information Technology".

McOmber (1999), focusing on recently developed technologies, offers a new perspective. In addition to instrumental and substantive theories he proposes a theory in which technology is perceived as "novelty" with the political, social and economic implications that derive from such a conception. Analysing technology as novelty, McOmber (1999, 143) explains that this perception shows a rhetoric of technological development that is neither continuous nor discontinuous, since today's technology has replaced an older one and that that same technology will be replaced by another one in the future. This, according to McOmber, results in an "ahistorical" (143) discourse about ICT which, on the one hand removes ICT from its historical and cultural setting and on the other hand, by reducing it to a mere revolutionary new technology, offers the opportunity to the oracles of technological utopianism to claim that all socio-political and economic problems will be eliminated (1999, 143). McOmber underlines another interesting feature of the novelty view, by suggesting that for those who espouse it, the novelty perception of technology also presents a tendency whereby it becomes a "synecdoche for entire cultures or subcultures" (1999, 143).

It would appear that both the USA, especially under the Clinton administration, and the British Labour governments, particularly in recent years, have deployed national and international campaigns promoting the unprecedented significance of ICT and the benefits it brings, promising more jobs, economic opportunities, better education, better entertainment; in other words, a better world. For example, as Birdsall shows, the creation of a National Information Infrastructure was such a priority for the Clinton administration that in 1993 a document of the Department of Commerce proclaimed that "America's destiny is linked to our information infrastructure".[11] Historical accounts of the Internet place its development in the early sixties and, according to Birdsall, the formation of the Ideology of Information Technology begins at the same time. Gradually, the notion that we move from a manufacturing economy to a "technologically driven information processing" one became a global phenomenon (Birdsall 1996). This amalgamation of ICTs, politics and economics in the USA was intensified by the works[12] of those who declared that technology was steering us from a "Second Wave industrial society into a high-tech, post industrial, Third Wave, Information Society" (Birdsall 1996).

A very similar discourse is found on the British government's website. At No 10, the view of the Labour government regarding ICTs, as well as ICTs' political, economic and social implications, changes and benefits, are clearly pronounced. Following America's fascination with ICTs, No. 10 advertises, explains, promotes and supports its adaptation of digital technologies, inviting all British citizens to be active members of the info-revolution.

Stating that

> The Internet is revolutionising our whole way of life. The way we
> work, communicate, shop, play and get the news are all being
> radically changed by the worldwide web (*sic*) (2000, http://www.
> pm.gov.uk/output/Page1.asp)

the governmental site, presenting statistics of UK household users, statistics of business users, the advanced services offered online by public
sector and the economic benefits and social changes for all, projects
exactly the same highly optimistic outlook on IT. Prime Minister Blair,
stating that "today we need the spirit of adventure more than ever"
(1999),[13] indicates that it is of paramount importance to be competitive
in the technological race and calls upon British entrepreneurs to follow
the example of Bill Gates and other Internet businessmen who operate
their business in "Internet years" (Blair 1999). The government's discourse, including its belief that both the national and international
digital divide can be diminished, clearly suggests that perhaps a possible
way towards socio-economic evolution is through ICTs.

Governmental views of ICTs, as well as the views of industrialists and
transnational entrepreneurs, on both sides of the Atlantic, are summarized in Winner's (1989, 105) notion of "mythinformation" which is

> the almost religious conviction that a wide spread adoption of
> computers and communications systems, along with broad access
> to electronic information will automatically produce a better world
> for human living.

These perceptions and convictions, as we have seen, result in the formation of particular ideologies. Barbrook and Cameron (1995) criticize the
ideals, principles and creeds of the computopian narrative of America's
West Coast—the so-called "Californian Ideology"—which, according to
the authors, link overexcited enthusiasm for electronically transmitted
forms of living with radical, right-wing libertarian ideas about the proper
definition of freedom, social life, economics and politics in the years to
come. The seemingly inexorable march of advanced digital technologies,
and their embracing, mostly by the western societies, poses a number of
questions regarding the face of cyberimperialism (Rusciano 2001).

The theoretical discourses presented here offer a variety of compre-
hensions and conceptualizations of technology and of technological
development, focusing their analyses on technology's socio-political and
economic implications, influences and changes. However, the implementation of a hermeneutical exegesis of discourses about ICTs, especially of cyberspace, indicates an emerging linguistic pattern of similes
and metaphors, highly invested with religious and spiritual meaning,

which assign the quality of the sacred to cyberspace in a significant way. Yet, these explicit or implicit discursive practices of the techno-philic digerati and popular culture are not expressions of an original and unconventional understanding and/or interpretation of technology, but, as the following section shows, continuations of a pre-existing religious and theological discourse surrounding technological advancements that dates back at least to the beginning of the Christian era.

Religion and Technology

Introduction

In order to establish the nature of religion as it presents itself within the domain of ICTs it is necessary to examine the relationship between religion and technology. Although the two might seem incompatible, a historical retrospection provides enough evidence to support Noble's (1997, 5) view that technology and contemporary faith are, and always have been, amalgamated; the "technological enterprise being, at the same time, an essentially religious endeavour". Moreover, Newman (1997, 1), stressing that the historical and prehistorical relations between technology and culture are usually ignored, states that for a number of cultural theorists, technology is perceived as having "more cultural significance than religion".

Contrary to the common belief that religion and technology are incompatible, evidence suggests that behind Western technological advancements there is a deep religious foundation which has motivated the development of both science and technology. In a sense, the relationship of religion with technology could be perceived as representing the effort to discover the Truth about the human condition, an effort which takes two different forms. On the one hand, there are those who are certain that the discovery of Truth will be achieved through the scientific investigation of phenomena, and, on the other hand, there are those who are certain that the Truth can only be discovered through absolute faith in divine powers and realms that cannot be reached via the senses.

Although the two approaches may appear to contradict each other, the works of Noble (1997) and Newman (1997) indicate that in reality the two are closely intertwined. This can be seen in the use of the latest technological tools for the promotion of religious ideas by different religious leaders, and by the scientists' and technologists' admissions that their efforts point to the pursuit of divine knowledge (Noble 1997, 3). Bauwens and Rossi (1999), in agreement with Noble, understand the technological quest to be a spiritual quest and base their view on the historical narrative of human civilization. The premise "the technological quest is a spiritual quest" is based on human desire to explore their relationship with the "totality" of existence, which, historically, Bauwens explains, has been defined by the opposing trends of "spiritual transhumanism" and "materialistic or technological transhumanism". While, initially, humanity's choice was that the transcendental "supernatural" reality could be reached by inner development, from the Renaissance onwards there is a shift in the Christian West, and instead of endeavouring to reach the transcendent through spiritual processes, the means of spiritual development became science and technology (Bauwens and Rossi 1999). Noble (1997, 9), who characterizes this cultural shift as "profound", locates it in the European Middle Ages and asserts that technological innovations began to be perceived as expressions of the transcendent itself.

This perception of technology, which, according to Noble, was exclusively Christian and elevated humans in the divine pantheon, may have its origin in the creation of the heavy plough that profoundly altered humans' place in nature, in that while humans used to be part of nature, now they became exploiters of it (White 1971, in Noble, 12). Humanity's basic yearning (Bauwens and Rossi 1999; Noble 1997) for the "supernatural" reality is interpreted by Miyake (2002) as "religious passion", embodied in the shaman or priest that existed in every prehistorical culture as the "person of religion", who was the only one having a specialized "job" in the primitive community. Thus, Miyake concludes, religions could be seen as the "earliest information business".

Anti-technological views

Technological advancements may have been perceived and promoted as aids to religious and spiritual ends at the beginning of the last millennium, or even earlier. However, in the first part of the last century a number of theologians and philosophers expressed a strong anti-technological discourse that Newman (1997) calls the "religious antitechnology movement". An extended analysis of the anti-technological discourses is beyond the scope of this study. It is useful, however, to have at least a basic awareness of the anti-technological tendencies that have been developed regarding issues arising from the intersection of religion and technology which may also be found in the contemporary discourses on religion and ICTs.

The primary figure in this movement is Jacques Ellul.[14] His work *The Technological Society* (1964) has been the most influential anti-technological study and has been used as a reference point in almost all works criticizing technology. Ellul's perceptions and critiques of technology are presented in all his works, in which he develops his theoretical anti-technological discourse. Briefly, Ellul (1964)[15] viewed technology as autonomous, that is, as a system with no regulation, within which "man has lost all contact with his natural framework" (ibid.). In summary, Ellul claims that the key characteristics of technology are rationality, artificiality, automatism of technical choice, monism and autonomy. Understood as such, technology is "more than a simple mechanism—it is a whole civilization in itself".[16] The object of his most forceful criticism is the "technician" who, because of his profession uses "technique", but in such a way that expresses his adoration which derives from the fact that for the technician "technique is the locus of the sacred" (Ellul 1964, 144, in Newman, 20). Ellul presents his theological understanding of technology in *The Meaning of the City* (1970 in Newman 1997, 22), in which he characterizes Cain as the "founder of craftsmanship", who by "carving stones thereby made them impure and unfit for use in an altar of God". However, it seems that Ellul disregarded the fact that this very same technical activity (carving stones), has been interpreted as the epitome of the relationship between religion and technology, as will be shown later.

The anti-technological literature offers a wide range of critiques deriving from theologians in which technology is understood: as society's "contemporary snake" (Schrader 1990, in Newman, 14); as a "demonic quasi-religion" (Thomas 1990, in Newman, 14); as "demonic" if it is not "tampered and shaped by religion" (Gilkey 1979, in Newman, 10); as the "force [which] is now at work to change the whole face of the earth and dehumanise and depersonalize man" (Berdyaew 1935, in Newman, 15). Yet, interestingly enough, these theologians, with their passionate writings about the destructive effects of technology on religion's cultural and spiritual importance, seem to have neglected to notice the fact that elaborate mechanical devices were used as torture tools by the Inquisition, which, as Newman (1997, 31) points out, could be seen as the ways in which "religion has corrupted technology".

Although religious anti-technological literature has an apologetic framework and perceives technology as creating deep social and moral problems, Newman (1997, 110) suggests that technology's contribution to the enrichment of particular categories of freedom and knowledge[17] offers the opportunity to think of technology as a collaborator, or even as a "substitution" of religion. This perception is supported by both Noble and Newman, whose heavily referenced works offer a wealth of information on the subject.

Technology and the Scripture

Historical accounts of different societies show that religion and technology were closely associated, if not completely amalgamated. For instance, in Mesopotamia the temple school educated pupils in both "mathematics and religious mysteries" (Forbes 1967, in Newman 1997, 113). Additionally, Forbes continues, the craftsmen, according to ancient texts, were members of guilds that were first and foremost "religious organizations devoted to the worship of the patron-god". Consequently, any technical "activities were joined to religious rites and ceremonies".

Religious scriptures could be characterized as being the first material evidence of the relation of technology to religion. Examples of such manifestations can be seen in the technology of writing on stone and on clay in Sumeria, and on papyrus in Egypt that were used for the production of holy books (Feibleman 1982, in Newman 1997, 113). Moreover, scholars who have been investigating various approaches of technological implementations, point out that the Hebrew Scriptures clearly reveal a positive attitude to technology. For instance, Florman (1976, in Newman, 115) emphasizes that the Bible is full of "walls, towers, palaces and gates"; that notwithstanding the fact of the desert environment within which the narrative of the Bible takes place, one finds a number of descriptions of "fountains, pools, wells and gardens". Furthermore, the detailed descriptions in the Bible of the construction of Noah's ark and of the construction of the Temple, according to Florman, support not only the acceptance of technology, but also a desire for exquisite craftsmanship and beauty.

The passages in the Bible are interpreted as signifying, on the one hand, that "human achievement is a sign of God's actions in the world" (Morel 1964, in Newman, 116) and, on the other hand, that "technology…is a sign of salvation"[18] (Schuurman 1984, in Newman, 116). Yet, as Newman indicates (117–18), although it is clear that the Torah is about God's commandments and laws, which people should follow, it also possesses another aspect that has been neglected; that is, that the directions provided in the Torah often take the form of the "master Creator-Craftsman" directing students and apprentices on how to perform tasks, both religious and worldly. Typical examples of such instructions can be found in Exodus,[19] where God himself "teaches" to man the insights and erudition for technological constructions.[20] It should be noted that the Torah begins by representing God as Creator-Craftsman,[21] who progressively creates an extraordinary and complicated Cosmos.

The Scripture also incorporates accounts of misuse and abuse of technological knowledge, in that certain technical activities, such as the building of the Tower of Babel[22] and the crafting of the molten calf[23] represent disobedience, disrespect and rejection of God, as well as "vanity, infidelity… [and] the diminution of the essential dignity of human achievement" (Newman 1997, 118). The construction of the idol—a product of human technology—underlines, according to Newman (119), that the urge and desire of humans to advance their knowledge and their power of creating can reach such levels that they believe that the spiritual context, within which their activities become meaningful, is no longer necessary.

As long as the spiritual context is intact, human creations, and consequently the technological means that facilitated their production, are acceptable and, to some extent, perceived as sacred works. This perception derives again from the Scripture and in particular from the passage of Genesis[24] which, according to Christian theologians, is the core of the whole argument about the relation of technology to Christianity, for it is usually interpreted as implying that God "hands over his creation to the human being, who enters into a partnership with God and 'finishes' or 'completes' the work of creation" (Hawking 1985, in Newman, 123). Such a perception is reinforced by the thinking of some Christian theologians[25] who, recognizing the development of technology and Christianity as being inseparably linked, based the justification of their claim in the person of Jesus himself, who in the New Testament is presented as a carpenter as well as one who was capable of performing "mighty works" with his hands (Mark 6:2–3). Furthermore, Newman (127) notes that the Jesus of the Gospel, who does not belong to the "class of priests and sages", is not so much a "philosophical thinker" but a "practical moral teacher who does good deeds and performs miracles".

If one follows the theological analyses in which technology is seen as a God-given means for the advancement of humanity's religious and spiritual levels, then technology itself becomes a religious expression. This, however, does not presuppose that "hand-made" objects are higher than mental, for technological objects result from "brain, mind and soul" activity (Newman, 148). The Decalogue could be seen as a characteristic example of the amalgamation of the physical with the mental. The Decalogue, consisting of God's moral teachings on how humans may live morally and ethically and in communion with God, is directly linked to God's craftsmanship, for its transmission was not only in oral, but also in written form, representing thus the "writing of God".[26] Through the stone tablets Newman (1997, 149) notes that God, apart from providing humanity with a conceptual and ideological framework in order to enable it to arrive at a meaningful existence in the universe, also provided "something" that would enable humans to "grasp" the real significance of a created product. This, Newman (150) explains, induced a realization and a deeper understanding of the relation between ideas and created material products, which in turn emphasizes that the "special ontological status of material products" derives from the mental process of the mind in both conceiving and producing them. In this sense, the created products, being the manifestations of mental, contemplative activity, evolve beyond the status of physicality—that is, being mere tools or artefacts—

and become means of comprehending, expressing and communicating the transcendent.

Technological quest as religious-spiritual quest

As noted earlier, historical evidence suggests that a cultural shift occurred in the Middle Ages which placed great emphasis on the religiosity and spirituality of science and technology. This shift initiated a departure from both traditional and mainstream Christian beliefs[27] in which activities other than intellectual were disdained, for they were associated with "manual labour, servitude and women" (Noble 1997, 9).

As one of the earliest references to that shift, in which technological advancements were presented as being part of Christian virtue, White (1971, in Noble 1997, 13) introduces a document from the Carolingian age which is an illustration of Psalm 63.[28] The illustration shows that in the preparations for battle of two armies—the one on the side of God and the other much larger one of the "ungodly"—the distinguishing element between the two can be seen in the process of sharpening of swords. Thus, while the "Evildoers" use the familiar whetstone, the "Godly" are using the "first crank recorded outside China to rotate the first grindstone known anywhere", which White (in Noble, 13) interprets as indicating that technological development is God's will. The illustration, which is infused in White's view by the particular ideology of perceiving technological arts as being spiritual ends, was produced by a Benedictine monk. As a number of scholarly works[29] demonstrate, the Benedictines' religious devotion, expressed through technological innovations,[30] reached such levels that Noble (14) characterizes it as the "medieval industrial revolution". Walton (2003) too, points out that the monasteries were the first places which offered the main interface between scholastic thought and the "useful arts".

For Noble (1997, 14), the creation and employment of technology by the Benedictines resulted, on the one hand, in the "useful arts"[31] gaining spiritual significance, which they lacked and, on the other hand, in the elevation of humankind above nature. This in turn presented humanity with the possibility of recovering its original "image-likeness of man to God" (Genesis 1:26) that had been lost by the Fall. This deconstructed view of the "useful arts", Noble (15) reports, gained full articulation in the ninth century by Erigena, who coined the term *artes mechanicae* to define all different technical arts and crafts. Erigena, though, apart from creating a new signifier, also elevated the status of the signified, thus distancing himself from the commonly held traditional view of the mechanical arts of that time.[32] Erigena raised the signified—*artes* mechanicae—by rewriting Capella's fifth-century work the *Marriage of Philology and Mercury*, in which, to the "liberal arts"[33] of the original, he added also the mechanical[34] ones giving them thus equal status and significance to the "celestial deities". By equating *artes mechanicae*, Noble notes (1997, 17), with the "liberal arts", Erigena connected the terrestrial to the celestial and consequently, technology to transcendence. Recognizing technology as being part of humankind's original God-like image, Erigena presented technology as a means of redemption. Noble (17) underlines that such a deconstructed and spirituality-infused perception of the mechanical arts sparked a "turning point in the ideological history of technology". Consequently, in the following centuries, the development of technology, as an assurance for humankind's restoration, became Christianized and a means for encountering the newly developed millenarian mentality (Noble, 22).

Bacon, the founder, among others, of modern science, who envisioned technological advances such as cars, submarines and aeroplanes, understood technological advancements not only as a means of restoration but also as a means of preparation for the kingdom to come, and as a clear indication that that kingdom was at hand (Noble, 26). Furthermore, Noble continues, the "Age of Discovery", that is, the exploratory voyages via the sea to central and east Asia, initiated and raised evangelical hopes. At the same time, the explorative endeavours themselves were seen as new ways of fulfilling the apocalyptic prophecies and therefore expediting the millennium. The discoveries brought about a new concept which significantly influenced the course of technology's development. For instance, while in the past restoration and returning to paradise was for humankind a vision, the New World discovered by Columbus gave substance to the vision and paradise became a physical place (38).

Equating the New World with the Garden of Eden, and other places, particularly islands, as the future sites of the Kingdom of God, resulted in uniting the worldly to the other-worldly and the present to the future, which in turn inspired a new apocalyptic vision of salvation based on both human ingenuity and faith. That vision was utopia (Noble, 38). The utopian ideology, promoted by key figures of the sixteenth and seventeenth centuries such as Luther, More and Giordano Bruno, placed great emphasis on the knowledge of craftsmanship which was clearly perceived as bringing humankind closer to God (Noble 1997, 39–40). The restoration process, however, was possible because God gave Adam and his descendants the opportunity to overturn the consequences of the Fall through rigorous labour (Webster 1975, in Noble, 46). Additionally, Webster defined the mechanical arts as "God's gift", through the mastering of which humankind could return to paradise.

Bacon, who comprehended Daniel's prophecy[35] as being of fundamental importance, was one of the most significant figures who shaped
and developed the mediaeval identification of technology with transcendence, which, in Noble's (1997, 53) view, has formed the "emergent mentality of modernity". Within the millennial teaching and its
theological analyses, the figure of Adam played a crucial role in the
development and understanding of his original status and consequently
that of the rest of humanity. Noble (45) states that the predominant perception about Adam was that he was the

> be-all and end-all of creation... By divine design and authority he
> enjoyed a superiority and dominion over all other creatures and
> complete control over nature.

The Fall's result, according to Bacon (in Noble, 51), was twofold. On the
one hand Adam lost his innocence and, on the other hand, he lost his
dominion over creation. In Bacon's understanding both consequences
could be altered, the first by religion and faith and the second by arts
and sciences.[36]

While up to the sixteenth century the focus was on the restoration
of humankind to its original status, Noble (1997, 57) suggests that the
scientific revolution of the seventeenth century brought about an additional shift in thinking and aspiring. This shift was characterized by the
scientists' desire to surpass restoring what had been lost and to reach a
new state which would go "beyond Adamic knowledge to the whole
of divine knowledge, beyond a restoration of original creation to the
making of a new creation" (57).

Spain may have been defined as the future site of the Kingdom of God
(Noble 1997, 38), but it is the US that kept and, to some extent, fulfilled
its characterization by Columbus as the "Garden of Eden". The writings
of R. W. B. Lewis and others of the seventeenth and eighteenth centuries
that promoted the colonization of the New World,[37] were depicting an
explicitly soteriological discourse in which the "American was the 'eternal
Adam' who would create 'an earthly millennium of perfect harmony in
the New World Eden'". The characterization of America as the place
where the "amalgamation of the City of the World into the City of God"
(Johnson 1628, in Noble, 89); as the "bulwark...against the Kingdom of
Antichrist" (John White in Noble, 89); and as the "most glorious state of
God's church on earth" (Edwards 1739, in Noble, 89), leaves no doubt
that in people's minds not only was millennial expectation "renewed and
reaffirmed", but also that America was the place where the "Millennium
seemed about to begin" or "already began" (Miller 1960, in Noble, 90).
These perceptions formed the ideological framework within which the
scientific and industrial revolutions took place.

The techno-religious ideology that prevailed in seventeenth- and eighteenth-century rhetoric surrounding technological advancements was enriched with new techno-religious affirmations as the development of new technologies progressed. For instance, the invention of the telegraph was seen as a divinely inspired process, the product of which facilitated the spreading of the Christian message[38] "farther and faster, eclipsing time and transcending space" (Carey 1989, 207). The telegraph, Carey (202–22) notes, generated a number of perceptions and changes of socio-economic, political and religious significance. The introduction of the telegraph employed to excess religious imagery and language which Marx (1964 in Carey, 206) termed the "rhetoric of the technological sublime". However, Carey and Quirk (1989, 206), taking into account that the telegraph was the first electrical engineering technology, altered Marx's term into the "rhetoric of the electrical sublime" to signify electricity's mystery that derived from its great forcefulness and invisibility. As Carey (206) explains, it was the invisibility of electricity that generated not only the religious connotations, but also raised the "mystery of the mind-body dualism and located vital energy in the realm of the mind". Within the ideological matrix of that time, electricity was perceived as "shadowy, mysterious [and] impalpable…livi[ing] in skies and…connect[ing] the spiritual with the material" (Czitrom 1982, 9, in Carey, 206).

The context, cultivating the rhetoric of the religion of technology in America, was enhanced, expressed and popularized by the utopian writings of Bellamy (1847, in Noble, 98), who declared that the "half-conscious God that is man is called to recognize his divine parts". In Bellamy's futuristic works, H. P. Segal (1988, in Noble, 98) stresses that the US of 2000 is portrayed as a technological utopia, that is, "an allegedly ideal society not simply dependent upon tools and machinery, or even worshipful of them, but outright modelled after them". This genealogical presentation of theoretical discourses about the relation of religion to technology has shown how the *artes mechanicae* were dressed with religious/spiritual significance by applying to them soteriological and millennial qualities, thus rendering them transcendent. This resulted, on the one hand, in the sacralization of technology and, on the other hand, as Noble (1997, 209), albeit in an appendix, points out, in the formation of a strong and everlasting framework within which technology is represented as uniquely masculine striving, evocative of masculinity and exclusively male. As has already been shown, the rhetoric about the restoration of humanity focuses entirely on Adam, which implies that the ideal of restored perfection was male. Moreover, all the promoters of the religious character of technology who are referenced are males and some contemporary technological achievements, such as the first manned spaceflight,[39] the seed programmes of Artificial Life (AL)[40] and the composite human genome,[41] have been named "Adam" (Noble 1997, 125, 171, 200).

It could be suggested that this focus on "Adam" may result from the perception that Eve—and consequently women—was not included in the restoration process[42] because, since Eve did not have God-likeness, she could neither lose it nor restore it; the restoration of perfection therefore became an exclusively male enterprise (Noble, 214). The identification of technology with men and the absence of women as active participants in technological progress, Stanley notices (1993, xxxvii, 747), are aspects of culturally created stereotypes, separating women from technology, which have their roots in the religionization of technology.

Conclusions

The fusion of technology with religious meaning and significance is not restricted only to theoretical and/or ideological levels, but is also manifested within the realm of physical activities. For instance, Babbage, the creator of the Calculating Engine that is considered to be the predecessor of the modern computer, used his device to demonstrate the "truth of miracles and the probability of the miracle of resurrection" (Noble 1997, 72). Religious relics were employed in 1958 by NASA engineers who wired a St. Christopher medal to a faulty rocket with the belief that the "Addition of Divine Guidance" would "repair" the rocket's inexplicable failures (Noble, 136). The deep religiosity of the technologists of the space program was expressed in the accounts of their religious experiences generated by their participation in space flights, as the astronauts of Apollo 8 in 1968,[43] declared. For one of them, the moon voyage was "the final leg in [his] own religious experience [during which] he saw evidence that God lives" (139). Perhaps the first religious ritual to be performed outside the earth's space is when Aldrin took communion in the Sea of Tranquillity (139).

This section has provided, on the one hand, a historical account of the development of the ideological matrix, which explains the amalgamation of religion and technology, and, on the other hand, a number of themes that can be identified in the discourses about ICTs and cyberspace in particular that are presented in the following section.

In the themes that emerge in this section technology is seen:

- as transcendence
- as the New Jerusalem
- as a means of expressing, communicating the transcendent
- as a means of restoration—return to Paradise
- as God's gift

- as a principle of social development and moral perfection
- as the new creation—completing divine knowledge
- as demonic and dehumanizing if separated from religion.

Theories of Cyberspace[44]

Introduction

The themes presented earlier have underlined the fact that despite industrialization of technological innovations, which labelled technology as a secular element of society, there were always implicit or explicit religious connotations behind both the development and the adaptation of technological apparatuses. As has been shown, these connotations, deriving mainly from Judaeo-Christian traditions, were extrapolated from the Bible's instruction to conquer nature, from the Protestant work ethic and from the millennialist vision of the restoration which promised the return and reign of the Heavenly City.

The metaphorical conceptualizations, techno-spiritual and techno-religious perceptions presented in this section indicate that the myth of a technological utopia continues to fuel the ideological mentality behind the discourses surrounding ICTs which, invested with soteriological rhetoric, promises to provide freedom, liberation, welfare, progress and advancement on both social and personal levels.

The drive behind embracing ICTs

Although technological developments have been continuously present in humanity's existence, the speed and magnitude by which the general public adopted ICTs is unprecedented. Wertheim's (1999, 28–29) explanation is based on notions of need and desire. A technological device, she asserts, succeeds when it is seen as fulfilling or satisfying a particular need and/or desire. However, she points to another factor which may also have been influential. As she notes, apart from desire for technology, the embracement of ICTs, in both conceptual and practical terms, also indicates a "profound psychological vacuum" that a number of netizens believe and/or hope that online existence might fill up. Winner (1986, 105) too, almost ten years before the mass availability and acceptability of ICTs by the general public, emphasized that those thrilled by the assumed redemptive qualities of ICTs are those who have become sceptical about social life. Additionally, Tatusko (2001) assigns the construction of ICTs to the desire to exchange information across vast distances. This, for Tatusko, is interpreted as a possible cultural response to the increasing fragmentation of culture initiated by print technology, reaching its peak in the division of labour and mass production.

A similar point is presented by Stone (1991, 95) in her analysis of the epochs[45] that signalled an intensified change in people's sense of communication. For Stone, the publication of *Neuromancer* was the "most significant event" in that it initiated novel and innovative forms of community, whose members were the "technologically literate" and "socially disaffected habitants" of Silicon Valley and other "electronic and industrial ghettos". The vision provided by Gibson's novel, Stone (1991, 95) explains, offered them a new, albeit imaginary or mythic social setting and a refigured community, promising the possibility of new social interactions. Furthermore, this cyberspatial social setting not only offers a limitless freedom to "be" whatever one wants to be, but also implies that the cybernauts connect to something greater than themselves (Tatusko 2001). If *Neuromancer* is taken as the exemplification of the myths of the twenty-first century, then the advocacy of cyberspace as the New Jerusalem should not come as a surprise, for as Benedikt (1991, 5) notes, myths both reflect the human condition and create it.

According to Davis (1998, 4), the ability of ICTs to create a new interface between the "self, the other and the world beyond [makes them] part of the self, the other and the world beyond". This interconnection of different concepts could be seen as explaining the mystical impulses that prevail in the Western world's obsession with technology, especially if ICT does indeed, as Davis suggests (4), form the foundation of the contemporary social construction of reality. Davis' observation could be expanded to include the forming of the foundation of a new religious/spiritual/philosophical—in one word, metaphysical—reality.

Definitions of cyberspace

The fact that ICTs allow people to "meet" anywhere at any time has been seen as the ultimate transcendence of the time-space singularity. Generally in narratives about ICTs, cyberspace is accompanied by adjectives, such as "new", "novel", "innovative", "revolutionary" and so on. However, Carey (1989, 2) emphasizes that, despite the changes that ITCs brought to notions of time and place, the discussions about the revolution and excitement of ICTs are no more than "the latest chapter in an old tale". Mosco (2000, 41) too, disputes such characterizations for, as he points out, cyberspace is not at all something new, but rather a deeper and extended evolution of existing communication spaces, which reached acceleration point with the telegraph, the telephone, radio and TV.

Perceived either as a new or as an extension of an old technology, cyberspace's capacity to reshape, reorganize and restructure every

aspect of both social and personal life has been the common denominator in the discourses. A typical example of both socio-political and
spiritual rhetoric, that in Herman and Sloop's view (2000, 81) characteristically illustrates the utopian cyberspatial discourse, is the Declaration
of Independence of Cyberspace authored by Barlow, the founder of the
Electronic Frontier Foundation (EFF).

> Governments of the Industrial World, you weary giants of flesh and
> steel, I come from Cyberspace, the new home of Mind... I declare
> the global social space we are building to be naturally independent
> of the tyrannies you seek to impose on us. You have no moral right
> to rule us nor do you possess any methods of enforcement we have
> true reason to fear... Cyberspace consists of transactions, relation-
> ships, and thought itself, arrayed like a standing wave in the web
> of our communications. Ours is a world that is both everywhere
> and nowhere, but it is not where bodies live... We are creating a
> world that all may enter without privilege or prejudice accorded by
> race, economic power, military force, or station of birth... We are
> creating a world where anyone, anywhere may express his or her
> beliefs, no matter how singular, without fear of being coerced into
> silence or conformity... Our identities have no bodies, so, unlike
> you, we cannot obtain order by physical coercion. We believe that
> from ethics, enlightened self-interest, and the commonweal, our
> governance will emerge... We will create a civilization of the Mind
> in Cyberspace.

The declaration[46] combines socio-political libertarian ideology with
implicit religio-spiritual undertones that present cyberspace as a distinct entity, parallel to the physical world, embodying the qualities
of decentralization, egalitarianism and transcendence. Furthermore,
Berland (2000, 236) opines that loci of public discourses, such as newspapers, magazines, TV and work places, to mention but a few, appear
to be dominated by "techno-evolutionism" and "cybertopianism".
The ideology of techno-evolutionism, in Berland's view, projects ICTs
as the force behind society's shifting movement towards a "postna-
tional", "postspatial", "postembodied" and "posthuman" form, which
eliminates distinctions between biological and technological products
–human/machine, between genders, between places and between
experiences. This shift, which is strongly reflected in Gibson's novel, is
suggestive of the craving for transcendence—the desire to experience
life beyond the boundaries of the physical.

Cyberspace is a term that is usually used interchangeably with those
of the Internet and the World Wide Web. The term was coined by
Gibson,[47] but since then it has become an autonomous entity, which,
having departed the confines of fiction, has entered into the vocab-

ulary, and into the thinking and living processes of the "connected". However, in the interest of historical accuracy, it should be noted that before Gibson's novel, and in particular in 1982, the first visual representation of cyberspace was offered in Disney's film *Tron*. As Manovich (2001, 250) comments, Tron's depiction of the users and their actions speeding through immaterial space outlined by lines of light is almost identical to Gibson's notion of cyberspace.

Cyberspace is a unique signifier, in that its signified neither really exists, nor can be located as occupying a physical dimension. Rather, it is a space that is "everywhere and nowhere, a place where nothing is forgotten and yet everything changes" (Benedikt 1991, 1). Yet, despite its immateriality, its presence is felt and becomes visible in the numerous diverse perceptions, characterizations and definitions that it has and continues to generate. Additionally, the heterogeneous definitions of and approaches to cyberspace illustrate the idiosyncratic character of the concept and, to some extent, explain the perceptions, attitudes and theories that it has initiated. Apart from definitions focusing on the technical side of its identity, cyberspace has invoked a number of descriptions that present its spiritual, metaphysical and ethereal side.

Technical definitions present the term as:

> the digital world constructed by computer networks, and in particular, the Internet. Whenever you hear the term "cyberspace", it generally refers to the online world, which is a place that actually exists, albeit as a communications medium rather than another galaxy. Perceived as an immaterial realm of data or some kind of virtual world, it is actually a physical infrastructure made up of the wires above our head, the cable beneath our feet, and the satellite dishes in the sky. Some people don't like this term because it's become commercialized, but at the same time, it represents the attitude of people who consider themselves wired or connected, for example.[48]

> A metaphor for describing the non-physical terrain created by computer systems. Online systems, for example, create a cyberspace within which people can communicate with one another (via e-mail), do research, or simply window shop. Like physical space, cyberspace contains *objects* (files, mail messages, graphics, etc.) and different modes of transportation and delivery. Unlike real space, though, exploring cyberspace does not require any physical movement other than pressing keys on a keyboard or moving a mouse.[49]

There are usually three variants of the generic term "cyberspace". In summary, they are: Barlovian cyberspace, virtual reality (VR), and Gibsonian. First, Barlovian cyberspace represents existing information and communication cyberspaces that are constituted by the Internet and telephone networks (Jordan 1999, 20). The term virtual reality (VR), coined by Jaron Lanier in the 1980s,[50] is defined as a computer-simulated multimedia environment in which the perceiver experiences "telepresence" (Steur 1992, in Featherstone and Burrows 1995a, 5). Similarly, Featherstone and Burrows (1995a, 5–6) define VR as a system which produces an authentic sense of being immersed in an environment. VR is an interface, which, by manipulating the senses, permits the user to be submerged in the simulated environment. Finally, Gibsonian cyberspace refers to the conceptual space described in William Gibson's novel *Neuromancer*, in which participants use VR to navigate the Internet creating a landscape comparable to a massive circuit board buoyant in space. Novak (1991, 225), in his definition, combines all the different conceptualizations, describing cyberspace as

> A completely spatialized visualisation of all information in global information processing systems, along pathways provided by present and future communications networks, enabling full copresence and interaction of multiple users, allowing input and output from and to the full human sensorium, permitting simulations of real and virtual realities, remote data collection and control through telepresence, and total integration and intercommunication with a full range of intelligent products and environments in the real space.[51]

Gibson's (1984, 51) most typical and widely cited description of cyberspace

> A consensual hallucination experienced daily by billions of legitimate operators, in every nation, by children being taught mathematical concepts… A graphic representation of data abstracted from the banks of every computer in the human system. Unthinkable complexity. Lines of light ranged in the nonspace of the mind, clusters and constellations of data. Like city lights, receding…

has been the foundation of the metaphoric conceptualizations of the Infobahn.

Tomas (1995, 35–36) interprets Gibsonian cyberspace as being "digitally and socially Durkheimian in the sense that it is both profane (a metropolis of data) and sacred (a cybernetic godhead)". Benedikt (1991) develops a number of definitions of cyberspace which describe it either in technical terms or in metaphorical/metaphysical ones. Thus, while he sees it as a "globally networked, computer-sustained, computer-accessed, and computer-generated, multidimensional, artificial, or 'virtual' reality" (1991, 122), he also understands it as

A new universe, a parallel universe created and sustained by the world's computers and communication lines. A world in which the global traffic of knowledge, secrets, measurements, indicators, entertainment, and alter-human agency takes on form: sights, sounds, presences never seen on the surface of the earth blossoming in a vast electronic night (Benedikt, 1).

And also as

The realm of pure information, filling like a lake, siphoning the jangle of messages transfiguring the physical world, decontaminating the natural and urban landscapes, redeeming them, saving them from the chain-dragging bulldozers of the paper industry, from the diesel smoke of courier and post office trucks, from jet fuel fumes and clogged airports, from billboards, trashy and pretentious architecture, hour-long freeway commutes, ticket lines, and choked subways...from all the inefficiencies, pollutions (chemical and informational), and corruptions attendant to the process of moving information attached to things—from paper to brains—across, over, and under the vast and bumpy surface of the earth rather than letting it fly in the soft hail of electrons that is cyberspace (Benedikt, 3).

Virilio (1995) identifies cyberspace as a new "form of perspective" which, not corresponding to any previously known audio-visual frames of reference, becomes a *"tactile perspective"*, for it enables the users to arrive at a distance, to sense at a distance. This, for Virilio, means that the perspective is moving towards a realm it did not include in the past: that of "contact, of contact-at-a-distance: tele-contact".

However, attention should be drawn to an additional issue that is altered significantly in the cyberdomain. As mentioned earlier, "being connected" presupposes the employment of technological interfaces in order to be transformed from an abstract notion to an actualized condition. The moment users start interacting with the interface(s) they move from the compounds of their commonly perceived "biological reality" to what Dyens calls "technological reality" (TR) (2003). While biological reality offers clear distinctions between humans and the material world, these distinctions seen through the lenses of technological reality become blurred and undefined. Although Dyens' analysis of TR focuses mainly on biotechnology—especially reproductive technologies—its consequences on ethics and morality, and the challenges that it poses on issues such as consciousness, intelligence, purpose and life's sacred nature, the term proves to be very useful in analysing the altered conditions humans face when they encounter themselves and their fellow humans in a completely new environment, within which their preconceived ideas about the self, time and space collapse, thus pushing them to reconfigure, reinterpret and redefine those long-ago established signifiers. Furthermore, they need to become aware of, to perceive and to understand that, being within the realm of technological reality of ICTs, they are no longer a centre but a node, a terminal, a component of the universal computing network (Dyens 2003).

Perceptions of cyberspace

This "existing", but simultanously "non-existing" space is a conceptual space; its future potential evolution, especially in the areas of virtual reality, telepresence and imbedded microchips carries a wealth of utopian promises. All this has encouraged the inception of a number of techno-spiritual/techno-metaphysical and techno-religious perceptions of and responses to it. Wertheim (1999, 21) stresses that the "spiritual" attractiveness of cyberspace may be explained as deriving from the idea of an achievable perfection through a secular technological product. For the connected, the "perfect realm", as Wertheim (p. 21) succinctly puts it, is not behind the "pearly gates" but beyond the network's gates such as ".com", ".net", ".org" and ".ac.uk".

Techno-metaphysical responses

Benedikt (1991, 4) compares cyberspace with Popper's "World 3".[52] The entities[53] of World 3 can be examined, evaluated, explored and discovered in ways that could be influential to the lives of all. Equally, World 3 entities can evolve—as the natural world does—and create their own autonomous issues, situations and advancements which, in turn, generate and guide happenings in Worlds 1 and 2. Within this framework Benedikt (1991, 4) suggests that cyberspace could be understood as "nothing more or less, than the latest stage in the evolution of World 3 with a ballast of materiality cast away—cast away again, and perhaps finally". The elimination of the material—in the case of cyberspace the body—has been a key issue in the narratives invested with religious, spiritual and/or mystical languages. Perceived as a "wavelength of well-being", where the second half of one's self[54] would be reached, cyberspace generates imagery such as Stenger's (1991, 50) in which people's

> minds [are] leaking rainbows of coloured imagination, soon [are] joined by innumerable rainbows that would embrace the earth and change the climate of the human psyche. Perception would change, and with it, the sense of reality, of time, of life and death.

Besides, Zaleski (1997, 236) stresses the liberating and healing properties of cyberspace as well as its capacity to facilitate self exploration and self discovery. Moreover, it seems that some of the users, fiction writers and theorists share a common perception of cyberspace which projects a future of "a space or a reality" that is presumed to be far more appealing than the tedious one that currently surrounds and contains humanity (Robins 1995, 135).

The spiritual and metaphysical rhetoric, in which cyberspace is presented, includes concepts such as: the "new bomb, a pacific blaze that will project the imprint of [people's] disembodied selves on the walls of eternity" (Stenger 1991, 51); "Platonism as a working product...suspended in a computer space, the cybernaut leaves the prison of the body and emerges in a world of digital sensation (Heim 1993, 89); the "Platonic realm incarnate"; as the "Pythagorean sacred mathematical language" (Cobb 1998, 31); "Like Indra's Net, each monad mirrors the whole world. Each monad represents the universe in concentrated form... Each microcosm contains the macrocosm" (Heim 1993, 98). This is not only almost identical to that of the writings of the seventeenth and eighteenth centuries, but this time the metaphoric and symbolic language corresponds not so much to a vision but to a feasible possibility which is "promised" by the "magical" powers of the new technologies.

Heim (1993, 85) asserts that people's fascination with technology, especially with ICTs, shows that there is a deeper underlying need to find a "home for the mind and heart". Wertheim (1999, 29) too, considers that cyberspace's appeal may derive from the western polarity between body and mind which differentiates physical space as the space of bodily existence and spiritual space as the realm within which "psyches" or "souls" exist. Furthermore, for Heim (85), these ideas indicate that people's fascination is more "erotic than sensuous, more spiritual than utilitarian". Consequently, people's relationship with ICTs is transformed from a superficial to a "symbiotic" one and "ultimately to mental marriage to technology". Within this framework then, cyberspace and everything that it incorporates (i.e. VR, 3D worlds, and so on) in Heim's (1993, 83) understanding is a "metaphysical laboratory, a tool for examining our sense of reality".

The ontological character of cyberspace, consisting of its ephemerality, immateriality and its capacity to shift in multiple directions and dimensions, offers an additional space for reaching mythical realities which to date, according to Benedikt (1991, 6), were restricted within the confinements of different material expressions such as the theatre, books and paintings that served as gateways. Interpreted as a gateway, cyberspace, Benedikt continues, can be seen as an expansion of people's capability and need to reside "empowered or enlightened" on mythic planes. The theme of the Heavenly City, discussed in the previous section, is also found in the contemporary writings on cyberspace;

only this time the approach, comprehension and analysis derive from a different stand point. For example, Benedikt (15–16) connects architectural constructions, such as those of cathedrals, the Taj Mahal and gardens of ineffable beauty with the desire of humans to create a place which would open the road of restoration. For Benedikt (16), the propulsion toward the Heavenly City continues to exist and now it can be realized through virtual reality. The notion of the Heavenly City, for Benedikt, not only implies that World 3 becomes "whole and holy", but also implies a "religious vision of cyberspace" (16).

Cyberspace's actual and potential capacity to incorporate *all knowledge* has resulted in views such as Heim's (1993, 85), who suggests that if perceived in the right way, cyberspace reflects the "same aura as Wisdom". This amalgamation of cyberspace and wisdom, which is materialized by the uploading of more and more libraries, museum collections and projects, such as the Gutenberg,[55] results in cyberspace becoming an "Ark of knowledge" (Wertheim 1999, 26). In addition, Benedikt (1991, 15) maintains that while Eden represents humankind's innocence, the Heavenly City represents humanity's state of wisdom and knowledge. The ontological character of cyberspace also incorporates the elements of connectivity, accessibility, openness, experience, communication and contact. These concepts, key components of human interaction, are reconfigured and transformed whenever the users are "shifting realities" and entering the cyber realm either in its simple form—by connecting to the Net, or in its more complicated and more seductive form—by immersing into a virtual reality. Thus, as Wertheim (1999, 22) points out, in cyberspace, cybernauts become "idealized beings, creatures of ether" because their physical attributes are removed. However, within a virtual reality domain, the users become ethereal beings because they are immersed within an ethereal, but intensely felt, environment where everything is possible. Virtual reality, Davis (1998) underlines, is the intersection between technology and human experience that results in a "state of holy being which reminds us that, indeed, we are all angels" (Pesce, in Davis 1996). Similarly, Stone (1991, 52) claims that "on the other side of our data gloves, we become creatures of coloured light in motion, pulsing with golden particles… We all become angels, and for eternity!"

Disembodiment

Freeing individuals from their distinct physical characteristics, cyberspatial interaction appears to occur between disembodied intelligences, minds or consciousnesses. What is astonishing about the idea of disembodied existence which prevails in techno-religious/spiritual discourses is, as explained by Wertheim (1999, 261), that while in the past the notion of overcoming bodily limitations was perceived as a "theological possibility", nowadays it is progressively understood as a "technological feasibility". This feasibility may be seen as deriving from what Cobb (1998, 51) calls the "sacred locus of computation", which she places in the interaction between hardware and software. Cobb characterizes the functionality of abstract mathematical algorithms used in computer programming, as "remarkable", for, when in action, their abstraction is transformed into a realm of experience. In other words, the process that takes place behind the screen, by which computational commands appear on the screen as meaningful, is perceived by Cobb (51) as "divine creativity in action". Furthermore, Cobb, defines the emanating relationship between hardware and software as being an "aspect of divinity itself", for, as she understands it, the "cosmic force" that rules reality is the same force that rules the everlasting "emergence of cyberspace" (1998, 51).

Cobb is not alone either in interpreting cyberspace through techno-mystical and/or techno-theological language, or in advocating it as an experiential realm (125). This excerpt,

> [l]et us begin with the object of desire. It exists; it has existed for all time, and will continue eternally. It has held the attention of all mystics and witches and hackers for all time. It is the Graal.

taken from Pesce's talk to a conference on cyberspace and virtual reality in 1997, is full of religious and spiritual symbolism similar to that found in the writings of mystics and yogis describing a mystical experience. In fact, Pesce himself describes his first contact with the idea of cyberspace[56] via Gibson's writings, as nothing less than the account of a mystical experience. In his own words:

> [it] left me dazzled with its brilliance, drenched in sweat, entirely seduced. For here, spelled out in the first paragraph, in the non-sense word "cyberspace", I had discovered numinous beauty; here, in the visible architecture of reason, was truth.

Pesce's experience of his "first contact", which Wertheim (1999, 252) characterizes as expressing an "almost ecstatic religiosity", would perhaps not seem surprising were it not followed by his assertion that such experiences are "the common element" shared by the community of ICTs' software engineers (Pesce 1997). Yet, Pesce's certainty is verified by Stenger's (1991, 52) narration of her first encounter with 3D computer-animated images in 1979. Like Pesce, Stenger felt that the computer animation was not a simple generation of moving images, but rather a "virtual world, populated by half-living entities, that [humans] would inhabit someday". Like others in the same line of work, Stenger (1991, 49–50) sensed that the hallucination behind the screen was just the first stage…, a rehearsal for a D day when the substance would finally escape and invade what we call reality… [The animation] had revealed as state of grace to us, tapped a wavelength where image, music, language and love were pulsing in one harmony. Inside the enclosed area of the computer something was calling us, inviting us.

Critique of techno-spiritual/techno-metaphysical responses

On the one hand, claims such as Pesce's and Stenger's could be seen as statements of a religiosity and/or spirituality that, despite their appearing to be outside "traditional" forms, in that in their portrayal a machine is perceived as the cause of their emergence, nevertheless express a *Weltanschuung* which cannot or should not be ignored. Rather, it could be considered as an additional dimension of religion, or as a religion in the making, which scholars of the field should monitor. On the other hand, however, such claims could be seen as the "digital equivalent of speaking in tongues" (Slouka 1997, 25), a point also made by Carey and Quirk (1989, 114) and Wertheim (1999, 254), who underline the secular religiosity that prevails in the semantic structure of narratives surrounding ICTs.

All these references, which clearly offer a utopian view of ICTs, demonstrate that the way in which the ontological structure of cyberspace is understood will determine how realities can exist within it (Heim 1993, 84). Moreover, Stahl (1999, 2) indicates that the languages used in discussions about technologies shape and define issues and problems. Additionally, the discourses on ICTs that have been invested with symbolic and mythical references have generated the rise of what Stahl (1999) calls "technological mysticism", that is, the implicitly religious understanding of technology which appears to have been developed in Western society. Another term for describing the proselytizational rhetoric of technological romanticism is what Winner (1986, 105) calls "mythinformation", that is, the "almost religious conviction" that an extensive worldwide adoption of ICTs will automatically result in a better world. Bauwens (1997) too, stresses the dystopian views on cyberspace in which human evolution is seen as deteriorating from the high levels of spiritual consciousness to today's end time, the "kali yuga"[57] or "Apocalypse". For some critics, Bauwens notices, ICTs, and especially virtual reality and artificial intelligence, will evolve into a "Machine-God", a Deus-ex-Machina, a kind of technological anti-Christ.

Heaven's Gate

The ideas and conceptualization of ICTs, already infused with notions of apocalypse and for some unwholesomeness, can be shifted even further towards either the utopian or the dystopian spectrum, by events which, although external to ICTs, have nevertheless been characterized as underlining their potential influence and impact on both religion and society. An example of such an event is the case of the mass suicide of the members of Heaven's Gate. Herman and Sloop (2000, 77–81) offer an analytical account[58] of the reactions of various media which provide valuable insights about the ways in which ICTs and their role in the event were interpreted. For instance, while some headlines referred to the event as "Net-savvy cultists"[59] and as "Inside the Web of Death",[60] others referred to the same event as the "First Web Tragedy'[61] and as a "Disturbance in the Field".[62]

Zaleski (1997, 249), examining the issue of cults and ICTs, not only embarks upon making assumptions about those who may be attracted to a cult's message,[63] but also emphasizes that the peculiarity of ICTs' functionality—via an interface with the physical presence absent—stimulates "fantasy, paranoia [and] delusions of grandeur". Such negative perceptions are reported by Herman and Sloop (2000, 80) in which ICTs are defined as "THE place for cult recruitment"[64] and as providing an open forum for "spiritual predators". Dawson and Hennebry (1999, 20), however, argue against such a possibility on the grounds that, as existing research on the subject suggests, the recruitment process of NRMs relies mainly on face-to-face social interactions and networks of relationships. Furthermore, the authors (19) pay close attention to the fact that there is limited—if any—data on the issues of cults' recruitment via ICTs.

Cultural lag

The case of Heaven's Gate is quite valuable in that, on the one hand, it offers a substantive example which can be used to support the conceptualizations of cyberspace as "liberating" and "freeing" humanity from the imprisonment of the flesh and, on the other hand, it offers an example which can be used to support the perceptions of cyberspace as threatening social stability.

The utopian/dystopian duality of responses to ICTs, which is ever-present in all discourses, narratives and rhetoric, being either socio-political, economic or religious, fits into Fisher and Wright's (2001) analysis of discourses on ICTs, in which they employ Ogburn's (1964, in Fisher and Wright 2001) notion of "cultural lag". The notion of "cultural lag" refers to the time elapsing between the invention of a technology, its introduction and distribution to a society and its cultural adaptation— that is, the social adjustment that follows (Westrum 1991, in Fisher and Wright 2001). Ogburn (1964, 134 in Fisher and Wright 2001) identified four stages to a "cultural lag": technological, industrial, governmental and social philosophical. Fisher and Wright, highlighting that different parts of a society accept and adopt a new technology at various speeds, point to industry as the first part which attunes to and obtains the newly created technology, followed by government and, lastly, by society. The history[65] of ICTs corresponds perfectly to this model. Created by the need of the military to develop an autonomous system of communication, ICTs were quickly adopted by industrial and commercial sectors and lastly by cultural institutions and individuals. Although from the moment of its conception and creation (mid sixties) to their mass adoption (mid nineties) there has been a period of thirty years, which some may see as challenging the theory of cultural lag, the reality is that ICTs were, for most of that time, the privilege of a small elite. When they reached the wider population, ICTs were already a sophisticated system of communication and distribution of information. Also, with increasing rapidity, new, even more elaborate tools were introduced to even more people who, although they used them, did not have the ability to comprehend them. This implies that there is time fully to grasp neither the technological devices themselves, nor the effects and impacts they may have on a society. Consequently, Fisher and Wright (2001) propose that utopian or dystopian narrations of technologies tend to be more the authors' personal, optimistic or pessimistic views on ICTs, rather than an objective evaluation of their effects and impacts. In this respect, "cultural lag" may be characterized as being responsible for the illusionary nature of both utopian and dystopian discourses in which the "satanic and angelic images" (Carey 1989, 2) of ICTs are found.

Noosphere[66]

Another metaphor invested with spiritual symbolism is found in the notion of "noosphere". The idea of the noosphere appeared, long before it was conceived by Teilhard de Chardin in 1955,[67] in Ralph Waldo Emerson's speeches in which he intertwines the technological developments of his era with transcendentalism. For instance to Emerson "[m]achinery and transcendentalism agree well... Our civilization and these ideas are reducing the earth to a brain. See how by telegraph and steam the earth is anthropologized (Carey and Quirk[68] in Carey 1989, 120). Although this statement precedes Teilhard's idea of the noosphere, it does nevertheless encapsulate its essence, that is, the connection of the whole planet via a "thinking layer" (Teilhard 1959, 182). In Teilhard's interpretation of the theory of evolution, the emergence of humans was not just the appearance of another species, but a consequential event for the planet, for it signalled the creation of the noosphere, which arises from people communicating with one other.

Seeing humans as the "center of the construction of the universe", Teilhard (33) was certain that humans' primal purpose was to conclude cosmic evolution. For Teilhard, Cobb notes (1998, 81), evolution was the key concept which he interpreted as being both a scientific and a holy process, or as he describes it "a light illuminating all facts, a curve that all lines must follow (Teilhard 1959, 219). In his understanding, the differentiating element between humans and other living beings is "reflection", that is, in Teilhard's (165) own words,

> the power acquired by a consciousness to turn in upon its self, to take possession of itself *as of an object* endowed with its own particular consistence and value: no longer merely to know, but to know oneself; no longer merely to know, but to know that one knows.

Consequently, through the reflection process, humans realize that they are *"nothing else than evolution become conscious of itself"* and that their consciousness is *"evolution looking at itself and reflecting upon itself"* (221). For Teilhard, therefore, the direction of human evolution, to reach that advanced level of consciousness—"noogenesis"—, was something that humans could determine. Teilhard's ideas and concepts have been employed as prophetic visions of the evolution and development of cyberspace as the manifestation of a "collective organism or mind". In fact Teilhard himself wondered what the outcome would have been for humanity, if, by "some remote chance it had been free to spread indefinitely on an unlimited surface" (Teilhard 1959, 240). It could be suggested that ICTs do indeed present humanity with that "remote chance" the result of which is, in Teilhard's own words, "something unimaginable, certainly something altogether different from the modern world" (240).

The application of Teilhard's noosphere is plentiful in the discursive spiritualization of ICTs. Examples of such applications include Barlow's (1994) conception of cyberspace as the "native home of the mind", as the realm where

> all the goods of the Information Age—all of the expressions once contained in books or film strips or newsletters—will exist either as pure thought or something very much like thought: voltage conditions darting around the Net at the speed of light, in conditions that one might behold in effect, as glowing pixels or transmitted sounds, but never touch or claim to "own" in the old sense of the word.

Kelly (1994), in his description of ICTs and their operationality, stresses the lack of any central authority and meaning and emphasizes that the repeating vision of netizens is that of "wiring human and artificial minds into one planetary soul". For Kelly, this emerging techno-spiritualism, along with new forms of socio-political and economic interactions, defined the exceptionality of ICTs because they were unpredictable and unexpected. Ronfeldt and Arquilla (2000), analysing noosphere, determine it as a spiritual concept which, when fully comprehended, will elevate humanity to a new evolutionary realm guided by a cooperative co-ordination of "psychosocial and spiritual energies and by a devotion to moral and juridical principles".

A prerequisite for this elevation is the presence of the noosphere, which, as King (1996) explains, appears when human communication attains adequate speed and sufficient critical mass. The issue of attaining "critical mass" underlines not only the importance of connectivity and communication, but also their dependency on the communication mediums. However, if the invention of the different communication tools is seen, as Kerckhove (1998, 145) suggests, as phases of one and the same technological lineage, then it is possible to identify the new and distinct features of each phase and their repercussions for the communication-connection activity, which, predominantly, is the immense amplification of the multilayered structure[69] of the communication. As already mentioned earlier, connectivity, or to use Kerckhove's term, "connectedness", is the fundamental feature of ICTS, for, within their domain, every thought links, instantly, one way or another. In this sense, then, connectedness can be defined as the inclination of unattached and formerly unassociated life forms to be connected by a link or a relationship (Kerckhove 1998, 144).

Evidently, the convergence of global ICTs and all broadcasting media is constructing an augmenting and ever-multiplying network of connected nodes which fuses both the physical and mental disparities of the connected into a "shared mind". Davidson (1995) stresses that the unprecedented capabilities of ICTs create a unique "satsang-like" quality for the netizens. Seeing virtual communities as "satsangs", Davidson highlights that these satsangs are united by spirit, "floating in the non-local domain of conscious space" and, by sharing "vision, beliefs, interests, passions, rituals and inquiry, they exist in the timeless, placeless, imperceptible, incorporeal and cosmic reality" of cyberspace that progressively acquires the qualities of consciousness itself.

All these accounts converge to a single point: ICTs, it is acclaimed, offer the perfect opportunity for the communication process to move towards an evolutionary stage, in which the earth gets a new surface layer, or better still, it "finds its soul" (Teilhard 1959, 183). Such an opportunity is presented to humanity for the first time in its history. The point made here is that communication and connectivity are bound to the limitations of the available communicative means at any given time. This, in turn, implies that, given King's preconditions, the creation of the noosphere, prior to the invention of ICTs, was an impossibility, because none of the previous communication means could reach either adequate speed or mass. This, though, indicates that one may view the techno-spiritual discourses, despite their hyperbolic and overenthusiastic tone, as exemplifying that the creation and constant development of ICTs, products of human ingenuity and invention, may be seen as epitomizing Teilhard's (1959, 224) assertion that the "spirit of research and conquest is the permanent soul of evolution".

Noospheric culture

Ronfeldt and Arquilla (1999), despite their acknowledgement of the spiritual nature of the notion of noosphere, also attach to it socio-political attributes and predict that the force that may create a global noosphere more probably originates from non-governmental organizations (NGOs), civil-society actors such as churches, schools and groups and from individuals advocating both the freedom of ICTs and the dissemination of ethical values and standards. Supportive evidence for this line of thinking derives from Boulding's (1982) work in which she differentiates the "global" from "planetary", in the sense that, while "global" refers to "systems of power", "planetary" refers to the sum total of human beings in their various social and personal activities. Perceived as such, Boulding proposes that the planetary may also be defined as "sociosphere"—the web of human connections which encircle the planet.

Ronfeldt and Arquilla (1999) see the "sociosphere" as the force which, stimulated by a "noospheric culture", could alter the way in which the world is governed. A characteristic example of noospheric culture could be the Open Source[70] software movement, in which software is not only available for free on the Web, but also people have unrestricted access to its code, thus enabling them to amend it and/or to improve it. This "gift-culture" (Ronfeldt and Arquilla 2000) among hackers occurs in the noosphere—the "territory of ideas, the space of all possible thoughts" (Raymond 1998). Examples relevant to the subject of this study—religions that exhibit signs of a noospheric culture—could be the cases of Falun Dafa, Partenia, the Israeli officers against the occupation of Palestine, and the Churches' coalition for social and economic justice. The common thread of these examples is the creation of connections of communication and connectedness, evoking thus the emergence of noosphere—the "ideational" (Ronfeldt and Arquilla 1999) realm of freely moving ideas, views, perceptions and thoughts.

Techno-religious Responses

Alongside the metaphysical and spiritual conceptualizations and interpretations of ICTs, there are also the approaches of representatives of
different religions, such as theologians, ministers and monastics, as well
as those of academics who examine the issues arising from the intersection of religion and ICTs. As mentioned at the beginning of this study,
the Web accommodates millions of sites that cover almost the entire spectrum of humanity's religious expressions. The sites of the Monastery
of Christ in the Desert, Hindu Net, Diocese of Partenia, Falun Dafa,
Western Wall live cam, Mecca, Buddha Net, Sivananda Yoga, Shinto
shrines, International Association of Sufism, Sikhism, and Wicca are
some examples of the diverse religious presences on the Web. In addition, the availability of specialized religious software, such as Arabic
tutorials and Islamic law database; online instructional Buddhist meditation; uploading prayers; online memorials, marriages and other
rituals; instructions for virtual rituals and Pujas, in other words the millions of different religious activities, are nothing less than, as Babin and
Zukowski (2002, 4) claim, signals of an inexorable craving for religion
and spirituality that is increasing within all cultures.

Zaleski's (1997) work is the first attempt which endeavours to offer
an exegesis of the adoption of ICTs by the major religions of the world.
Although it may be outdated and limited, it does nevertheless offer
some valuable insights. Zaleski discusses with his interviewees both
technical and religio-spiritual issues, such as the design and uploading of websites; the possibility of ICTs serving as a holy end (20); the
spiritual presence behind the websites (61); authority and hierarchy
(100–108); disruption of peoples' "pranic" system (211) and the possibility of God manifesting on the Web (214). Also, the works of Babin
and Zukowski (2002), Hammerman (2000) and Groothuis (1999), who
examine the relation of religion and ICTs, offer some intriguing views
of confessional approaches and responses to the effects and impacts of
ICTs on both practical and theological issues. The illustrative examples
which follow should not be taken as representing the view of each tradition, but as pointers to the multiplicity of understandings that appear
not only between traditions, but within each tradition as well.

In an article in 1995 about the website of the Zen Mountain Monastery,
Victoria Hosei Cajipe (1995, in Zaleski 1997, 164–65), the monastery's
webmaster, published three claims about ICTs. The first was that the
Net is in the process of constructing Teilhard's notion of noosphere, the
"planetary mind"; the second was that the units of multimedia information on the Web and their flow are similar to the "contents and flow

of those of the mind"; and the third was that Abbot Loori of the monastery has integrated the duality of 0s and 1s of the computation language as "skilful means for communicating the Dharma". Moreover, the Abbot (in Zaleski 1997, 166–67), underlines the importance of skilful means and asserts that the Buddha himself would use computers to disseminate Dharma. While acknowledging that communication and interactivity through any means, apart from face-to-face, may lack intimacy, the Abbot also acknowledges that words can be transformative, if they are "live –if they have chi". "Live" words, according to Abbot Loori, can have a "turning effect" on people in every form they appear. However, although the Abbot (172–73) emphasizes that the energy that flows from teacher to student cannot be transmitted through the Web, he maintains that the websites should be conceptualized as "pointers to sacredness" rather than being sacred in themselves.

Venerable Pannyavaro (1998), the founder and webmaster of Buddhanet, echoes Abbot Loori in the utilization of ICTs in spreading the Dharma and in the belief that the Buddha would be a cybernaut, but expands the intersection of Buddhism and the Web beyond the notion of skilfully employing all available means. In his view ITCs' decentralized character and freedom from any kind of control offer a new opportunity for all perceptions, opinions and voices to be equally expressed. This, for Venerable Pannyavaro (1998), is the true essence of ITCs' nature, which favours neither a particular religion nor a particular branch of a religion. In this way, he continues, the Dharma, as always, can only be identified through the "genuine experience of individual practitioners and not by any arbitrary authority". The worldwide connectivity offered by ICTs is understood by Venerable Pannyavaro as an opportunity for the creation of an "online Buddhist community of practitioners". It is imperative, for Venerable Pannyavaro, that the "Cyber Sangha", who will provide the "dataline to Enlightenment" consists of computer-literate monks and nuns "if Buddhism in the 21st century is not to be left behind as a museum piece".

A similar concern is put forward by Babin and Zukowski (2002, 64) regarding the modernization of the Catholic Church in respect of employing ICTs for spreading her message. Conveying exactly the same thought as Pannyavaro, they highlight the possibility of the Church cutting herself off from a historical moment. Zukowski (2002) takes a step further and proposes that the catechetical ministry for the twenty-first century should follow Disney's example in creating a team of "imagineers". Like the Disney counterparts, the Church's imagineers should be engaged in continuous creative thinking about their work, which, in the Disney work environment, is supported by "dream retreats". The purpose of "dream retreats", Zukowski explains, is to place the participants in an environment of new ideas which may generate innovative solutions to existing problems.

For Babin and Zukowski (2002, 4–5), the Catholic Church faces a number of challenges deriving from the new concepts brought forward by ICTs. For example, they recognize that nowadays a new realization of the "sacred, of the Totally Other, of religious tradition and of the spiritual life" (5) is emerging. They also notice that people are being immersed in a spiritual restlessness resulting from their incapability to relate their new religious experiences to the traditional concepts of Church teachings. As ICTs reach a wider spectrum of users, Babin and Zukowski (2002, 7) indicate that it is necessary for the Church to develop an awareness of how the reality of both believers and non-believers is affected, influenced and reformed by the new environment with which people interact. In order to compete in a highly technological and commercial world, Babin and Zukowski (2002, 107) emphasize that the Church needs to engage in a "dynamic dialogue", which has to be characterized not by "passive tolerance", but by "activity, compromise, knowledge of one's partners, of their history, of their psychology and their positions". For the authors (167–69), cyberspace, an increasingly expanding novel cultural space, has its own "creeds, codes and cults" and its culture is characterized by interactivity which triggers the "dynamics of inter-personal relationships and the formation of new virtual communities". Websites, according to Babin and Zukowski (2002, 169), are not only places for interactivity, but also places and spaces for attracting and capturing the imagination of netizens, who either just explore or search for spiritual meaning. The way, therefore, in which the Church perceives and places herself within this multidimensional space is quite important. Being just another node among millions of others, within an anarchic milieu, the Church loses any sense of control over both the surfing and the experiences of her followers. This may prove problematic for those who are accustomed to be in control (Babin and Zukowski 2002, 170). The Church, the authors (170) suggest, in order to move to the twenty-first century, has to train her ministers according to the demands of ICTs' diverse sphere of action.

This is also highlighted by Fajardo (2002), whose understanding of evangelization and missionary work within ICTs offers an additional dimension to those discussed by Babin and Zukowski. For instance, while recognizing the need for the missionaries to "read the Signs of the Times" (Fisichella 1995, in Fajardo 2002) and be creative, Fajardo emphasizes the importance of reaching the poor. Cyberspacing Popular Mission, for Fajardo, has a twofold result. On the one hand, it demonstrates that the ability to make present "God's Reign in a click, is a real evidence that the Kingdom of God is not only an image in cyberspace, but is ACTUALLY a reality unfolding in Cyberspace". On the other hand, it announces the subjugation of ICTs in the service of the poor, marginalized sector of society, which, in his view, "bridges the global Digital Divide". An example of such creativity may be the CBCPNet[71] (Catholic Bishops' Conference of the Philippines), an Internet service provider in the Philippines established by the Catholic Church in 1999. CBCPNet provides, on the one hand, a filtered access that blocks pornographic sites and, on the other hand, affordable access which implies that the poor areas of the Philippines will have the opportunity to get connected. This initiative corresponds to Fajardo's (2002) vision of the Church's active engagement in wiring the poor and also to Babin and Zukowski's (2002, 171) view in which the catechists, missionaries and strategists of the Church

> [n]eed to consider [themselves] as artists of faith in the media-sphere. [They] have new tools that offer [them] creative opportunities to pioneer within the new frontier. This is not the time for lone rangers, but for collaborators and innovators.

Swami Atma (in Zaleski 1997, 209), the webmaster of the Sivananda Yoga site, believes that God does manifest on the Web, when God is thought of as being pure consciousness. In this sense God is everywhere. However, the Swami stresses that the energy that passes over in a living relationship between disciple and teacher cannot pass through cyber-space. Sheikh Hisham Muhammad Kabbani (in Zaleski 1997, 54–62), though, believes that when people log on to the Haqqani site and engage with its content, they receive some energy which then can be further developed to higher levels through practice and meditation. In fact, for the Sheikh, ICTs are energy which can be enhanced by peoples' meditative experiences, when these experiences are "saved" in a computer and shared with others (64–67). In this sense, ICTs can be understood as a force which not only connects people but elevates humanity. A similar framework of thinking is expressed by Rabbi Kazen (in Zaleski 1997, 17), responsible for the Jewish site Chabad.org which belongs to the Hasidic branch of Judaism that emphasizes one's relationship with God and devotion to others. A series of talks, given by Rabbi Schneerson between the late sixties and the early eighties, inspired an essay entitled "Modern Technology and Judaism" (in Zaleski 1997, 19) in which it is stated that

> [t]he advance of scientific understanding is increasingly revealing the inherent unity in the universe, as expressed in the forces of nature. Being aware of this can serve as a preparation and prologue to the Era of Mashiach, for at that time the Creator's simple uncompound unity will become evident.

Although Rabbi Schneerson was referring to radio and TV, Rabbi Kazen affirms that, not only is the concept of inherent unity in the world reinforced in ICTs, but they can also be seen as "holy technologies", as serving a "holy end", for they can bring humanity together and consequently, they can unite the "good and light" that exist in the world (in Zaleski 1997, 20). As such, for Rabbi Kazen, ICTs are a means toward the Era of the Mashiach. By uploading the Hanukkah—the Festival of Light—in 1996, the Rabbi believed that he was utilizing the "power and realm of the Internet to raise the moral and ethical barometer of our planet". The availability on the site of the link "ask the Rabbi" has proved an invaluable tool, not only for doctrinal guidance but for the creation of deeper and closer relationships between the Rabbi and his congregation.

Hammerman (2000, 129–32), a Rabbi himself, identifies the interconnection between the concept of God and ICTs. Highlighting that Christianity, Islam and Judaism are centred on the sanctity of the written word, Hammerman analyses the term "Word" that is exemplified in John's Gospel (1:1). In his analysis, Hammerman employs the Oxford Annotated Bible (John 1) in which "Word" is interpreted as being "God [himself] in action, creating, revealing, redeeming", and suggests that God is experienced within ICTs through the word. On a personal level, the Rabbi (133–38) presents the experiences generated by communicating with his ministry by email, through which, opening new channels of contact and new, freer and constructive forms of communication, he reaches deeper levels of connectivity with his congregation. This ability offered by ICTs for a wider, more intimate communication between a minister and his or her congregation and between colleagues is a repeated point. The Presbyterian minister Henderson (2002) too, proclaims that online connectedness was "a life-transforming experience", which not only eliminated any feelings of loneliness but also developed a new kind of collaboration between ministers that would not have been possible without ICTs.

Concluding his search for the digital God, Hammerman (2000, 208) proposes two ways in which God can be found online. The first is to look for "God on the Internet" and the second is to see "God as the Internet". While the former refers to the search for "divine messages, sacred inspiration, interpersonal and communal connection and theological education", the latter refers to the acknowledgement that cyberspace as a whole can "bring us closer to understanding and experiencing the sacred". Hammerman's model, despite its theological character, encapsulates the essence of ICTs. If, however, instead of the word God, one uses words such as "the Other", "Reality", "Enlightenment" and so on, then Hammerman's model expands its applicability to all religious/spiritual/metaphysical traditions.

Final Remarks

All these different theoretical perceptions, approaches and ideological positions surrounding the ontological character of ICTs and their metaphorical/conceptual part—cyberspace/Infobahn/noosphere—not only reveal the extraordinary ways in which the medium can be understood, but also the diverse variety of ways in which it can be used.

The role of the digerati may appear to be just a theoretical one. However, as Slouka (1997, 29) indicates, some have not only the financial means but also the technological knowledge and expertise to create and develop their theories, thus giving substance to their utopian and prophetical views and visions. The members of this elite, Jordan (1999, 129) maintains, control cyberspace by exercising their cyberpower which, generated by their advanced technical knowledge, allows them to alter from within the "thingness" of the technological apparatuses that construct the online experience. Consequently, Jordan stresses, this elite has the capacity to produce, adjust, transform and control the possibilities of cyberspace. This can be seen not only in the research projects of different, highly technologically orientated institutions, such as the MIT, but also, as will be shown in the following chapter, in the formation of totally new cyber-religious utterances, such as the Church of Virus, Technosophy and Digitalism, among others, whose founder(s) belong to the community of computer scientists.

This theoretical presentation of both techno-metaphysical/techno-spiritual and techno-religious conceptions is by no means a detailed or an in-depth one, for three reasons. First, such a detailed account, due to its sheer size, cannot be incorporated as part of a study but has to be a study in its own right. Second, to date, there is no study that has addressed the topic in a systematic way; therefore, there are no data (maybe for conclusions?). Third, the purpose of the presentation is, on the one hand, to offer a snapshot of a vast and unexplored area of theoretical discourses, and, on the other hand, to provide possible methodological signifiers, in that, as Markham (2003) and Stahl (1999) indicate, different discursive choices have constructive and significant repercussions on the form and perception of ICTs. Extending this point, it is suggested here that the discursive choices also may determine the ways in which ICTs are employed and used, either traditionally or innovatively. This, in turn, may further facilitate the monitoring, investigation and understanding of the purpose, functionality and meaning of religious websites.

The point made here is that cyberspace, as has been shown, has the capacity to be perceived as a sacred space, as a spiritual space and as a socio-political space. As such, it not only carries institutionalized, non-institutionalized religions, NRMs and, as Zaleski (1997, 4) points out, "a worldwide hearing of every voice within these religions", but also, an exceedingly unimaginable and immeasurable wealth of people's religious expressions, as well as novel religious and spiritual utterances. From the discourses presented in this section, it appears that two responsive models are emerging. On the one hand, it is the utilitarian responses that interpret ICTs in terms of their unique capacity to disseminate, globally, the doctrinal, ethical, mythological and social dimensions of a religion, and, on the other hand, it is the metaphorical/symbolic responses that interpret ICTs in terms of their unique capacity to generate new avenues for the experiential and ritual dimensions of a religion.

In the themes that emerge in this section ICTs and their conceptual/metaphorical derivatives are seen as:

- Heavenly City
- The new home of Mind
- Platonic realm incarnate
- Realm of "psyches" or "souls"
- Wisdom
- Disembodiment
- Generator of mystical experience
- noosphere
- Skilful means
- Means toward the Era of the Mashiach
- Cyber Sangha
- God.

Perhaps most of all, the rewording of Psalm 139[72] shows the result of the intersection between religion and ICTs, for, as Drees (2002, 646) comments, new expressions that move beyond traditional religious imagery are important. The significance of novel utterances and imageries lies in their "realism about human nature", that is, their ability to convey and reflect the "way things really are" (Drees 2002, 647).

> O Lord, You have searched me and You have accessed me
> You know my logging on and my logging off.
> You discern my outlook from afar.
> You mark when I surf and when I download,
> All my cache lies open for You…
>
> If I take the links of AltaVista
> And dwell at the innermost ends of the Net
> Even there your cookies would find me
> Your mouse hand holds me fast…

O God that You would slay the viruses
Keep away from me hacking hands
With deceit they act against us
And set our hard drives at naught...

O scan me God, and know my directories
Defragment me and know my files
See that I enter not the wrong password
And highlight for me the paths of life eternal.

Although this cyberPsalm does not reflect humanity's reality, it nevertheless presents the new conceptualizations of cybernauts' reality and their technological ability to amend that reality.

5 Research Process and Method

My method of identifying a representative sample of websites involved repeated searching of the Web, using keywords and hyperlinks, over almost the whole period of preparation of this thesis. I could have approached this theoretical study by identifying, in advance of any empirical examples, "types" of websites which would represent different poles of expression within an overall religious discourse in cyberspace. For example, I might have presupposed that Buddhist websites would be very different from Islamic, and so on. However, this approach would have produced findings which simply reflected my naïve assumptions. Instead, over a period of years I explored the Web, gradually building a sense of what is to be found in cyberspace, and from this knowledge I developed a series of experimental typologies (discussed in detail in the Introduction). The most recent of these typologies presented here is not the final word, but allows me to present a genuinely varied sample of websites, differentiated not by sectarian or doctrinal characteristics, but by aspects such as authorship, "voice", variability over time, utilization of Web technologies, discursive formations, etc. (see Chapter 6 on Methodology).

My prior involvement with ICTs, mostly the Web, proved to be both beneficial and disadvantageous, in the sense that while offering me a base upon which I would develop and expand my research, it also created a number of presumptions, especially regarding certain aspects of my field. My interaction with ICTs can be divided into three different stages, each of which reflects my relationship first with ICTs and, later on, with my research field and subject. I would describe the first (at the beginning of the nineties), as the stage of "naivety". This period was characterized by unquestioning enthusiasm, wonder and fascination for the recently developed and intricate technological advancements in communication and dissemination of information. At that time, I perceived ICTs as a "miracle" of human invention, and their conception and design as the epitome of humanity's development of communication and knowledge-sharing tools. My second stage (mid-end of the nineties) was the "hypothetical", during which my experience of "being online" initiated a number of assumptions that later on proved to be false. These assumptions were a result of the way in which I experienced my "online journeys": for instance, I was able to have the latest technological infrastructure (hardware and software), to use efficiently those available "tools" and my capability to surf the Web—in other words, my advanced computer skills. The thought that all these instantly placed me in a privileged "class" never occurred to me. Instead, I assumed that, like me, everybody was able to experience the novelty.

Consequently, I embarked on my research in September 2000 believing, with a high degree of certainty, that: (a) the community of cybernauts consisted of the majority of the human population. This in turn implied that (b) having a website was a matter of choice of a religious body; therefore (c) all religious bodies could/would exist on the Web. This, again, produced a series of assumptions regarding the Web's retrieval systems and search processes. My impression was that finding a particular site on the Web was a straightforward process that depended solely on the researcher's ability. In other words, I believed that everything on the Web is just a "click" away.

In summary, prior to 2000, my interaction with ICTs was characterized by a number of presuppositions deriving from my *Weltanschauung* which was marked, to a great extent, by my exaggerated over-utopian understanding of the medium.

However, a number of factors contributed to movement from the "naïve" and "hypothetical" frame of mind to the adoption of a critical approach, which was the last and final stage of my interaction with the Web, and which remained with me for the whole duration of my research. All my preconceived ideas were demolished as soon as I announced to family and friends the subject of my thesis and what it entailed. Their reactions and questions, such as, "What is the Internet?", "What do you mean, you connect?", "What if you do not have the Internet?", among others, surprised me, placing a considerable question mark on all my previous claims about religious discourses, or any other discourse, in cyberspace, and underlining the indispensability of investigating and including the issue of access into the thesis. Investigating the issue of access revealed that my knowledge of the field was not only quite limited, but what I thought I knew was a biased and very narrow "slice" of a vast area of which, in reality, I knew nothing. Questions such as, "Who participates in religious discourse in ICTs?"; "Is cyberspatial religious discourse an essentially elitist discourse (articulated by religious leaders) or it is also formed at the grass roots?", seemed to form an essential part of the thesis.

Additionally, re-addressing some of the points that I had underlined in the nineties,[1] it became apparent to me that the main issue of the study should be not so much about classifying the different cyberreligious discourses, but about addressing/investigating the subject and its relation to the field within which it appears. This realization generated further questions which expanded the horizon of my thinking, and initiated the adoption of a broad approach to the field that led to connecting the e-religious discourse's presence with the wider sociology of the Web, as this was shaped by the Web's epistemological and theoretical formations. Consequently, a number of points were identified as being fundamental to the thesis. For instance:

a.   A deeper understanding of my research field was essential for the construction of a methodological approach.
b.   Techno-religious theories would facilitate the identification of the different usages of the Web.
c.   A methodological set of tools would enable multiple ways of exploration, investigation and study of e-religion in its different forms.
d.   No predetermined methodological apparatus would offer freedom and flexibility to recognize and explore emerging concepts and issues.

Thinking critically about my field enabled me to develop an in-depth knowledge about its operational, functional and structural properties which, in turn, allowed me to identify the parameters that influenced my research process.[2] For example, I am well aware of my impact on the results of my research and that my contributions to the construction of my data were determined, to a great extent, by particular capabilities which were decided by a number of factors, such as adequate technical infrastructure, ability to operate hardware and utilize software, linguistic capabilities and socio-cultural frameworks.

Additionally, I am also aware of the limitations of my study that result precisely from my socio-cultural circumstance and my linguistic capabilities. For instance, although the technical tools available to me were well advanced, which meant that I was able to discover any available site, I was capable of analysing and incorporating into the study only those that I could understand, i.e. those that were either in English and/or Greek. For example, sites such as those of the Holy Resurrection Cathedral in Tokyo, Islamway and hindu.dk, despite the fact that I was capable of recognizing their "identity" (i.e. Japanese Orthodox Christian church, Islam and Hinduism), through their symbols (due to my academic upbringing in the study of religions), could not be included because their texts were in Japanese, Arabic and Danish respectively. Thus, while in some respects I was well "equipped" to identify religious sites, in some other respects I was "disabled". Linguistic barriers meant that a substantial number of sites which could have enriched my types and provided an additional perspective to my findings had to be excluded. In other words, my study suffers from the absence of a number of universes that could neither be explored and studied, nor be integrated into the thesis, because of my multilingual inabilities. However, it should be noted that what I was able to discover, study and include in my findings was not always dependent on my technical and linguistic capabilities, but also on external circumstances.[3]

Moreover, it is suggested here that if this study were conducted by one who lives in a western country, speaks English, but has different technical infrastructure,[4] or by one who has the latest technical infrastructure but lives in a non-western country and speaks no English, then it is very likely that he or she would have understood and presented a different e-religion from the one presented here. In other words, this study reaffirms that "what people (the 'seekers') are able to find on the Web determines what the Web consists of for them" (Introna and Nissenbaum 2000, 25).

Process and Method

Investigating the Web and its features resulted in the formation of some questions, such as, Whose religion is expressed in the websites? How is this religion manifested? What are its characteristics? What perceptions initiated such conceptualizations and contextualization? What new issues, conceptions and usages are emerging and what new religious expressions are formed? These questions, as well as this study's overall directions, issues and considerations,[5] reveal, on the one hand, my understanding of e-religion and, on the other hand, how this understanding was developed. In order to answer the above questions, and also taking into consideration my previous experience, I decided that my "fieldwork" would provide a much wider sample of sites if it was based more on the motto "go boldly where no one has gone before" and implementing a multidimensional research approach rather than having a specific plan. For instance, I could have continued my research focusing on particular religious keyword queries and on the directories' categories, but this would reveal only the "obvious" sites, while the "hidden" and "unexpected" that I assumed existed would have remained concealed.

My research was built on the following steps: Firstly, I created a database of URLs which was divided into different categories. For example, primary resources (i.e. religious sites) and secondary resources (i.e. academic and non-academic works on cyberspace in general and on religion online in particular). The in-depth knowledge of search engines' and directories' operationality[6] that I had acquired, and also the accelerating numbers of results showed that my research could not rely only on a keyword search of the Web. Thus, in order to increase the spectrum of my results, I created a network of sources:

- Search engines
- Web rings
- H-links
- Directories in both surface and deep Web
- Journals, books, newspapers, magazines (in both off and online forms)
- E-zines
- Radio
- Mailing lists, discussion forums and chat rooms.

which I was searching every day for several hours. Another source that proved quite valuable was the cultivation of "social capital". Friends, colleagues and my students were passing on to me the URLs that they came across.

My keyword searches were divided into two types. First, I was using a specific keyword such as "Islam", "Judaism" etc., and second, a general keyword such as "religion" or "church", "synagogue" etc. The specified keywords provided the "obvious" results, such as the sites of the C of E, the Vatican, the Islam Page, the Hindu Universe or the Ecumenical Patriarchate and pages about Islam, Hinduism and so on that were uploaded from a wide variety of sources (i.e. academic, media, individuals, governments). The "obvious" were usually found on the first page of the results. The general keyword searches proved to be quite problematic, in the sense that the number of hits was of such a considerable size (usually in the region of millions) that it made the exploration of them very time consuming. Thus, in order to discover as much as possible about the presence of e-religious discourses, I conducted a series of Web searches using various combinations of keywords. For instance: "Religion and the Internet"; "religion and the Web"; "religion and cyberspace"; "religion online"; "religion in cyberspace"; "cyberreligion"; "religion and technology"; "technoreligion/ous". The same procedure was followed for other terms (i.e. "church and", "church of", mosque, synagogue, temple, monastery, clergy, imam, priest, rabbi etc.). From the results pages of each search, a number of pages were randomly chosen (i.e. from 1 to 6, to 11, to 19, to 36, to 78 and so on) the hits of which were explored and the selected site(s) were added on to the database.

Directories provided a valuable number of sites, especially in terms of religious expressions unknown to me, and also those related to cyberculture. In order to have representative a sample as possible I searched two directories of the surface Web (Yahoo and the Open Directory Project dmoz) and one directory of the deep Web (Complete Planet). Cross-referencing sites between the directories offered me an insight into the differences of cataloguing and classifying various sites between the directories. For example, if one clicks Yahoo's category "Society and Culture" then "Religion" then "Faiths and Practices" then "Cyberculture Religions", one will discover Digitalism, Cosmosophy and the Church of Virus. In order to find cyberreligions in the dmoz directory, however, the path is totally different. For instance, despite my efforts it was not possible to find any of the cyberreligions listed in Yahoo. By performing a keyword search, though (a facility provided by dmoz), I finally discovered the Church of Virus, which I would have discovered if I had taken the following steps: from the category Society, to Religion, to Humanism, to Groups, to Online Groups, where the Church of Virus is listed.

Mailing lists were an indispensable source of academic works on my subject and discussion forums provided some important ideas and concepts, such as online Eucharist, online weddings and e-rituals in general. Web rings and H-links were other sources that proved valuable in discovering "hidden" sites.

Some examples of the ways in which certain sites were accessed may elucidate the research process and method. For instance, the Holy See, C of E, and Ecclesia (the website of the Church of Greece) were found through specific keyword search.

"Digitalism", "Technosophy" and "Cosmosophy" were found in Yahoo's directory. The "Church of Virus" was discovered through a keyword search ("church of") and it was found on results page 12. "Virtually Zen", an Israeli Zen site, was found by a Web ring; "Skate Church" was discovered through H-links; the site of the "Church of Fools" was accessed after reading an article in an offline newspaper. The "here-and-now" site was discussed in a chat room and the "Brotherhood of the Crossed Circle" was suggested to me by a colleague.

My fieldwork activity and experience emphasized and confirmed not only the versatility of the Web and the important role that issues such as time and hypertext links play in its overall structure, but also their consequential ramifications in the research process and in the construction of the proposed methodology.[7] For instance, the above mentioned examples on the one hand demonstrate that a versatile field such as the Web requires a flexible and multifaceted research system and, on the other hand, they underline the dynamic role of hypertextuality, in the sense that it may function not only as an indicator of navigationality and/or referentiality, but also as an "unintended" locating/explorative research facility.

The multidimensional approach to researching the Web resulted in the accumulation of a considerable number[8] of sites which were added to the database. As mentioned earlier (see Introduction), the realization that my field was in a constant flux played a crucial role in the formation of the methodological apparatus. In order to overcome the changes that were occurring in my field, especially those observed through time, the problems deriving from sites that were either "lost" or "revised" were resolved by implementing specified software that enabled me to save selected sites on the hard drive, keeping thus their initial design and format. This method of preserving samples of sites enabled me to observe possible changes, and also the extent to which the sites were either developing and expanding, or decreasing and decaying.

For the examination of sites, Bainbridge's (2000) dual ethnographic method—*observation ethnography* and *informant ethnography*—was employed as being the more appropriate. While observation ethnography concentrates on static examination of websites—involving no interaction with the owners—informant ethnography involves dynamic examination, requiring communication and interaction. Consequently, for sites belonging to the spatial categories and those under synchronic investigation, observant ethnography—in having no predetermined focus—is more suitable, for it allows the sites under investigation to "speak for themselves". The investigation and analysis of New Cyberreligious Movements (NCRMs), and the nature of the diachronic examination, however, requiring contact, communication and interaction with both the owners of the sites and, possibly, with other participants, demanded the employment of informant ethnography.

Thus, by utilizing, whenever possible, the "contact us" link, I engaged in a "conversation", via email, with the persons/individuals responsible for Digitalism, Technosophy and the Church of Virus, aiming to ascertain specific information that was not revealed on their website. The questions I asked each informant were:

- What is the country of origin of Digitalism/Technosophy/Church of Virus (D/T/CoV)?
- Personal information regarding the founder(s) (age, education, occupation)
- Does D/T/CoV exist purely online or does it also exist in the offline world?
- Would you characterize D/T/CoV as a religion, a philosophy, a spiritual path or something else?
- What was the driving force behind the formation of D/T/CoV?
- Do people respond to D/T/CoV? Do they find the ideas/concepts/ philosophy/etc. of D/T/CoV appealing?
- Could you say that there is a community around D/T/CoV?
- How do you perceive the relationship between D/T/CoV and cyberspace?

- Are you aware of other religions/philosophies/spiritual orders/etc. that exist purely online? If yes, could you name them?
- Are there any plans for expanding D/T/CoV (e.g. practices, festivals, rituals etc.)?

The responses I received, which were at times quite lengthy, revealed a great amount of valuable information, not only regarding these NCRMs, their beginning, the founder's visions, their theoretical foundations and so on, but also unexpected information which enhanced my methodological perspective and analysis.[9]

6 Methodology

Introduction

The diversity and wealth of the existing body of literature suggest that the Internet provides us with a profusion of research areas, by offering an infinite variety of issues, concepts, ideas and perceptions for investigation in both online presences and interactivities.

The question of methodology within the general field of cyberculture studies has, to date, been explored and presented primarily in terms of utilizing the Internet to conduct surveys, to collect data, to publish online survey reports and to study communities, MOOs, bulletin boards (BBs), peoples' online interaction and online social networks (Garton et al. 1999; Mann and Stewart 2000; Jones 1999a).

The currently proposed methodologies for researching either the whole (the Internet), or any of its parts, suffer from the dominance of functionalist perspectives which give prominence to the design of research models that would provide efficient, successful and effective results in the area of quantitative research. The majority of these works, by using the Internet as a data collection and/or publication tool, reduce it to a mere instrument.[1] This, however, has been contested and as Poster (1995b) and others (Dawson and Hennebry 1999; Ward 2000; Mann and Stewart 2000; Markham 2003) have emphasized, the Internet is also a social space, an environment, which has the capacity to initiate new forms of interaction and new types of relations of power between participators. Furthermore, different technologies should not be seen simply as aids to human activity but also as influential forces acting to reshape that activity and its meaning (Winner 1986). Such a perception clearly underlines the paramount importance of researching religious, or any other, activities within the sphere of ICTs. It also underlines that the way in which the Internet is perceived and understood influences the process of choosing an adequate methodological approach for its investigation.

This chapter presents a critical evaluation of different methodological approaches, identifies the elements of the field (website), proposes a methodological framework and presents illustrative empirical evidence.

Researching Religion on the Web

Systematic works that have examined different methodological approaches related exclusively to the subject of religion and the Web are those of Bedell, Bainbridge, Helland, Horsfall, Mayer and Introvigne in the Hadden and Cowan (2000) collection; Frobish (2000) and Karaflogka (1998, 2002). A general discussion on methodological issues and research strategies is offered by Dawson (2000).

Approaches and issues

Conceptual generalism

A critical analysis of the works in the Hadden and Cowan collection, related to methodological enquiry, reveals two interrelated issues. The first, which may be called "conceptual generalism", refers to the choice of words used within the various methodological, theoretical and/or descriptive studies relevant to religion and ICTs. For instance, the constant interchanging of the terms "CMC", "the Internet", "the Web" and "cyberspace", which prevails in most works (Dawson 2000; Helland 2000; Introvigne 2000; Bedell 2000; Horsfall 2000; Karaflogka 1998, 2002), presents a conceptual generalization of ICTs that proves problematic for both theoretical and methodological frameworks, for it implies homogeneity.

However, as stated elsewhere in this study,[2] in order to avoid possible ambiguities of perception, differentiation between the Internet's different applications is essential, since such applications—emails, chat rooms, forums, BBs, MOOs, blogs or websites—are diverse "Internetopoi"[3] each functioning within different spatial, temporal and contextual frames/models, provoking and facilitating specific and largely unique expressions, activities and interactions. These Internetopoi, being diverse, require diverse methodological models which will take into consideration the various features and qualities of each.

Equally problematic is the excessive use of the term "religion". References such as "religion and the Internet", "religion in cyberspace", "online-religion" and so on, imply that religion is one comprehensive entity that can be studied as such within the domain of ICTs. Yet, as is well known, there is neither one definition of religion nor one religion.[4] Moreover, even if the term "religion" is accepted, one has to consider the different components that constitute the concept "religion", such as, for example, Ninian Smart's (1969) seven dimensions of religion. Smart's dimensions are used here not as exhaustive but as representative cases, for other issues and/or concepts could be added as being parts of a religion. For instance, what the author calls "Web facets of religions"[5]

could be characterized as additional components of the notion of religion. Each dimension of a religion embodies a set of distinct characteristics that form its nature. As such, not only does each dimension have
its own distinctive characteristics, but also its own function and usage
in both the offline and online worlds. Within the environment of ICTs,
the dimensions are enhanced by the mediums' unequivocal peculiarities. For example, ritual and practical dimensions are articulated dispa-
rately in a chat room, on an academic site, on a blog and on a website
of either a religious system or an individual. The disparateness is observable in both content and method of presentation. For instance, while
in the first applications (chat room, academic, blog), the notion of ritual
appears as a piece of information disseminated almost exclusively tex-
tually, in the latter (website), ritual may move beyond the textual form
to become an animated action that the user can participate in and/or in
which he or she can interact with other users. This is possible because
of the Web's capacity to support specially formatted documents, including graphics, 3D environments, audio and video.

Methodological exclusivism/reductionism

The second issue to be unpicked is what the author calls "methodological exclusivism/reductionism". The term refers to research methodologies that are highly specific in their focus, and, as a result, propose only
selected aspects as their areas of investigation. Such an approach is valuable when its focus is clear and its subject-matter is distinctly orientated,
as in the cases of the exceptional study of Frobish (2000), which offers
a critical analysis of the content of the site of the Church of Scientology;
Bedell's (2000) qualitative research of people's usage of ICTs for either
enhancing their spiritual life, or participating in spiritual communities;
Horsfall's (2000) comparative study and suggested descriptive typology
of the ways in which different religious organizations and/or groups are
using the Internet; and Bainbridge's (2000) excellent study of the ways
in which religious movements compete with each other on the Web.
Similarly, the works of Mayer (2000) and Introvigne (2000) that concentrate particularly on "cyberspace propaganda wars" and on "anti-
cult terrorism via the Internet" respectively, offer constructive aspects of
e-religious utterances related to New Religious Movements (NRMs).

The usefulness and value of these works is that, regardless of the conceptual amalgamation and, in cases, as for example in Horfall's study, total
absence of research methods, the authors offer investigations of quite specific research areas that facilitate substantially the basic understanding of
the intersection between religious discourses and the Web in particular
cases. In the cases of Helland (2000) and Karaflogka (2000a, 2002), who
attempt to provide a general methodological platform for studying reli-

gion on ICTs, the term "methodological exclusivism/reductionism" refers to a narrow view of both religion and ICTs that results in the formation of a methodology, which, on the one hand, excludes parts of ICTs and, on the other hand, reduces religion by excluding aspects of it.

For instance, Helland (2000, 205) states that his work entitled "Online-Religion/Religion-Online and Virtual Communitas", provides a "heuristic device for a general classification of religious and spiritually focused Web sites". In Helland's view, "religion on the Internet manifests itself in two forms" (205), namely "online-religion" and "religion-online". Helland grounds the "online-religion" category on Turner's (1969) notions of "liminality" and "communitas" (214–15). Employing Turner's types of communitas (existential, normative and ideological) he divides "online-religion" into three types of communitas and offers examples of "online religious groups" (216) that fit the profile of each type. Thus, for Helland, "online-religion", on the one hand, represents a "direct reaction to religion in the secular world, allowing for a new manifestation of religious interaction, participation and community" (205), and, on the other hand, being "anti-structured", unregulated" and "unsupervised" may offer a "low commitment form of religious participation" (219). "Religion-online", in Helland's understanding, represents characteristically "institutionalized religious structures" and their usage of the "medium as a traditional form of one-to-many communication" (205). As well as some conceptual generalism that prevails in Helland's study, there are also signs of contextual and methodological confusion. For instance, while for his first category Helland uses as examples chat rooms and forums,[6] for his second category he uses websites. Yet, even if Helland's usage of two completely different parts of ICTs as examples of the particular "heuristic device" is accepted, his analysis of "religion-online" remains restrictive and reductionistic, in that, as typical examples of "religion-online", he offers the websites of the Vatican and the Church of Jesus Christ of Latter Day Saints (LDS). As he points out, websites of the "religion-online" type "have retained complete control over the belief system and present it to their practitioners without allowing for any reciprocal input" (220). This, however, is only partially accurate, because although the official site of LDS does not provide a link for interaction between the site and its visitors, other LDS sites do.[7] Regarding the Vatican site, Helland seems not to have taken into account that apart from being the official site of the Catholic Church, Vatican.va is also the site of an independent state, which implies that online communication and interactivity with the Vatican would most likely follow those of the offline type that are characterized by formality and bureaucratic procedures. One can communicate with the Vatican via the site, as long as one knows precisely whom one needs to contact and for what reason. For example, contact can be made with the Office of the Cardinal-Secretary of State, General Affairs, Relations to the States, Congregation for the Evangelization of Peoples and Congregation for the Clergy, and a number of Pontifical Councils focusing on various issues such as culture, family, youth to mention but a few.[8] In fact, since August 1998, connected Catholics have been able to follow the Pope's weekly audiences and special masses in real time. This was made possible by the launching of the Vatican's website and the total wiring of the Vatican which is supported by three Net servers that the Pope (allegedly) has personally named Michael, Gabriel and Raphael.[9] Moreover, both Catholics and non-Catholics have been uploading websites in which they may inform, support, challenge, confront, debate or even condemn the teachings of the Church.[10]

Karaflogka's (early) (2002) methodological apparatus, despite offering an analytical and comprehensive typology of Web religious expressions, also suffers from methodological exclusivism. For instance, while the distinction between religious expressions "on" and "in" ICTs is quite valuable for the study of e-religion, the typology of the "religion on" category proves exclusivist and reductionist. Its weakness is found especially in the "confessional" type in that this type cannot accommodate all websites deriving from a confessional perspective. Denominational disparities are not the only aspect that needs to be considered. A religion is not a coherent entity expressed in one way, but rather is multifaceted and manifested in a multiplicity of ways. Moreover, religion appears as having a more dominant and influential role in one location than another, and one can detect different degrees and patterns of interrelation between religion and other social institutions in one location or another. Therefore, the examination of sites of religions requires one to take into account the differences of a religion that result from a number of factors located within the sociology of each site's location.

For example, the Greek Orthodox Christian sites of Greek dioceses are different from those of the diaspora. Hence, although they could all be characterized as belonging to the same religion (in this case the Greek Orthodox Christian tradition), each site represents a particular perspective of the tradition as this is shaped by the cultural, political, social and economic dynamics arising from the locality from which each site originates. This framework could be applied to all religions—institutionalized, non-institutionalized, NRMs—and to different religious expressions such as doctrinal, social and/or experiential. Thus, it could be suggested that a comparative study, similar to that of Bainbridge (2000), or Horsfall (2000), conducted in a different social setting (e.g. in Europe), would perhaps provide different results.

Dawson (2000, 26), in his work "Researching Religion in Cyberspace: Issues and Strategies", quite rightly proposes that a research scheme for studying "religion on the Internet" has to incorporate the issues that derive from the "general sociology of the Internet". Within this framework, he identifies as "key substantive concerns" identity and community (31) and as "more specific concerns" the issues of "recruitment, conflict, authority and experience" (42). Dawson's "issues and strategies", while exceedingly helpful in establishing a basic model for investigating religion on ICTs, need to be expanded and/or amended if they are to be included in the investigation of websites.

Dawson (32), emphasizing the importance of identity and its relation to and ramification on an individual's religious life, focuses his attention on the construction of identity within the context of synchronous communication (MUDs, chat rooms and forums). However, the issue of identity within ICTs is far too complicated to be investigated only within the realms of MUDs and chat rooms.[11] Asynchronous communication also offers grounds for expressing one's identity, as is the case with personal websites which can be perceived as reflecting the construction of their producer's identities (Chandler 1998). Moreover, personal sites not only function as "self-publishing" mediums for "self-advertisement" (Chandler 1998), but also as "windows to the innermost sphere of an individual— that of their religious beliefs" (Karaflogka 1998), beliefs which, exposed to the public, offer themselves to the scrutiny of others. Seabrook (1995) notes that while one of the purposes of the physical homes is to keep the world out, personal sites are like slits people make in their real homes to let the world in. In addition, as will be shown later, parts of the design, structure and presentation of the websites of religious organizations, institutions, groups and so on, also reflect their owners' identity.

A further angle, through which the question of identity within ICTs could be examined, is offered by Zurawski (1999) who suggests that, instead of investigating the influence of ICTs on identity, one could investigate how culture and identity influence both the use and perception of ICTs. Such an approach may provide valuable indications, on the one hand, of the relationship between ICTs and the "outside world" of which they are an integral part (Zurawski 1999) and, on the other hand, of the relationship between a particular religious expression and ICTs. The examples of wide-ranging confessional perspectives that have been discussed in the previous chapter[12] highlight, not only the diversity of ICTs' function and usability, but also how problematic can be the chosen terminology, not least regarding the word "religion".

Final remarks

Broad, general and unspecified usage of the word "religion", found in most works on this topic, creates a number of questions which deserve attention and invite deconstructive and exegetical analyses. One may start, for example, by asking when scholars refer to "religion on/in/ and the Internet", whose religion do they refer to? Which religion do they mean? As has been shown, ICTs are a compilation of different applications within which one can find a profusion of diverse religious utterances and occurrences generated by officials, semi-officials, self-proclaimed theologians and spiritual experts, practitioners and laity, whose scope is to present, advertise, sell, caricature, celebrate, evaluate, attack or support particular religious causes.

Therefore, it could be suggested that the various methodological approaches and typological examinations presented in the previous section, notwithstanding that their contributions are in many respects of considerable value, remain restrictive for two reasons. Firstly, those who do refer to the Web seem not to have taken into consideration issues such as ephemerality, hypertext links and hypermedia that form distinct and exclusive characteristics, and the important role they play in the construction, formation and dissemination of e-religion. Secondly, the multimedia-mediated environment of the Web, which offers distinctive opportunities for disparate forms of usages, undertakings and performances, has been largely ignored. Consequently, it would appear that an area of considerable size, with accompanying heterogeneous theoretical and practical utilizations which significantly contribute to and enhance its content, has not been acknowledged. This means that (a) values, socio-religious and politico-religious dynamics, power relations, evolution and development, collaborations and co-operations, adaptation or abolition, utilization or manipulation of the Web from established religions, NRMs and individuals; and, (b) most importantly, the emergence of novel religious phenomena, at both theoretical and practical level, are largely excluded from the investigative process.

These issues, however, are important because (paraphrasing Poster's evaluation [1995b] of the Internet), although it seems that at present the Internet extends existing religious functions in new ways, the ways in which it may introduce new religious functions are far more persuasive as possible long-term effects. An additional element, which has not been addressed in any previous study, and which contributes substantially to users' "getting connected" activity, is that of the shifting between realities[13] that users experience when they are online, and its ramifications—if any—for the users' embracing and employing of different media offered by the Web, such as virtual reality, which, in turn, may encourage the creation and development of new religious structures.

The multidimensionality of both the medium (ICTs) and the subject (religion) indicates that the researcher is faced with excessively large and rhizomatic research areas. As such, each area may require a particular method for its study which may not be suitable to another area. Moreover, because certain types of online activity among users generate particular forms of involvement and interaction, they enable the acquisition of insights into specific issues. For example, while chat rooms, forums, MOOs and virtual communities offer data for studying social relationships and the representation of identity and gender, websites, having a different lifespan and a multimediated character, thus being a multifarious field (Wakeford 2000, 31), offer opportunities for investigating aspects related to linguistics, semiotics, aesthetics, symbolic representations and audiovisual effects.

Identifying the Elements of the Field

All the above-mentioned issues, concepts and aspects call for a methodological approach which will take into account their dynamic interrelation and influential part in the structure of the field's ontological character. As stated elsewhere in this study (see Chapter 4 on Theory) the different ways in which the medium is perceived, not only affect the ways in which it is utilized by the users, but may also shape the researchers' investigational processes and analyses (Markham 2004).

The medium's capability to be perceived in multiple ways (Markham 2004; Jones 1999a; Mann and Stewart 2000) is repeatedly emphasized in this study because it is considered to be fundamental. Thus, a methodological model for investigating websites has to include a number of elements which enable the identification of the different perceptions as these are reflected on a website. Such elements are hypertext/hypermedia, hypertext links and time which have at least a dual character. On the one hand they are integral parts of the field,[14] namely they belong to the field's infrastructure and as such they constitute the field as a whole. On the other hand, however, being also independent from the whole, that is, being themselves subjects of study, their inclusion or exclusion in a site determines, defines and to some extent affects the site's content and classification[15] which, in turn, provide valuable insights into the status of e-religion.

A metaphor that would elucidate the point is that of the planetary ecosystems. While air, water and soil constitute the planet's ecological infrastructure, each one thus contributing explicit biospheres to the whole, each supports its own ecosystem, which, being distinct and unique, enriches the diversity of the whole. For example, water sustains the planet as a whole; it has its own ecosystem (which is subject to investigation, study, categorization and so on); and its presence or absence from an area defines the ecosystem of that area (e.g the Amazon and the Sahara desert). In similar terms, hypermedia, hypertext links and the transcendence of spatio-temporal understanding are not only parts of the World Wide Web's infrastructure and themselves subjects of investigation and analysis,[16] but their presence or absence, as will be shown later on, determines the character, presence and type of the website under investigation. Consequently, a website methodology is bound to include in its investigational structure the issues of hypermedia, hypertext links and time.

Furthermore, the introduction and mass adoption of technological devices in any area of human activity, expression and experience (professional, social, educational, religious), redefine and transform, on the one hand, the meaning of the activity/expression/experience, and, on the other hand, the way in which this very activity/expression/experience would be perceived in the future (Winner 1986, 6). For instance, today, the word "communication" cannot be defined without reference to the Internet. Moreover, people's perception of "communication" will always include, at least, emailing and chatting online. The Web, as a technological system that relies solely on humans for its operationality, reconstructs its users' subjectivity in fundamental ways, for it "will not work unless human behaviour changes to suit its form and process" (Winner 1986, 11). This change of behaviour can be observed in the tsunami of religious websites (and in the use of all other Internet applications for that matter) which may indicate that, at least for seasoned netizens, online activity has become "second nature" (Winner 1986, 11). This in turn implies that "being connected" is one more part of people's everyday activities like walking, talking, working and so on. Consequently, since religious occurrences may be an integral part of users' everyday living, it makes sense for the "connected" to express and execute both their beliefs and practices in a wide variety of different forms that are only possible through the multimediated character of the Web. The point made here is that the website, apart from being seen and studied as an easily accessible form of "publishing", can also be seen and investigated as a "visible artefact" (Markham 2003) in which institutions', groups' and individuals' religious subjectivities are manifested, negotiated, altered and evolved. Hence, meanings and people's behaviour, within the cyber environment, could be seen as being in a constant state of flux, which has to be taken into account.

All new concepts and experiences made available by "being online" draw attention to the question of whether they may have an impact on users' religious perceptions, attitudes and activities and what that impact may be. However, as Winner (1986, 55) indicates, in the context of the relationship between technology, socio-political structures and democratic procedures, the question is not so much about impact but about evaluating the different infrastructures created by particular technologies for life's activities. These infrastructures may include religious ones. In the same way, Levy (2001, 8) rejects the process of analysing the impact as faulty and he replaces it with that of

> "identifying the points of irreversibility", [namely the points where] technology forces us to commit ourselves and provides us with opportunities of formulating the projects that will exploit the virtualities it bears within it and deciding what we will make of them.

Both these authors stress the importance and necessity of examining the extent to which Web technologies have added "fundamentally new activities to the range of things human beings do" (Winner 1986, 13). Within the sphere of religion, this means the ways in which institutionalized religions and NRMs employ the Web; the new religious infrastructures that may have been created by users' interaction with the Web; the communication process between content providers and receivers, namely the provision or not of possibilities for interactivity; and finally, the "points of irreversibility"—if they exist—in religious terms.

Religious websites open new research opportunities to a range of subjects and analyses which may be seen as offering new paradigm shifts not only in the areas of the established religions, but, more importantly, in the emerging areas of e-religious presences. These newly developed "techno-religious spaces" (Kong 2001, 405), when regularly updated, provide both immediate and direct access to materials, thus enabling people not only to bypass commentators, analysts, catechists, evangelists and missionaries (Soukup 1999), but friends, neighbours and family members. Authoritative figures such as imams, bishops, priests, rabbis and sheikhs are "competing" in the digital arena with individuals who may support, challenge or dismiss their teachings and guidance. Religious websites facilitate grass-roots ecumenism, interreligious and interfaith dialogue, potentially, on a global scale, and exchange of personal beliefs, perceptions and experiences among individuals, whether believers, followers, sympathizers, objectors, critics or polemicists. Equalizing hierarchies and status, websites allow netizens to surf freely and to engage in conversation, debate and discussion with religious "leaders", clergy and academics (O'Leary and Brasher 1996, 252). The contextual character of the Web, therefore, is as rich as the number of its netizens and diverse as their universes of meaning.[17]

Hypertext-hypermedia

Some methodological challenges of researching the Web are related to its distinct characteristics. The ontology of the Web, apart from its spatial and temporal qualities, also encompasses physical attributes, such as the sites, hypertext and the hypertext links which construct the Web's "infosphere" (Johnson 1997, 110). This infosphere and its features—the issue of time, the structure of hypertext and the dynamic role of hyperlink—constitute its multidimensional structure, its multiple functionalities and its polymorphic character. Therefore, a critical methodological approach has to consider those issues and the role they play in the construction of a website's subjectivity.

The idea of hypertext is usually attributed to Ted Nelson, who in the late sixties defined hypertext as a "body of written or pictorial material interconnected in such a complex way that it could not conveniently be presented or represented on paper".[18] However, the idea of hypertext can be traced back to Vannevar Bush, who in 1945 proposed a kind of hypertext device—the "Memex"—in which "an individual stores all his (sic) books, records, and communications, and which is mechanized so that it may be consulted with exceeding speed and flexibility" (Bush 1945). In essence hypertext is a specialized database in which different objects such as texts and pictures can be connected to each other (Webopedia 2002). In its current state, the term hypertext is used synonymously with the term hypermedia which is effectively an extension of hypertext that supports the connection between still and animated images, graphics, sound, and video components (in one word multimedia) in addition to those of text.[19] Hypermedia can be understood as a means of organizing and presenting multimedia, the elements of which could be divided into two major categories, that is, audio and visual. The audio incorporates sound that can be found either as a single, non-rhythmical tone,[20] or as a musical piece which may begin—by default— the moment a website's main (home) page is launched, or it may be an indicated link to a sound (song, chanting, music) that has significance for the religion presented on that specific site. The visual element incorporates images in all different forms, namely graphics, video, pictures, and text.[21]

All these points suggest that within the realm of the Web's multimodality, the "text", with or without the prefix "hyper", is no longer just "written words", but becomes a vital analogy for any sign system formulated by humans (Titon 1995, 434). Consequently, as Titon asserts, the signifiers that surround humanity are not confined to written words but incorporate the "entire universe" (1995, 434). Likewise, Strate highlights that the multifaceted character of hypertext transfigures text from being an "object held by a reader into an environment through which the reader navigates" (2003, 372). These idiosyncratic qualities of hypertext allow the readers to "move" freely within the textual environment thus making their own choices, which in turn constitute the identity of the text (Joyce 1991; Titon 1995, 441). On the other hand, the presence of a multiplicity of simultaneous texts on the screen and their interconnectivity to each other, and also to texts outside the domain of a given website, indicates that there is no definite finish, no definite end, apart from the readers' decision to stop (Titon 1995, 443).

Although the concept of hypertext is an intriguing one in terms of its technical character, as well as its role in transforming the "art" of writing and reading, within the context of this study it is considered solely as a methodological element.[22] As such, it contributes two key elements to the subject matter (the website) of this chapter, namely multimedia and hypertext links. Hypermedia bring to the investigational process a number of critical issues such as the use of colour, symbolic imagery and sound effects that cannot be ignored. Rather they should be acknowledged, included, evaluated and analysed, for, as it has been pointed out, their presence or absence significantly affects the presentation of a website's transmitted message.

Hypertext links

Hyperlinks (hereafter H-links)—an additional feature that is of concern here—have been characterized as the "cornerstone of the Web" (Shields 2000, 145). Their power, influence and fundamental role in the construction and retrieval of a website are reflected in the number of works[23] that investigate the notion, its functions and its significance for the websites.

Before commencing an analytical presentation of H-links there are two undeniable facts that need to be documented: the first is that every act on the Web is associated and executed utilizing a H-link.[24] The second is that the motion of "clicking" H-link A instead of H-link B, or C, is a choice made explicitly by the users (Mitra and Cohen 1999, 184), which has a twofold effect. On the one hand it enables the users to depart from any predefined area of a website (Shields 2000, 149) opening thus avenues of exploration, both within and outside the domain of the visited site. On the other hand, it changes the flow, structure and consequently the meaning of the reading (Titon 1995). This is due to the fact that every hypertext embodies multiple possible ways of navigation, each one of them presenting the reader with a number of choices (equal to the number of H-links) not only of different ways of reading, but also what to read and what to ignore. Yet, in Tosca's (2000) perception, H-links, instead of interrupting the flow of meaning, make it more exciting because they insinuate a "suspended meaning" waiting to be discovered. This results from the absence of meaning of H-links, in the sense that H-links themselves do not have an obvious meaning of their own, but they function just as indicators (Tosca 2000) inviting the reader on a journey into different meanings.

The interplay between text and H-links and between authors and readers forms a lattice of relationships which Harrison (2002) divides into two types. The first is what she calls "relationship potential" and refers to the author's choices of creating and/or adding H-links in order to develop their text; the second is "relationship actuality" and refers to the readers' choices of which links to follow in order to investigate the connections created between those texts. Harrison follows Burbules (1997) who, in his detailed analysis of H-links, identifies three key aspects one of which is interpreting the inherent attributes of the relationship between texts implied by H-links. As the second aspect, Burbules describes H-links as signifiers that proclaim the hidden biases, motivations and assumptions of the author of a hypertext. His final aspect, which is in accordance with Titon, is the power of H-links over the act of reading and understanding the text (Burbules 1997). Shields (2000, 145–46) interprets the presence of H-links as disruptive, for not only do they break the flow of the text but they also "force" the readers to move to another text, which diminishes the control the author has over their text.

Accessing Web materials is characterized primarily by movement that derives on the one hand from the co-existence of different elements and on the other hand from H-links functioning as "indexes— semiotic pointers" indicating further explanations and presentations (Shields 2000, 146). Burbules too, points out that H-links construct texts as "semic Web[s] of meaningful relations" (1997), a point made also by Harrison (2002), who concludes that irrespective of how links are perceived and interpreted, their predominant principle is that they are "semantic by nature". At the same time, however, Burbules (1997) also sees H-links as "rhetorical moves" that have "non-neutral signification". For instance, as Harrison (2002) emphasizes, the intention of most websites is to convince viewers that the information provided is trustworthy, significant and useful. Seeing H-links as part of this intention, one therefore can critically question their meaningfulness, their hinted choices, assumptions and ramifications (Burbules 1997).

If one considers the millions of sites available on the Web, then the need for an "advanced rhetoric of persuasion" becomes apparent. This comes as a consequence of a probable clash between two opposite poles. On the one hand is the abundance of diverse data on the Web, and on the other hand is the personal belief system of each viewer, which creates a dialectical discursive activity between the two, in which the viewer decides whether to accept the validity of the information or to dismiss it and why (Harrison 2002). This process of evaluating and deciding about the credibility of a single piece of information or a whole philosophical, religious or spiritual system has an impact upon the viewer even if her final decision is to ignore what she has encountered. As Slevin (2000, 24–25) suggests, this is because the choice to dismiss the information will be the result of a thinking process during which the viewer exercises judgemental procedures while being conscious that there are multiple ways of "getting things done". Website designers employ a great number of means for enhancing a site's presentation, increasing thus its "life-span" and popularity, in terms of attracting as many visitors as possible. Since the role of the design is not only to attract visitors but also to sustain their interest, it is more than apparent that the rhetorical competition among websites becomes so intense that Lanham (1993, 117–19, cited in Harrison 2002) proposes rhetoric, within ICTs, to signify "the economics of human attention-structures". All these points stress that H-links, apart from being semantic by nature, are also "rhetoric in purpose" (Harrison 2002).

Yet, regarding H-links' rhetorical character, Manovich (2001, 77) brings to the debate a different approach, in which he suggests that the acceptance and exaggerated utilization of H-links epitomizes a contemporary and ongoing general reduction of the field of rhetoric. This stems, in Manovich's view, from two factors. The first is the H-links' capability to connect one text to another but in no particular order, which in turn means that there is neither a hierarchical relationship between the connected texts, nor a dominance of one text over the other. This, he claims (Manovich 2001, 76), corresponds to

> contemporary culture's suspicion of all hierarchies, and preference for the aesthetics of collage in which radically different sources are brought together within a singular cultural object.

The second factor is related to the way in which Web texts are presented to the viewers. Contrary to printed materials which guide the readers step-by-step through structural, argumentative, contextual and conceptual analyses, the Web inundates users with all information instantaneously. Consequently, and in agreement with Manovich (78), it can be concluded that the rhetoric of the Web is defined by the selection process of what is to be included and what is to be excluded from the entire collection presented[25] in one Web "place".

A recapitulation therefore of the concept of H-links would identify their dual character. On the one hand, the H-links of a website, because they join together different internal and external texts, function as navigational tools; on the other hand, because they specify and call viewers' attention to another "presence", they are also referential tools. However, H-links' functionality expands beyond the borders of mere navigationality and referentiality. Since H-links primarily join texts together they ascribe to the Web the characteristic of connectivity. This term, within the Web, apart from being central to the construction of the "state of being connected" (Oxford Dictionary), is also central to the construction of cultural and ideological Webbing. In view of the fact that the vast majority of websites are interconnected to a plethora of other sites, then the following emerge: First, and in terms of ranking, the position of each site is determined by the number of its incoming H-links; second, the outgoing H-links of a site transform the identity of the site from being independent to relational (Shields 2000, 150). The point made here by Shields is that the information or the discourse of a site is neither self-defined nor autonomous; rather it incorporates elements from the network in which it participates (150).

If H-links are perceived as references corresponding to a citation, then the H-links of a site A correspond to a recognition of the connected site's B relevance to the discourse of site A (Rogers and Morris 2000, 154). In addition, apart from relevance, H-links from site A to site B also imply a sense of acceptance and respect of site's B validity and reputation (154). However, as presented in Chapter 3, the linking activity's dual character, namely "link to" and "be linked", designates an overall planning and a number of issues that the owner of a site has to consider carefully. For instance, as Rogers and Morris (2000, 154) suggest, the main questions an organization or individual would face concerning linking are:

> In which discourses or spaces shall [I] or [we] desire to be present? What sorts of politics of association may the linking structures around [my/our] organization imply?

Consequently, in Rogers and Morris' observation, H-links reveal "belonging" (154), but, it could be suggested that they may also demonstrate socio-cultural affiliations, ideological fellowships and compatibility of beliefs.[26]

Time[27]

Historically humans have produced various material means, such as writing, buildings, artefacts and technological objects, through which different generations and, in cases, different historical periods stretching through millennia, are connected (Finnegan 2002, 245). This connection, which occurs via cultural, religious, intellectual and commercial products, demonstrates and informs the ways of life of humanity in different temporal settings. Time is a fundamental constituent in the formation of cultures, identities, communities and meanings (Strate 2003, 361), for both people and societies are embodied time (Castells 1996, 429).

Computers—a technological medium of communication—have introduced to humans a new sense of time, for they have potentially an abundance of different times ready to become real (Stenger 1991, 55). These endless possibilities of times are made possible by the manipulation of the software responsible for the computer's time frames. Thus, Virilio speaks of a concentrated time that is not intact but forever broken into as many "instants, instanteities as the techniques of communication allow" (Virilio 1987, 20, in Stenger 1991, 55). At the same time, however, the computer also embodies "real time"—30 fps[28]—that, as Stenger notices, corresponds to Eliade's definition of sacred time, which is "circular, reversible, and recoverable, a sort of eternal presence" (Eliade 1961, in Stenger 1991, 55). Computer's "real time",[29] Stenger continues, is also an "eternal presence of symbols reversible and recoverable, an ontological time...that does not participate in the profane duration" (55). In the same vein, Rushkoff interprets virtual time as a form of "sacred time, a mystical Zen-like experience" (Rushkoff 1994, in Strate 2003, 381), which, in Strate's understanding, indicates on the one hand a state of timelessness and on the other hand time's limitless expansion in non-linear forms (381).[30]

Castells too, in his detailed exploration of time in which he investigates the relationship between time and society, underlines that—within the sphere of the "networked society"—the perception of time as a measurable, linear and predictable notion has been overturned (Castells 1996, 433). Castells, in accordance with Strate, states that this transformation of time develops a new concept of temporality that he terms "timeless time" (434). This metaphysical interpretation of time is the result of a combination of factors that are found in technological, sociological, political and economical analyses of time. For example, Castells analyses time historically and he associates the changing of the notion of time with the international political and economic changes of the last century, as well as with the changes brought about by biotechnology and advances in medical sciences. For instance, transfer of capital, expansion of reproductive capabilities of women, flexible working hours, instant wars and so on, have substantially contributed to the modification of people's perception of time (Castells 1996; Cooper 2002).

Strate, emphasizing the distinction between natural/biological time and that of computing, invents the term "cybertime", and he examines the concept as both a measuring and as a representational device (Strate 2003). As a measuring device "cybertime" refers to computer's ability to generate its own time, which is different from the time of the outside world. To illustrate, the computer clock measures time length, determines any present point in time, determines the computer's speed of processing and displays the time of the outside world. The computer's "inner clock", however, generates time for the computer's internal world (Strate 2003), thus the computer includes both traditional temporal modes and those of cybertime. As representational apparatus "cybertime" refers to the computer's functionality as a medium which can represent and communicate time in a symbolic sense and which also can produce an entirely different sense of time via virtual reality (Strate 2003). Strate employs Hall's term "metatime" (1984 in Strate) to define cybertime as the time that "includes all other concepts and representations of time" (2003, 370). When perceived as "metatime", then, as Strate suggests, cybertime would include the idea of sacred time (380). Strate employs Hall's term "metatime" (1984 in Strate) to define cybertime as the time that "includes all other concepts and representations of time" (2003, 370).

Another alteration of peoples' perception of time that ICTs have brought about is related to simultaneity (Castells 1996; Cooper 2002) and immediacy (Cooper 2002; Strate 2003). In particular, while communication tools, such as newspapers, telephone and the telegraph, enabled the perception of simultaneity, which in turn made visible the concept "global" (Kern 1983, in Cooper 2002, 9; Castells 1996, 461), Internet technologies proffer immediate access to both people and/or objects "at any time"[31] (Cooper, 8), as well as to socio-political events and cultural utterances[32] (Castells 1996, 461). This form of instantaneity is directly related to the speed by which technologies store, process and access information, which in turn, according to Cooper, shifts the value of things, namely from their content to their structure, valuing thus the speed by which they can be made to function and/or by which they can be accessed (2002, 121). This modification on the one hand affects people's traditional perception of time, so the experience of cybertime, induced by people's interaction with and utilization of computers, is characterized by "temporal dislocation" (Strate 2003, 381) in that it eliminates the differentiation even between day and night (Cooper 2002, 121). On the other hand it creates new temporal entities, such as the "electronic day" and "Internet time",[33] which reconstruct time in correspondence to an "artificial technologically-rationalised sequence" (Cooper 2002, 121).

Examining time outside the metaphysical and technological realms, and in terms of its relationship with the Web in particular, it appears that speed also has to be investigated as a methodological issue. As such it embodies two aspects. The first is the continuous and speedy change of technology itself (Sudweeks and Simoff 1999, 31); situating technology's change into a methodological framework presents two issues that have to be accommodated in the methodological design. For instance, in the not so distant past, computers, let alone the Internet, were solely in the hands of a skilled minority. The development of more user-friendly software, such as GUI, opened the use of both computers and ICTs to the public (Sudweeks and Simoff 1999, 31). This in turn meant that the public's interactions, adaptations and creative utilizations of PCs and Internet applications created new and multifaceted research areas not available in the past. Additionally, developments, changes and technical advances of ICTs, such as the creation of HTML language, audio, 3D, animated graphics and so on, also meant that each gave rise to new utilizations, which, in turn, generated a plethora of concepts, ideas, expressions and activities that cannot be ignored, for they are intrinsic parts of the field under investigation. The second aspect is the speed by which new information is added, and old updated (Finnegan 2002, 257), and/or information disappears (Mitra and Cohen 1999, 191). Both aspects highlight that all ICTs applications are primarily characterized by ephemerality. This idiosyncratic feature of ICTs is particularly visible on the websites. As Finnegan (2002, 258) and others (Mitra and Cohen 1999, 190–92) have indicated, ephemerality is a critical issue that can substantially alter the research process and its results, if its consequences are not included in the methodological design.

Iconoclastic Approach

The proposed methodology is the outcome of the dynamics of a two-part process.

The first part of this process was formed through reflection on the strengths and weaknesses of previous studies, identifying and selecting some of their proposed issues and extracting notions and principled explanations from the theory and epistemology chapters of this study. The second part was formed by the dialectical discussion which took place between the proposed issues and the principled explanations (theoretical analyses). The result of the dialectic is the synthesis of an "iconoclastic methodological approach". The term "iconoclastic" is used here to emphasize the need for a paradigm shift in methodological perspective, and refers to a critical, multidisciplinary and multi-perspectivist methodology, which (a) detaches itself from existing studies that focus almost exclusively on notions of community and identity; and (b) makes allowances for future developments in the field of e-religion, especially within the ritual and experiential dimensions.

As stated elsewhere in this study,[34] the two fundamental dimensions of human experience—time and space—are altered considerably when encountered within ICTs. The entire Web is characterized by movement

(Levy 2001; Mitra and Cohen 1999) and websites are in a constant cycle of regeneration, evolution, change and transformation. Furthermore, appearances and disappearances of sites are so common that the "404 error file not found" has almost become itself a signifier of the Web's culture (Mitra and Cohen 1999).

Taking therefore into account:

(a) the unconventional relationship between the Web and time;

(b) the multifaceted relationship between the different elements of the Web and its sites;

(c) their repercussions on the explorative and analysing processes; and

(d) the various theoretical approaches to and perceptions of ICTs

the methodological model is dichotomized into spatial and temporal categories which are bisected. The spatial is divided into "cartographic" and "topographic" analyses and the temporal is divided into "synchronic" and "diachronic". In the spatial category, the first application—cartography—is the formation of a typology of the diverse categories of religious sites. The second—topography—is a presentation of the elements of a website. The synchronic analysis, which reflects the issues of ephemerality and impermanence, is concerned with the ontological status of religious affairs within a given time. The diachronic analysis acknowledges the efficacy of time and investigates the effect that it may have on the discourse of religious websites.

This section provides therefore a methodological construction for investigating, monitoring, analysing and studying the polymorphic religious information found on the Web. The scope of such a construction is the development of specific tools that would enable: (a) a systematized study of e-religion; (b) the exploration/investigation of new religious, spiritual and/or philosophical formations that emerge from the interaction of the notions of religion, spirituality and philosophy and advanced digital technologies; and (c) the identification and examination of e-religious practices.

Spatial Categories

Cartography of religious websites

The different terms used to describe religious beliefs and structures, such as totemism, shamanism, ancestor worship, nature spirits, tribal religions, denominations, ancient religions of Egypt, old Arabic religions, Babylonian, Greek religions, Confucianism, Judaism, Islam, Kami traditions (the list is almost endless), emphasize the diversity that characterizes different religious perceptions, conceptualizations and contextualizations that have existed, exist and may continue to exist in humanity's constant quest for existential answers. The Web offers an unprecedented opportunity, potentially to the whole of humanity, to publish views, opinions, beliefs and expressions. A cartography therefore, of the multifarious religious landscapes as they appear on the Web, is still necessary and appropriate.

Past studies (Karaflogka 2000a, 2002) have offered the dichotomy "religion on cyberspace"/"religion in cyberspace" to differentiate between the uploaded information of religious expressions and information which is totally virtual, in the sense that it has no presence outside the domain of the Web. However, both the dichotomy and its typological categories are reconfigured when the qualitative differences between the notions "the Web" and "cyberspace" are taken into consideration. While the former is the domain content/context of information, the latter is the conceptual, metaphorical and metaphysical domain of connectivity and interactivity. Furthermore, the issues deriving from conceptual generalism must also be taken into account. Therefore, the dichotomy becomes "religious discourses *on* cyberspace" and "religious discourses *in* cyberspace". The rationale is that the term "religious discourses"[35] better encapsulates the diversity of religious utterances and occurrences, in that it implies both conceptual and contextual plurality. In addition, the term, perceived as an "extended interactive communication", may be also used for investigating the practical and ritual dimensions that are emerging in imaginative and innovative ways. Finally, the term "cyberspace" was retained for two reasons. Firstly, although any uploaded information exists on the Web, in order to reach it one has to enter cyberspace via the interface of a Web browser. Secondly, the term "cyberspace", as has been shown, is being highly invested with religious, spiritual and metaphysical metaphors. Employment of metaphors, in Markham's (2003) and others' (Stefik 1996) view, is a process in which people associate a new and, to some extent, foreign concept with something known and recognizable. The discursive choices people make in describing or discussing cyberspace, Stefik notes (1996, xvi), have significant ramifications on both the perception of the term, and on the ways in which people interact with and respond to it. Thus, Markham (2003) points out, the metaphoric contexts[36] used not only define the understood reality of cyberspace within these contexts, but also set the contextual parameters for new users. The point made here by Markham is that when new users are introduced to the new experience they may understand and interpret it through the already developed terminology.[37]

The different understandings, interpretations and usages of the medium are reflected in the ways in which the content of a website and its overall structure are presented. The distinction between the two forms of e-religion—religious discourses *on/in*—is imperative in that:

(a)   it facilitates the investigation and analysis of the status of a particular religious discourse as this is reflected in its website;
(b)   it enables monitoring of the creation of new and the development of existing techno-religious constructions;
(c)   it offers a "map" for identifying NCRMs; and
(d)   it facilitates the identification of the discourses' relationship with and utilization of cyberspatial technology, to mention but a few (Karaflogka 2002, 2003).

Religious discourses on cyberspace

This category refers to information uploaded by any a-religious or religious agent (institutionalized or non-institutionalized), church, individual, group or organization, which also exists and can be contacted in the offline world (Karaflogka 2000a). The category consists of three types: confessional, subjective and scholarly (Karaflogka 2002). The author is well aware of the debatable nature of the term "subjective". For instance, one could argue that both the confessional and scholarly types, in a way, represent a subjective conception, in that the former represents a subjective religious/spiritual/philosophical system and the latter the subjective approach and examination of a topic/issue/question. This, however, entails an in-depth analysis of both the nature of religion and the ongoing debate of the objectivity of the study of religions which is beyond the scope of this work. The term is used here instrumentally, as a facilitator, for the development of an e-religious landscape. Despite its weaknesses, this categorization, as will be shown, offers valuable insights into a number of different areas of e-religious discourses.

Confessional. As noted earlier, the confessional type, as presented by Karaflogka (2000a, 2002) proved problematic, in that it was ambiguous and reductionist in its generality. As Sharot (2001, 12) points out, an examination of a religious discourse would most probably show that there is significant difference in the ways in which it is understood and expressed between the "masses" and the religious "elite".

Hence, it could be suggested that since each website is like a fingerprint—unique in design and content—each site projects the way in which its subject is perceived by its leader(s)/follower(s) and how it conveys this perception. The site may be seen as reflecting the identity and mentality of the religious discourse it carries, and clearly illustrating what the leader(s)/follower(s) think that the essential message of the site should be (Karaflogka 1998).

Consequently, within each religious discourse there is an interplay of contrasting mentalities that is found:

- in disparities between how beliefs and practices are interpreted
- in how conceptions and impressions are understood, and disseminated
- in variable degrees of reaction and response to social and political issues
- in variable degrees of interrelation between the "speaker" of a religious discourse and the technology.

Therefore the confessional type, in order to become more "inclusive" and/or reflective of the plurality and diversity of religious manifestations, has to be deconstructed. One way of fragmenting the type into sub-categories/types is by implementing an amended form of Sharot's (2001)[38] sociological model. The amendments result from two factors.

Firstly, the conceptual differences of the different distinctions (i.e. "great/little traditions", "official/unofficial" and "elite/popular") were taken into account. For instance, Sharot (15) interprets "elite religion" to be that of the religious elite of a religion. This elite, Sharot explains, is usually seen as being formed by the hierarchy of a religious system, or by those who are recognized as "exemplifying the highest values of the religious system". Hence, for Sharot (15), while "great tradition" signifies the elements (doctrines, norms and rituals) that the elite/hierarchy of a "religious cultural system presents and interprets as [forming] the authentic religious tradition", the "official" category consists of the elements that the religious hierarchy of a religious system accepts as justified or legitimate, within the parameters, of course, of the system they represent.

In Sharot's (2001, 15) view, "little tradition" reflects the understandings, adaptations and uses of the "great tradition", as these have been constructed by those outside of the hierarchy, corresponding to their regional and community concerns, and "popular religion" reflects the formations between the little tradition and other elements that are not associated with the hierarchy's regulations. Sharot (16) points out that the "unofficial religion" consists of the beliefs and practices of popular religion which are not accepted or tolerated by the elite.

The second factor that led to the modification of Sharot's model concerns the unique characteristics of the setting in which his categories would be applied. The reason is that while Sharot deals with the world's religions[39] within the physical world, this study deals with the

world's religious discourses within cyberspace, which implies different paradigms of relationships between the "elite" and the "popular"
types, one of which is the equalized presence of the discourses by the
medium.[40] Thus, while Sharot's model fits perfectly his particular sociological analysis of world religion's interaction with hoi polloi at a particular time, in this study it is modified. Firstly, the distinction between
"elite" and "popular" is chosen as being more appropriate to represent
the diverse utterances and occurrences of e-religious discourses. The
rationale is that the particular connotations that the terms "elite" and
"popular" carry (i.e. elite is associated with power, higher educational,
social and economic status) are particularly helpful for distinguishing e-
religious discourses, for as has been shown earlier there are a number
of factors that affect the accessibility and usability of the medium.

Secondly, this dichotomy, being polarized, does not offer a middle
ground which would accommodate the discourses which, on the one
hand represent the official beliefs and practices of a religious system,
and on the other hand also incorporate elements deriving from and relevant to the physical socio-cultural setting that the site corresponds to.

That being so, a third type, termed "formal", is used to classify the
"between" discourses. The term "formal", being in "accord with established forms and conventions and requirements",[41] denotes "acknowledgement", "acceptance", "approval" and "accreditation". As a result,
the confessional type is divided into "elite", "formal" and "popular".
The categorization of sites is based on the ways in which they present
themselves which may not correspond to that body's status in the eyes
of the world.

Elite. The characteristics of sites belonging to the "elite" category are: (a)
they represent the official teachings of a religious system; (b) they represent its hierarchy; (c) they provide its leadership; (d) they assure its
authenticity; and (e) their authority is undisputed. Understood as such,
the "elite" category, then, could incorporate sites of both institutionalized and non-institutionalized religious expressions, as well as those of
NRMs. Additionally, the "elite" sites, by design and content, present a
transnational discourse, in the sense that their disseminated information appears to be targeting the global audience and not only the audience of a particular physical place. An "elite" site may be consulted by
both the officials and the believers of its religious system for authoritative guidance and perspective, decisions and strategies related to either
religious, or secular aspects and, more importantly, to issues of controversy. To the seekers—those who are searching for a religious system to
be affiliated to—"elite" sites provide the "main entrance" to all dimensions of the system they present.

Although each of these sites could be the subject of an in-depth analysis, only some indicative/initial observations that are of interest are presented here. The "elite" sites share some common characteristics, the most prominent one being the absence of external links that has been termed by Rogers and Morris (2000, 153) as "the style of net omnipresence". However, creating a website denotes participation in, and possible influence of, the "organic construction" of the medium (MacDonald 1995). "Granting a link" and "receiving a link" (Rogers and Morris 2000, 150) are key parts of the construction process that result in the formation, expansion and evolution of the Web's "variety of continua" (MacDonald 1995). As discussed earlier, H-links, apart from being central to the construction of the "state of being connected", are also central to the construction of cultural and ideological Webbing, in that they reveal "belonging" (Rogers and Morris, 154) which may demonstrate either socio-cultural affiliations, or ideological fellowships and/or compatibility of beliefs.

The elite sites, therefore, by "granting no links"—offering no external links—on the one hand expect the viewers to remain within their domain and, on the other hand, denote a certain view that the owners of the sites hold about their religious system. However, despite the implicit sense of "self-superiority" reflected in the design of the elite sites, by default they are connected to and interact with both the medium and all other sites that they share it with. Moreover, if one examines the discourse of the "elite" sites in terms of how the owners perceive and use the technology of the Web, then from the perspective of the interrelation between the "speaker" (the site) and the medium, it appears that the "elite" sites demonstrate an instrumental view of the Web and a perception of communication which focuses solely on transmitting their message.

A brief analysis of two example sites, the Transcendental Meditation (TM) and the Ecumenical Patriarchate of Constantinople, will illustrate the above features of elite sites.

TM represents the official teachings of a religious system. The main page of the site offers analytical presentations of TM programs and their benefits to both individuals and society. The site is massive, incorporating several hundreds of pages which present TM's solutions to various social problems, such as crime and conflict, and the advantages of TM's practices towards an individual's physical and mental improvement. Additionally, the site offers information on a number of other activities in which TM is involved, such as its educational institutions, Maharishi's solutions to war and terrorism, and the achievement of world peace.

The TM site, by design and content, is transnational,[42] targeting a global audience not that of a particular physical place. It may be consulted for authoritative guidance and, to seekers, the site provides the "main entrance" to the TM system.

Like other elite sites, TM eschews external links, thus expecting viewers to remain within its domain and, also, presenting an undisputed leadership in relation to other TM localized sites, as for example TM Netherlands, which are linked to it. By offering no interactive facilities to visitors, the TM site demonstrates an instrumental view of the Web which emphasizes transmission of a message from the centre.

The site of the Ecumenical Patriarchate of Constantinople (EPC) presents similar characteristics. This site is also of substantial size and it offers a biography of the current Patriarch, a list of all the Patriarchs beginning with the founder, St. Andrew the Apostle, Synodic decisions, patriarchical encyclicals, news bulletins, theological articles, activities of the Patriarch related to ecological issues, conferences and the Creed of faith, among others. The site is offered only in English and Greek, but the Creed is offered in a number of languages. The contents indicate that the target audience is not so much individual seekers, for there is no analytical presentation of the Orthodox faith, but rather the site's primary function is to provide authoritative information about the Patriarchate's and the Patriarch's religious and political activities, news and encyclicals that the global Orthodox clergy/community may consult.

As with TM, so the EPC site adopts an instrumental view of the medium by allowing no interaction between itself and its visitors. However, it should be mentioned that the EPC site acknowledges—by linking itself to them—the Patriarchates of Alexandria, Antioch, Moscow, Serbia and Georgia, among others, as well as the autocephalous churches of Greece, Albania, Poland, Finland, Czech–Slovakia and Estonia. It is worth pointing out that while the sites of the Patriarchates fall into the elite category, for they all demonstrate an authoritative presence on the Web, the sites of the Churches would be placed in the formal category. As appears in a number of cases, the involvement of the leader of a religious system in social and political activities and the reporting of news items considered important or relevant to that system are common features of the elite sites. For instance, one of TM's issues of concern is that of global peace and the positive impact of TM on individuals and societies. In TM's "global good news" link, one can be informed about what TM characterizes as "Positive trends", such as the peace talks between Taiwan and China; "Successes", as for example medical studies proving the beneficial effect of TM on life expectancy; and "Flops", such as the current turmoil in Nepal.[43] The Ecumenical Patriarchate's news focuses mainly on reports about Turkey's relation with the EPC, human rights violations in Turkey, inter-religious issues, and the annual report of the Patriarch to the Archons, among others. In a separate link, the site's visitors can be informed about the activities and speeches of the Patriarch on ecological issues.

Other examples[44] of "elite" sites are those of: the Diocese of Partenia; the Jodo Shinshu Honganji school; the Ecumenical Patriarchate of Constantinople; the Islam Page; the Holy See; the World Jewish Congress; the Unification Church; the Worldwide Buddhist Information and Education Network; the Church of Scientology; the Cao Dai; the Hindu Universe; the International Shinto Foundation; the Transcendental Meditation; the Sikhism; the Islam World; the Jehovah's Witnesses; the Church of England; the Branch Davidians; the Church of Jesus Christ of Latter-day Saints; the Baha'i World; the Falun Dafa; and the Office of Tibet, the official agency of His Holiness the Dalai Lama.

Formal. This category incorporates the sites that present a discourse which most likely has the approval of the elite and embodies elements of local orientation and interest. This category contains sites of dioceses, churches, synagogues, mosques, monasteries, centres; sites with specialized content; sites of special events and interests.

Apart from providing aspects of beliefs, the "formal" sites also provide information about the community to which they belong; information about worship, rituals, services, events, contacts; and in some cases views on national and/or local, social and/or political issues. They may include links to the church's radio or TV stations and magazines (if available) and their external links connect to sites with which they share either ideological affiliation and/or collaboration. Some sites may offer free sacred books or teachings (Bible, Buddhist texts) and there may be requests for donations, email contact(s) and, in some cases, the presence of a bulletin board or discussion forum provide a local communicative space for their congregations. Thus, for the members of their communities, these sites represent a focal point, a source of information, of contacting and connecting with the site's leader(s) and with fellow believers. For the local seekers—those not yet affiliated—the "formal" sites provide a starting point for exploring the activities and the overall character of the church/synagogue/mosque/ temple/centre. "Formal" sites, to a greater or lesser degree, employ the Web not as a mere instrument but as a socio-cultural environment which, being utilized in various ways, may promote, support and enhance their purpose. Furthermore, communication, within the "formal discourses", appears to be perceived as a "ritual" (Craig 1999, 124) denoting shared beliefs (Carey 1989, 18), encouraging and enabling the development of fellowship and participation.

Examining the sites of the Temple Beth El in Providence, USA (which belongs to the Reform Jewish Tradition), the Buddhaland Buddhist Centre in Athens, Greece and the Birmingham Central Mosque in the UK, which may be characterized as typical examples of the "formal" category, one may identify the above-mentioned features.

The Temple Beth El's opening page welcomes the visitor by offering a brief account of the temple site's purpose, timetable of worship services and special events. Through the provided links, visitors can explore the history of the temple and the different "identities" it has obtained throughout its existence. For instance, the temple is presented not only as a house of worship but also as a house of study, of assembly, and as an "eye to the future". Presented as such, the temple becomes a religious as well as a social, educational and cultural institution in the service of its community. The site not only reflects all these aspects but, to some extent, facilitates and encourages their development among the congregants. By offering in great detail information about its structure, for example, the clergy, the various committees (e.g. financial, fine art, music, Minyan, interfaith family, social action etc.), auxiliaries (Sunday school for children while adults enjoy the newspapers at the temple's "Bagel Café") and organized groups (e.g. brotherhood, sisterhood, youth etc.), the site functions as a "gathering" point, as an information provider, and as a supportive "environment" for the community. The site also offers, in full length, the *Shofar* (newsletter) of the temple, which covers the life of both the community and the temple.

The Birmingham Central Mosque's opening page offers current news in its main body, address and contact phone numbers and a number of links related to news, events, services, media, resources and information. The site is quite similar in content to that of the Temple Beth El, in the sense that it provides an informative space for the local Muslim community. The structure of the site is built around aspects of the community's life, these being religious, familial and social, as well as political aspects that the Muslim community as a whole faces. For instance, the news reports on the opening page are about Eid al-Adha prayer times, the funds the Mosque has raised for the tsunami appeal, the Mosque's new calendar and the visit of the police force to the Mosque in order to discuss ideas and exchange information on how the relationship between the police and the Muslim community will continue to strengthen. The "news" page offers, apart from the main stories, accounts related to Ramadan, research on the history of the Mosque, announcements for family support and counselling services, and community features such as the "joy of Eid", "cycling for peace" and so on. The "events" page informs about public talks on "the war on terror, racism and attack on civil liberties" and on "Shakespeare and Islam?", and gatherings such as Tafheem-ul-Islam Meetings, and Birmingham Muslim-Quaker Peace and Social Justice Group's dialogue to explore Muslim and Quaker perspectives on faith-based schools. These, along with the information about services that the Mosque offers for marriages, divorces, funerals and "embracing Islam" ceremonies, and the resources and literature it provides to visitors, underline that the focus of the site is the physical local community.

Formal sites are, perhaps, the key place for one to discover and identify the issues and problems that a particular religious institution and/or community faces locally and, in some cases, nationally or internationally. The content of the formal sites is very often bilingual, in the sense that it is presented in the language of the country in which the physical community resides, but with some or most of it in the original language of the religious system, where this is different.

Further examples of "formal" sites include: the Council of Sikh Gurdwaras; the Birmingham Central Mosque; the directory of Baptist Church websites; the Pagan Federation; Soundvision; the Hare Krishna Movement; the Metta Forest Monastery; the Church of Greece; Jewish resources; the Catholic Church in England and Wales; The Pastor's Helper; Mount Athos; the Buddhaland Buddhist Centre in Athens, Greece; the International Association for Religious Freedom; the Temple Beth El; the Centro Israelita Sionista de Costa Rica; the Byzantine Catholic church in US; the Hare Krishna temple in Pietermaritzburg, South Africa; ISKCON in Cardiff, Wales; the Church Army; the Ise Jingu shrine in Japan; the Tharpaling Buddhist Centre in Corfu, Greece; the Tao Te Ching online; the Skate church; Islam101; Falun Dafa UK; Virtually Zen (an Israeli Zen site) and Holy Trinity Church in Frome, Somerset (UK).

Popular. The "popular" category is understood here to refer to sites that incorporate those elements of the religious system proclaimed by its elite and prescribed by its officials, as they are interpreted, adapted and applied by the common believers. The "popular" interpretations may incorporate elements that are not recognized by the elite; may present an amalgamated and/or an acculturated form of a religious discourse; or may present a form of a religious discourse deriving from syncretistic processes.

"Popular" sites are quite variable in their contents, but common features are inclusion of: their own online shops or links to external e-shops; testimonies and stories of their members; classifieds about jobs, classes, courses, retreats or meeting people; petitions either to support a cause or to condemn an event; radio programmes either of or about the discourse of a site; film announcements and reviews (e.g. Gibson's *Passion*); advertisements about companies who sponsor a site; members' books and art works; events and trips related to sacred places of significance to that particular site; a membership page and donations. This type also demonstrates an approach in which the Web, perceived as a multifaceted space, offers a mixture of opportunities for communicating a discourse in various beneficial ways rather than simply disseminating its message.

For instance, the Kataragama-Skanda site provides to its visitors a vast space in which they are able to find almost anything about the Kataragama cult. The site incorporates an extensive number of links organized in several categories such as: the different religious traditions in which Kataragama is found (Buddhist, Hindu, Islamic and Vedic); "historical accounts" of the cult in different geographical locations, as for example Sri Lanka, Ceylon and India; "sacred spaces" which offers links to the sacred geography of the Kataragama shrine and analyses of the oriental cosmography that the shrine represents. The "feature articles" links incorporate a wide variety of topics and themes, including: personal testimonies, photo galleries, facts about Kataragama, biographies of Swamis and so on. The "Pada Yatra" links inform the visitors about the pilgrimage over the years and the various organizations that support it, such as St Johns Ambulance Brigade. The site also includes academic works concerning Kataragama such as, "Dionysious and Kataragama: Parallel Mystery Cults". In addition, there is an extensive list of temples, such as the Ruhunu Kataragama Maha Devalaya built around 160 BC, the Selvasanniti Murukan Temple and the Batticaloa Tiruchendur Murugan Temple, which was destroyed by the tsunami, among others. In the exhaustive list of links the visitors can also find Bhakti centres, Sages of Kataragama, festivals, interviews, weather forecasts, maps, rest houses, TV documentaries and Yahoo groups; they can purchase screensavers, books and CDs and offer donations.

Another site that fits the "popular" profile is the Khanaye Doost, dedicated to Iranian lesbian, gay, bisexual and transgendered (LGBT) women. This site, focusing on a very specific subject, incorporates a substantial number of links that direct the visitors to key areas that the content designers thought to be of interest and/or useful. For example, the opening page links to: articles, lexicon, forum, Iranian LGBT links, general LGBT links, women's links, chat room, books, the Homan magazine, news and announcements, guest book and "email the site". The main page also includes links to: a commercial site that sells posters; suggestions and comments about the site; a research study on relevant issues; and to *Persian Mirror*, a magazine for Persian weddings, cuisine, culture and community. Although the majority of themes and topics are around homosexuality, bisexuality and transgendered issues the site also covers women's affairs in general. For instance, the women's link directs the visitors to: webwoman.info, an online community that promotes professional development of Afghani and Iranian women; Bagjens, an Iranian feminist newsletter; Radio Ghasedak; Afghani women links and articles, and Amnesty International Women's human rights, among others. The site is exceptionally informative, not only because it analyses a wide variety of topics, but also because it offers links to relevant organizations dealing with the particular subject from either religious or social angles.

The site, as well as others of the popular type, provides a space where the seekers can be informed, but also communicate, interact and socialize with fellow "believers" within an environment they can trust and feel safe and free to express themselves. Through the information offered a number of theological questions are answered related to sexual orientation and to women's social status in general within Muslim communities, thus dissolving its visitors' feelings of isolation and outcast.

Additional examples of "popular" sites are: Burning Man; the Church of Almighty God; the Church of the Lukumi Babalu Aye; the Hollywood Jesus; the Buddhist Kataragama; Rael; the Brotherhood of the Crossed Circle; the Urantia Book; Theonomy; the Peyote Way Church of God; the Yoruba; the cult[45] of Mary in Croatia; the Hermetic Alchemical Order of the QBLH; the Virgin Mary's End-times Prophecies; Here and Now; Summum – The Millennium of Reconciliation; the Cosmic People; THELEMA.

Subjective. Apart from the "elite", "formal" and "popular" discourses, the Web also includes sites of individuals, as well as those of groups that comprise the "subjective" type for they correspond to an idiosyncratic point of view (Karaflogka 1998). The "subjective" type is the discourse produced by the perception that some people have about a religion other than their own; or a critique of their own religion or of a national/ international religious event; or a happening or incident that in peoples' opinion is closely related to religion (Karaflogka 2002). It includes personal sites uploaded by individuals who want to share their beliefs, to communicate with other fellow believers, to exchange ideas and experiences and sometimes to debate the doctrinal dimension of their own or another religion (Karaflogka 1998).

"Subjective" sites project the personal perception and understanding of a particular system of belief; they may explore and communicate a unique religious experience or praxis; they may project the views of a person or a group about a socio-religious situation; they may criticize a current or a historical event, or a television programme; they may present socio-political interpretations of a religion, the religious reactions that an event generated, and so on. It could be suggested that the "subjective" sites exemplify the existing tensions between religious discourses and social discourses; interreligious tensions; antagonistic tendencies; hatred and detestation. At the same time, though, they also exemplify interreligious acceptance; tolerance; cooperation and respect. "Subjective" sites share almost the same features of the "popular", in that their main menus incorporate links to: internal texts, publications, various modes of contact (email, forums, chat rooms), feedback, donations, analysis of topics, references to other media (newspapers, magazines, radio and TV), projects, updates of issues of concern, personal profiles, calls for action, prayer requests and external links to associative sites. In the "subjective discourses", as well as in the "popular" and "formal", the Web is viewed and approached as an evolving set of structures that enables various kinds of online action, interaction and active participation.

The Corrymeela Community site could be seen, perhaps, as a representative example of the subjective type. The site represents a group of people, from all Christian traditions, committed to the "healing of Social, Religious and Political divisions that exist in Northern Ireland and throughout the World".[46] The aims, objectives, projects, activities and history of the community are among the themes provided on the site. The visitors can access Corrymeela's magazine, *Corymeela's Press*, publications, articles and important addresses. In the Knoklayd link, one is informed about the community's place of events and "retreats", and the current list of open events such as "studying the scriptures in a special way", "a weekend devoted to explore and share the grief journey", "gardening", "photographic skills" and "Easter celebrations", among others. The site also offers "search the Bible", "contact us", "feedback form" and "support groups and contacts" links which encourage interaction between the community and online visitors. Visitors can purchase books or make a donation. However, apart from financial support, the site invites its online visitors to get involved in the community's work, either as members, or as volunteers. The "links" section incorporates a number of external links to sites and organizations that Corymeela is associated with. These links are divided into categories corresponding to local groups, for example, "Mediation Network for Northern Ireland", "Irish Council of Churches Peace Education Programme" and the "Glencree Centre for Reconciliation"; to religious directories that include the sites of "Christian Resources on the Internet", "Christianity. Net" and "Global Church Web Pages International". The national and international category offers links to "European Platform for Conflict Prevention", "Minority Rights Group International", "Peace Brigades International" and so on. The Corymeela opening page is covered with current comments, politics, events, debates, news and stories.

Another "subjective" site that is in direct opposition to the elite's proclaimed position is the Catholics for a Free Choice (CFFC). CFFC focuses on an issue which is not only totally unacceptable to the elite (the Catholic Church) but also controversial to all religious systems and societies. The home page of the site offers links to: News, *Conscience* (CFFC's magazine), media, youth, articles and publications, CFFC

USA, CFFC international and Catholic health care. The "news" cover the latest events (e.g. the death of Pope John Paul II, the new Pope, etc.), interviews and press releases of CFFC's president, selected articles from the magazine and action alert. The "action alert" link, at the time the site was visited (May 2005), presented the US Department of Justice medical guidelines for treating sexual assault victims that did not include emergency contraception. In CFFC's view this "puts sexual assault victims, especially those who seek services at Catholic hospitals, at risk of unintended pregnancy",[47] and calls on the public for immediate action. Other links include information about contraception, sexuality, "Bishopwatch" and CFFC's international partners in Bolivia, Brazil, Mexico and Costa Rica. The "youth" page, apart from information on several subjects, also offers a "get involved" link which provides access to a number of lobbies and organizations that campaign on issues such as "condoms 4 life", "Catholics for contraception", "change the status of the Roman Catholic Church", "call to accountability" and "work with CFFC". The "information for Catholic women" link is about the abortion decision. The motto "you are not alone", as headline of the text, underlines that the abortion issue is not just one woman's problem. On the contrary, the statistical data that the text offers indicate that the majority of Catholic women around the world have faced/are facing this question. The text answers questions related to theological matters in conjunction with abortion. For example, "What is the Church's teaching on abortion?"; "Will I be excommunicated if I have an abortion?"; and "After all is said and done, how do I go about making up my own mind?" The answers given are as comprehensive as possible and also in the text visitors can find liturgies for "Responsible Reproduction", for "Seeking Wisdom", and of "Affirmation for making a difficult decision". In the same page, other links connect to the "history of abortion in the Catholic Church", "a brief liberal Catholic defence" and "reflections of a theologian". While the first two documents present analyses from a historical and a doctrinal perspective, the latter is the personal account of a Catholic, male theologian's exploration of abortion and the experiences and insights he gained throughout his "journey". Both sites reflect the efforts of some people to address social and/or political issues that are intertwined with religion. They offer information, support and a point of view which, although does not correspond to that of the elite, remains within the belief. At the same time, these sites function as examples of the utilization of the Web as a communicative place/space in which netizens are able to access more than a simple message.

Further examples of "subjective" sites are: Jesus is Coming Soon; the Spiritual Sanctuary; the Spiritual Quest; the Voice from the Throne;

numerous sites on the "Eastern Lightning" cult in China, including personal testimonies; Asia Harvest's report and the China for Jesus extended analysis on different "heretical sects". Other sites deriving from a particular perspective are: the Apologetics Index; the Interfaith Alliance; the Promise Keepers; the American United for Separation of Church and State; the Shinto and Buddhist Corner; the altreligion.about; the World Jen Chen Buddhism; American Atheists; the Karmapa controversy; Catholics against Vatican II; the Jesus Puzzle; the Energetic Matrix Church of Consciousness; the Cult of Mary; Worthy News; the Catholics For Choice; Kahane.org; Kobo Daishi; and Janna: Muslim Women.

Sites uploaded by individuals presenting a wide-ranging variety of standpoints, issues and cultural approaches are countless. Some samples are: the Unvarnished Truth About Religion, Christianity and Spirituality in 2004; an individual's site about Druse, Mowahhidoon; Jesus Christ is the ONLY Way to God; the Spiritual Quest; Access to Insight; the Spirit Wheel and Earth Portals.

Scholarly. This comprises the Web pages of universities, institutions, academic journals and personal pages of scholars, such as: the California State Polytechnic University's page on Chinese Folk religion; Web Missiology; the Wabash Centre; My Jewish Learning.com; the International Association for Religious Freedom; Ontario Consultants on Religious Tolerance; Academic Info Religion; the Religious Movements Homepage Project! (sic). Sites particularly relevant to ICTs are: the NUA (statistics); the Pandia Search Central (all about search engines); CMC Magazine; Cybersociology; and the Recource Center for Cyberculture Studies.

The "scholarly" sites are informational and their content is presented primarily as text. Usually they incorporate internal links, but in some cases they may include external links to sites that are closely associated with the subject matter. For example, the Web Missiology[48] site grants links to a number of similar sites including SEDOS (Service of Documentation and Studies on Mission) and IAMS (International Association for Mission Studies). Web Missiology offers a novel implementation of linking by incorporating Google's results on missiology as an external link. Additionally, they may also include links to online academic works, journals, conferences, courses and gateways. Sites that do not exist under the auspices of an educational institute may include links to "sponsored"[49] sites such as online bookstores, or software companies' sites that promote their subject matter.

Religious discourses in cyberspace

The "religious discourses *in*" category propounds a novel dimension which demands the investigation, exploration and analysis of new

e-religious discourses that flourish within the milieu of this global innovative medium (Karaflogka 2003, 195).

'Religious discourses *in"* has been divided into two different expressions, namely, "cyberreligions" and "New Cyberreligious Movements"
(NCRMs) (Karaflogka 2000a, 2002, 2003). The first refers to a completely new phenomenon that: exists exclusively in cyberspace; has a
founder or founders; introduces a new insight into post-modern religiosity; and addresses issues closely related to ideas including cyberspace as a sacred space, the metaphysics of virtual reality, immortality,
disembodiment and cybernetic spirituality/religiosity (Karaflogka 2002,
284; 2003, 196). The medium's structural and operational characteristics, which diminish any sense of central authority and hierarchy, offer
opportunities for the creation and development of cyber-communities
and movements that have their own rules, agendas and codes of practice. Karaflogka places (2002, 286) NCRMs within this framework, and
she justifies her invented term as: "new because they address issues
using a new medium and introducing new possibilities; cyberreligious
because they mainly exist and function on-line; movements because
they can, potentially, mobilize and activate the entire human population". As characteristic examples of NCRMs, Karaflogka suggests Falun
Dafa and Partenia (2003, 196–97).

Although the differentiation between discourses *on* and *in* is a helpful
methodological tool, it requires deconstructive intervention for, in its
present form, it proves to be problematic and exclusivist for a number
of reasons. Firstly, the division between "cyberreligions" and "NCRMs"
implies that cyberreligions are conventional forms of religious discourses.
However, the interpretation of the term as "a new phenomenon", and
also the theoretical and applied formulations that cyberreligions present
in their discourses, signify that cyberreligions have not yet been recognized as "accepted", let alone regarded as standard forms of religious
expressions. Secondly, taking into consideration the interpretation of the
term "NCRMs", the division implies that cyberreligions do not incorporate any of the characteristics of NCRMs. This, however, proves to be
a contradiction in terms, in the sense that, as Karaflogka (2002, 2003)
suggests, cyberreligions use a new medium, introduce new insights,
new issues and new ideas such as that of cybernetic spirituality/religi-
osity, and NCRMs, too, address new issues, new possibilities and use
new media. Thirdly, the division, especially regarding NCRMs' potential
capability to mobilize, motivate and involve some or all netizens in an
activity, whether virtual or physical, removes from cyberreligions such a
capability. However, such a prospect, being a significant component of
e-religious discourses, as the cases of Falun Dafa, Partenia and Jediism
have shown, has to be available to cyberreligions. Fourthly, the issue

of utterances and occurrences that are "between" _in_ and _on_ has to be taken into account.

Consequently, it is proposed here, that the religious discourses in cyberspace (RDIC) category may be comprised of NCRMs and mainstream e-religious manifestations (MEMs), such as cyber-churches, cyber-synagogues, cyber-mosques, cyber-events, cyber-practices and cyber-rituals. Although MEMs (apart from a few exceptions) do not exist exclusively in cyberspace, they are placed under the RDIC heading, for their proficient utilization of cyberspace as a communicative space for followers, sympathizers and polemics; as an informative and "action-taking" place in which people can learn about, act towards and interact with any form of MEMs; and as a place of virtual practising. The proposed dissection of religious discourses _in_ cyberspace (RDIC) enables the investigation and study of NCRMs and MEMs and also makes allowances for possible future developments of its elements.

NCRMs. A search using "cyberculture" or "virtual religion" as a keyword provides a list of sites which exhibit some of the features of religions, but may seem more or less unusual by conventional standards (Karaflogka 2003, 196). Several are actually intended to be satirical, if not cynical, while others are quite serious (Dawson and Hennebry 1999; Karaflogka 2003). It could be said that these examples illustrate a wide range of human motivations and attitudes concerning religious thinking, emotions, beliefs, impulses, practices and responses to the religious reality, as the creators of these sites perceive it to be.

A characteristic expression of this type is the "Church of MOO".[50] Dawson and Hennebry (1999, 35), in their detailed analysis of the Church, point out that the site reveals "an elaborated development of alternative sets of scriptures, commandments, chronicles, mythologies, rituals and ceremonies". The size of the website is vast (around 800 pages) and the discourse published shows an acute appreciation of religious history, comparative beliefs and practices, and some real knowledge of philosophy, anthropology, and sociology of religion (Dawson and Hennebry 1999, 35). The founders of MOOism, according to Dawson and Hennebry, are attempting to devise a "self-consciously post-modern, socially constructed, relativist, and self-referential system of religious ideas" (35). In MOOism's discourse there are elements that suggest a connection to neo-paganism, and the "religion" could be characterized as representative of what is coming to be called Techno-paganism (Dawson and Hennebry, 36). The Church of MOO is presented on the "Unusual Churches" site as being a

religion created to meet the unique needs of postmodern society. It has been designed to break your brain out of routine modes

of thought and restore you to the truly human mode of functioning which was once practiced by the Ancient Atlantean Adepts. It
stands opposed to such sinister forces for mind control as Alien Psy-
chomorphic Satellites, The Ancient Atlantean Adepts, Cheese, Bob
Dole, and International Squid Biscuits.

The site of MOOism has remained the same since its creation in the
early 1990s and despite sophisticated statements—used occasionally—
such as:

Among other things, MOOism has been called the Negativland of
religion. Not only does it irreverently (and sometimes irrelevantly)
sample innumerable other religious traditions, it uses recontextual-
ization and paradoxical framing techniques to prevent minds from
settling into orthodoxy. Paradox and radical self-contradiction are,
in the postmodern context, the most reasonable way to approach
the Absolute.

its overall intention is about having "fun" with the notion of religion
(Dawson and Hennebry 1999, 36). Whatever MOOism's initial objective, its creation signifies the advent of a novel religious framework generated by ICTs and facilitated by the Web itself. Further examples of such
emerging conceptual creations that appear either as religious/spiritual/
philosophical/mystical "teachings" and/or as practical guides that exist
and operate exclusively in the cyberdomain are: Cosmosophy, Digitalism,
Technosophy, and the Church of Virus among others. Although an extensive analysis of these discourses in terms of their philosophical ideas, their
structure, the sources that played an influential part in their creation and
development, the intertextuality of their conceptual construction and the
novelty and/or relationality of the theoretical aspects of their discourse, is
beyond the scope of this study, some points that may form the basis for
future research are presented here.

NCRMs may express the ideas and conceptions of a group (as in
the case of the Church of MOO) or of an individual (as in the cases of
Cosmosophy, Digitalism, Technosophy, and the Church of Virus). NCRMs'
sites are characterized by the use of extensive texts and minimal or total
lack of external links and their design varies from being just plain, monochrome text, as Cosmosophy's, to the elegant, quite sophisticated format
of the Church of Virus. They all appeared on the Web in the mid nineties
and all sites are still available today (as of May 25th, 2004). Digitalism,
Technosophy, and the Church of Virus have one common denominator:
their founders are computer scientists.[51] It could be suggested that the
creation of NCRMs in a way substantiates Slouka's (1995, 29) assumption that some technologists have not only the financial means but also
the technological knowledge and expertise to create and implement their

theories, thus giving substance to their utopian and prophetical views and visions. The theoretical frameworks presented in the sites of NCRMs seem to be the result of a process of amalgamating concepts from different religious systems with notions deriving from the fields of computing and ICTs, such as virtual reality (VR), nanotechnology, and memetics. NCRMs, by using the Web as an environment where human imagination and creativity can be easily presented, deconstruct established sociocultural concepts and reconstruct religious, spiritual and philosophical ideas and practices. It could be suggested that NCRMs may challenge, not so much the status quo of institutionalized, hierarchical and established religions, but rather the notion of religion itself, in the sense that NCRMs, being interpreted as the manifestations of the implicit/explicit religious/spiritual/metaphysical connotations that surround technological discourses, transform these connotations from being potentialities into actualities. This in turn implies that any future reference to the notion of religion may include NCRMs as an integral part of it.

MEMs. The "mainstream e-religious manifestations" type consists of the virtual expressions of established religions, such as virtual churches, synagogues, mosques, temples, pilgrimages and rituals. There are three different types of cyber-presences:

(a) those created for educational purposes (i.e. religious education classes), such as Rabbi Scheinerman's Synagogue and the Virtual Mosque Project;

(b) those created to provide a space for cyber-devotional practice (worship, meditation, prayer), such as the Alpha Church, Buddhanet; the First Church of Cyberspace; the Online Meditation of Zen Buddhism; the Zarathushtra temple; the Virtual Church, and the Mountains and Rivers Order of Zen Buddhism; the Church of Fools; the i-church and the Web Church of Scotland.

(c) the "virtual tours" of places of worship, places of pilgrimages and sacred places, such as Durham Cathedral; Mecca, the live cam in the Western Wall; the virtual Pilgrimage to Fatima and the Kumbha Mela 2001. A number of MEMs, such as the Universal Life Church and Bible Sermons Online, among thousands of others, focus on the clergy and offer online ordinations, ministry products, sermons and seminars. Access to virtual practice is not always open and free. For instance, the Masonic Cyber Temple requires the visitor to fill in a registration form before entrance, and the i-church requires the completion of a membership form in order to join the community. In some other cases entrance is totally blocked to unidentifiable IP addresses,[52] which implies that the cyberchurch/temple is accessible to members only.

Different MEMs, especially those that offer the possibility for virtual practice, participation and interactivity, present significant differences in their scope and variable degrees in using ICTs' technological capabilities such as multimedia.

For instance, while the scope of the Alpha Church and the Church of Fools is to provide a place of practice, the scope of Buddhanet and the First Church of Cyberspace (FCC) is to provide both a place of informing and of practising. However, the weight of the First Church of Cyberspace is placed more on the informational aspect of the site, whereas Buddhanet, Alpha Church and the Church of Fools tend to concentrate more on offering an experiential space. These differences, attested by the technical choices that the owners make on how better to present their discourses, reflect each site's rhetoric, that is, the systems of discourses the owners use, on the one hand to build reciprocal relationships and experiences in a new domain and on the other hand to renegotiate and redefine established elements of religious practice.

For instance, while the First Church of Cyberspace primarily uses hypertext (but experiments with Java Theology[53]), the Alpha Church enhances its discourse by incorporating audio and visual. Buddhanet moves a step further and presents its material in a multimedia context which encompasses audio-visual in a plurality of different forms such as video, films, virtual tours, cartoons, interactive tours of Buddhist teachings, talks, chanting, songs and meditation instructions to mention but a few. The Church of Fools, on the other hand, offers a "real", though virtual, church in which visitors do not participate, but "are there" in the Sunday service, listening to the sermon and communing with the rest of the congregation. The Church of Fools is the UK's first 3D virtual church,[54] which is activated when one "enters".[55] The church activity is monitored by "wardens" who can intervene and block access to those who fail to comply with the "house rules". The Alpha Church, the Church of Fools, Buddhanet and the First Church of Cyberspace are some examples that indicate: (a) the versatility of the Web; (b) the extent to which different religious bodies are willing to embrace its possibilities; and (c) the variable degrees of implementing these possibilities for building/creating novel forms of religiosity.

It could be suggested here that the categories, issues, ideas and examples presented in the Cartography section represent Feenberg's (1991, 14) interpretation of technology as a "parliament of things on which civilizational alternatives are debated and decided". Furthermore, Cartography may also be seen as reflecting Feenberg's (1991, 92) principles[56] (the "principle of the conservation of hierarchy" and the "principle of subversive rationalization"). For instance, while the "elite", "formal" and "scholarly" types support and sustain the notions of hierarchy and authority, the "popular" and "subjective" subvert them by giving voice to those who are marginalized. On the other hand, NCRMs and MEMs reconfigure the concepts by developing, proposing and applying alternative views and practices.

Topography of websites

The content of a site and the way in which it is presented are two key issues in researching e-religious discourses. A site reflects the identity and mentality of its discourse; it clearly illustrates what the leader(s) think, on the one hand, the essential message of the page should be and, on the other hand, the best possible ways to present it. This is achieved by the morphology of the idiosyncratic language employed in electronic discourse which is far richer than its linguistic content alone, for a new possibility—multimedia—is involved. This new field of visualized information—the product of an imaginative approach in Web designing—is an integral part of the study of e-religious discourses.

This section, therefore, is concerned with the semantics of sites— ways in which information is presented in different sites; how the design of the sites reflects the owner's perception of and attitude towards the technology; the extent to which the unique characteristics of the Web are included in, or excluded from the design; the levels of interactivity between the "speaker" (site) and the technology; between the "speaker" and the audience; and amongst the audience themselves.

Elements of a site

Hoffman and Novak (1995) distinguish two types of interactivity via ICTs. On the one hand it is "interactivity through" the medium and on the other hand it is "interactivity with" the medium. The authors note that while the former implies that the medium is perceived as a tool of connecting sender and receiver, the latter signifies a relationship between both sender and receiver with the environment with which they interact. Hoffman and Novak (1995, citing Steuer 1992) emphasize that because of this interaction the sender is also a receiver, and information is not simply transmitted but rather "mediated environments are created and experienced". Examples of such created environments may be found in sites that offer to the visitors the possibility of participation in a synchronous and/or asynchronous communication and interaction, in which their perceptions, concerns, questions, doubts, agreements, gratitude and challenges become part of the content of the site. Therefore, by being part of the content they enhance it and eventually contribute to the discourse's subjectivity. In such cases the triad (sender/receiver/medium) creates a place of symbiosis for the discourse and its followers or critics.

The use of multimedia in a site's design, in both static forms such as text, still images and graphics, and dynamic forms, such as audio, video, animated images, texts and graphics (Bornman and von Solms 1993) is an additional aspect that a methodological framework has to incorporate, since multimedia play an important role in the presentation of the content. The point of presentation has been highlighted by Mitra and Cohen (1999, 181) who suggest that one way of understanding Web "texts"[57] is through "critical/cultural textual analysis". In their view, such an analysis not only reveals aspects of the content, but also reveals the effectivity of the text and what it says about those who designed it and those who interact with it. Hence, they propose three key elements through which a website could be analysed: the formal features of the site and its signifying strategies; the intertextuality of the site; and the role of the readers who through reading the text acknowledge its very existence and make it meaningful.

A number of works (Chandler 1998; Tate and Alexander 1999; Agre 1998; Frobish 2000), addressing the issue of generic features of a website, have formulated different sets of criteria for, either evaluating the information of a site, or identifying its genre, or how to design it. For instance, Tate and Alexander (1999, 37–47) suggest six basic elements of a website: authority (site level and page level), accuracy, objectivity, currency, coverage and intended audience. Authority, for Tate and Alexander, is related to who has published the site, that is, an institution, organization or individual; accuracy is the degree to which information is trustworthy and free from errors; objectivity is the extent to which the site expresses facts without personal biases; currency refers to the site's regular updating; coverage reflects the variety of topics and the depth to which they are examined; and the intended audience is the people for whom the site was created. Chandler (1998) who focuses on personal websites proposes the following features: identity, form of content, technical features, iconography and targeted audience. Agre (1998) examines the features of a website within the context of design and among others he suggests the following questions as being of importance: Who is the site for? What is its purpose? What activities does it offer to visitors? What questions may the visitors have? How up to date is the visitors' hardware? What type of Internet connection do they have (modem, ISDN or B-ISDN)?

These compilations highlight that while some criteria apply to different types of sites, some are applicable to all. For example, while Tate and Alexander's list is suitable for sites such as the Religious Tolerance, Web Missiology and the International Association for Religious Freedom, it is not suitable for sites such as the Holy See, Hindu Universe or Understanding

Islam for a number of reasons. First is the issue of authority. The notion of authority has been a prominent one in many works and is considered to be a key indicator of a site's credibility. However, as has been discussed in this study, the very existence of the Web depends on its users who provide its content. Moreover, as Mitra and Cohen (1999, 196) and others (Kinneya 1995, 764; Babin and Zukowski 2002; Venerable Pannyavaro 1998) emphasize, the Web has challenged the notion of authority. Thus, questioning the authenticity of the voice the very rationale of the Web is compromised and its purpose undermined. Secondly, "accuracy" and "objectivity" could not be applied to sites such as the Burning Man, or the Big Mystery, because these sites, or any religious site for that matter, present a unique *Weltanschuung*, which cannot be juxtaposed to another similar in order to measure its accuracy and objectivity. However, the features of currency, coverage and intended audience should be taken into account when a site is investigated, for they indicate the owner(s)' perception of and relation to their site's purpose. This depends, though, on the overall format and objective of the site. For example, in the Bible Gateway, or in the Holy Qur'an Resources on the Internet , obviously, the sacred texts do not change, but new commentaries, translations, essays and special features (i.e. subject index) enrich the site's coverage and expand the range of its usability (e.g. to believers, to researchers, and/or to for-whatever-reason-seekers). Chandler's list, although compiled specifically for personal sites, incorporates elements that can also be applied to non-personal sites.

For instance, in the theme "who am I?", that refers to the presentation of the identity of the owner, Chandler (1998) includes, among others, issues such as: personal statistics, biographical details, ideas, values, beliefs and causes, friends and acquaintances. The "forms of content" theme includes: personal advertisement, commercial advertisement, frequently-asked questions (FAQ) and structural organization (i.e. index, contents page). The theme "technical features" is formed by: links, access counter, frames, forms (i.e. guestbook, feedback), email and chat room. "Iconography" consists of elements related to aesthetics such as: colour, typography (font size, colour), graphics, sounds and the overall style. Regarding the "intended audience" Chandler (1998) lists friends, intimates, colleagues, peers and employers. Some of Agre's (1998) features overlap with those of Tate and Alexander's and Chandler's, therefore, from his list, the features of activities, site's purpose and consideration for the visitors' hardware are worth considering.

Themes and features

The above presented lists, although they overlap in places, clearly underline that no "one size fits all" approach is adequate for analysing the diverse array of Web pages (Tate and Alexander 1999, 3). For example, a commercial site's objective, which is to advertise and promote a sell-able product or service, is quite different from that of an anti-global-ization group, therefore, the design of each site would be structured in such a way as to best reflect and maximize the purpose of the site. As Tate and Alexander (1999, 3) eloquently express it, "a news page is significantly different from a personal page created by an individ-ual who merely wants to share photos of the family pets". Likewise, e-religious discourses present both contextual and conceptual disparities. For instance, the difference of objectives between the site of the Zen Buddhist Order of Hsu Yun and that of Amber's personal site is illus-trated in the size, design, content and presentation. While the former includes fifty-six links, the latter offers only seven, one of which con-nects to the Jehovah's Witnesses official site (Amber's religious affili-ation). The site of the Order, by providing the contents of its site in eleven different languages, targets an international audience, whereas Amber's site remains accessible only to an English-speaking audience. However, these sites share some common features, such as they both present their historical background, include family pictures and photo-graphs of friends.[58]

Websites, according to Babin and Zukowski (2002, 169), are not only places for interactivity, but also places and spaces for attracting and capturing the imagination of netizens. Additionally, Miller (2000, 17) suggests that the aesthetic represents an attempt to join creator and visitor in time and space so each can "dock alongside the other in cyber-space". Therefore, it makes sense to suggest that semiotics, both textual and visual, should be included in the methodological apparatus. In fact, Codognet (1996) and Moriarty (1994) have both stressed the impor-tance and power of semiotics as a tool for examining communication within the Web. Furthermore, the multiplicity of media which form the message of a site, according to Mason and Dicks (1998), signifies a shift in the relationship between text and image, in the sense that the "let-tered representation" does not solely carry the meaning of the message. Rather, the authors point out, the images' function is not restricted to that of accompanying illustrations, but they become active participants in the construction of meaning. Moriarty (1994) also emphasizes the importance of visual communication in the construction of meaning and proposes "visemics" as a distinct field of studying visual commu-nication employing theories of semiotics. Moreover, Codognet (1996) suggests that the ability of ICTs to manipulate pictorial information, on the one hand transformed the previous human-to-computer and human-to-human (through computer) interactions limited to the alpha-numeric set, which, in his view, is directly related to the explosion of the Internet and, on the other hand, it made the Web a mesh of icons, indexes and symbols that act both as navigational tools and as symbols of homogenization of the appearance of a website. Visual information is subject to more active personal interpretation (Moriarty 1994) which, this study would contend, is influenced by culture. This in turn draws attention to the importance of aesthetics, iconic symbolism, symbolism of colour and semiotics of sound/music within a particular cultural and/ or religious system.

Socio-political configurations. The lists of the elements of a site could be placed under the theme "composition" and subsumed under the features: content, aesthetics, activity/interactivity, accessibility (intended audience), hypertextuality and intertextuality. However, analysis of an e-religious discourse should not be confined only within the parameters of content and its presentation, but it should also include the investigation of the wider social, political, cultural, economic and historical frameworks and motives that may have determined and influenced, to a greater or lesser degree, both the circumstances of its creation and its content. Therefore, socio-political configurations may also be an additional generic theme whose inclusion in the investigational process may further advance the understanding of an e-religious discourse.

For instance, Frobish (2000) examines the site of the Church of Scientology in the context of how its Web presence may overturn the obstacles Scientology has faced regarding its credibility and ethos. The purpose of the excellent composition and presentation of Scientology's site, Frobish (2000) asserts, is multifaceted, in that the site's objectives include: to keep its visitors entertained and absorbed in a number of activities; to build a sense of trust between itself and the users; and to present a socio-political and religious image by associating itself hypertextually and intertextually to accredited sources. In this way, Scientology, through highly proficient use of the Web, produces and communicates "a credible religious ethos" (Frobish 2000). Such an examination of a site enables the identification of either implicit or explicit political agendas, affiliations, objectives and nationalistic ideologies. Examples that may be considered as implying such socio-political configurations include the sites of the Presidential Prayer Team, the Anti-Defamation League, the Nation of Islam and the Hizbollah Movement.

Composition/design. Contextual and/or conceptual dissimilarities have already been identified as issues that need to be considered. However, other factors may also play a determinant role in a site's composition and overall appearance/image. An exemplification of this would be if Amber's site is juxtaposed to that of R. Grant Jones'.[59] Visually, Amber's site is rather simple. The site's design consists of a black border, shaped as an upside-down L, placed on the left-hand side and top of the screen, with a white background. A contrasting effect is achieved by using white fonts on the black border and black fonts on the white background. The links are the typical blue of hyperlinks and in the middle of the page there is a photograph of a sunset. The only indication of Amber's religious beliefs is the link to the Jehovah's Witnesses site. R. Grant Jones' site is substantial in size (twenty-one links in the front page, the majority of which link to massive texts). The front (home) page is divided into two parts: a narrow section on the left and the main one. At the top of the left-hand section there is a Byzantine icon of Jesus, and underneath it, Grant has placed an extract from St. Basil the Great's *On the Holy Spirit*. This pattern (i.e. an icon followed by an extract) continues until the end of the page. The central space of the page is devoted to the purpose of the site, the beatitudes, internal and external links and the Symbol of the Orthodox faith. Although the site is in English, the beatitudes and the symbol of the faith are in both Greek and English. The background of the site is a darkish burgundy wallpaper which complements the colours of the icons and the fonts, which follow a colour scheme (headings soft green, main texts light blue, extracts pale cream) and the links are orange instead of blue.

From this short description, the following dissimilarities are noticeable between the two sites. Regarding the identity feature, Amber includes an "about me" link, and a "family" link in which she provides information about herself, her religious affiliation, her interests, her family and friends. Grant, however, does not offer such links in his site; information about him or his family and friends is excluded from the formal features of his site.[60] Taking into account these differences, it would appear that while Amber presents her religious belonging as just one aspect of her identity, Grant presents his religious belonging as the only aspect that best defines who he is.

Regarding the structural organization, there are significant differences in: (a) size: Amber's site consists of seven pages; Grant's site, by far larger, consists of twenty-one second-level[61] pages, some of which lead to "third-level" pages; (b) aesthetics: Amber's site is aesthetically indifferent, in that it has a plain design, almost monochrome, but the few photographs improve the overall appearance of the site. Grant's site is aesthetically more appealing, in that its design is more sophisticated and colourful, and the Byzantine icons enrich the overall impression.

However, an important point is that the size and design of a site are contingent upon a number of factors that need to be included in the evaluation and analysis process. For instance, while the size depends on the slice of "cyberspace"[62] that the owner of the site can afford to purchase, the design depends on the means by which the site is produced. These means may be either a website design software package, or a professional website designer, or an individual's personal effort using the freely available tools on the Web. Furthermore, the space and design are not independent from one another, but are interconnected in a relationship of mutual dependence, in that the available domain space can determine the design—the more elaborate and complex the design, the more spatial resources it demands.

Cost. Therefore, both features—key elements of a site—are intertwined with cost which is not an issue only faced by owners of personal sites. Rather, financial resources should be seen as an influential factor that governs, to a great extent, not only the presence in, or absence from, cyberspace of a religious discourse in any of its forms,[63] but also its spatial dimension and presentational configuration. Studies[64] (LaRue 1999; Thumma 2002) on the interrelation between finance and technological equipment and Internet usability found that churches with an annual budget under $100,000 are less likely to have adequate hardware infrastructure. In particular, LaRue notes that 73 per cent of those churches own one computer, while wealthier churches own two or more depending on their budget. As one may have guessed, LaRue (1999) found similar disparities regarding software usability and access to ICTs.[65] Thumma's research,[66] conducted in 2002, highlights that in 2001 only 43 per cent of churches in the US had uploaded websites. 60 per cent of those with an annual income of $1,000K and above have a site, while only 10 per cent of those with an income of less of $99K have a site. Cost, undoubtedly, is a decisive factor in engineering a website, therefore although there is a wide range of advanced tools in Web designing which can produce aesthetically alluring and stimulating sites, they are, at least at the moment, available only to "megachurches" (Thumma 2002) which can afford both their implementation and the spatial resources they require. The issue of financial resources is clearly illustrated in the size and design of sites such as the Holy Trinity Church in Frome, UK; the Temple Beth El in Stamford, US; and Global Good News[67] which is one of many very impressive sites of Maharishi Mahesh Yogi's organizations.

Content analysis. The objective of a site is demonstrated in both textual and visual form. Thus, one has to consider the manner in which a site's textual information is, through linguistic practices, formulated. The investigation of the textual part of a site may be performed through interpretive textual analysis[68] which includes semiotics, rhetorical analysis, ideological analysis and psychoanalytic approaches, among many others. Interpretive textual analysis of a site allows the researcher to approach its text from a number of different perspectives, which in turn enables the identification of its key elements and its dynamics.

Questions that may facilitate the basis of interpretive textual analysis include: What is the purpose of the text? What was the exigency behind the creation of the particular text? What is the social, cultural and political standpoint of the "author"? Who, on the basis of the style, content and emphasis of the text, seems to be the intended audience? What discourse community does the text seem to be part of? What issues are addressed? In other words, analysis of lexical and structural semantics[69] and pragmatics[70] of the textual part of a site(s) offers invaluable and constructive information which, in conjunction with the other elements of the site, provides a holistic view of the presented e-religious discourse. An example that illustrates the importance of semantics and pragmatics is DharmaNet International. The "about" link reveals the purpose of the site which is to provide

> gateways for Buddhist study and practice resources. It is home to Dharmanet's own in-house databases and collections, as well as providing links to all online Buddhist resources, large and small. DharmaNet offers this www/ftp site freely in hopes of helping Buddhists and other interested individuals around the globe to find Dhamma teachings and teachers, to help support Dhamma centers in all traditions, to promote dialogue and communication, and to help build a vital and cooperative online Buddhist community.

The site offers a substantial number of links to centres and practice groups, Buddhist studies resources, various personal and non-organizational sites, newsgroups, lists, and chat, Dharma teachers, Buddhist products and commercial services and publishers and bookstores, among others. At first sight DharmaNet International appears to be an informative Buddhist mega site devoted solely to Buddhist information. However, if all links are activated, then the Engaged Buddhism link reveals a page whose entire content focuses exclusively on socio-political issues. What the visitor sees on that page is, at the top, the Tibetan flag and a short text explaining that

> DharmaNet International is flying the Tibetan national flag here in acknowledgement of Tibetan sovereignty in an occupied Tibet. May the Dharma prevail on the "roof of the world" for the benefit of all beings. Long life and success to the Dalai Lama. May the atrocities of the Chinese government end soon. May injustice and unkindness toward all beings everywhere end soon.

However, the page's key piece is the links to Vote to Impeach and Censure the President that are in picture form. The page offers an immense amount of links, under themes such as education, environment, hospice, gay and lesbian, prisons, volunteerism, women, Tibet, and non-Buddhist peace and human rights sites.

Aesthetics. As noted earlier, websites are compilations of a number of different elements such as texts, graphics, pictorial signs, still and animated images, symbolic representations, audio and video. In other words, most of the time a website is the product of a combination of colour(s) and symbol(s). What the user then encounters, when a site appears on the screen, is a collage of diverse features that constitute the whole, which initially is an image. Taken as such, and before the user deconstructs it into its different parts, the site conveys a visual message. This message is formed by the interaction that occurs between its different elements (texts, colours, indices, symbols etc.) that reflects the site's cultural heritage which is not static but dynamic—it changes and evolves through time. The point made here is that the design of a site reflects the past, present and to some extent the future of its discourse.[71] For example, while the texts and teachings of Buddhanet, the Church of Fools and the Alpha Church sites reflect their historical tradition, the implementation of advanced software reflects the sites owners' desire to bring their discourses into the current socio-cultural matrix. Regarding the future development of these discourses, taking into account their present status, one can only speculate that they might embrace future technological advancements.

Another part of the aesthetic aspect of a site is colour. Colour is a significant component of Web design, almost as important as content and navigation, for it is a powerful communicator (Morton 1998). Colour symbolism is significantly meaningful in religion, art, politics, and ceremonies, as well as in everyday life. The large numbers of online website design companies[72] offering advice and analysis of the meanings and cultural differences of colours demonstrate the consequence colour may have on a site. Colours not only add visual attractiveness to a site but also determine its message, for they embody symbolic meanings that are interpreted diversely by different cultures, ages and genders. For instance Ensenberger (1997) points out that some languages do not contain separate words for green and blue, or for yellow and orange. Yet, Eskimos use seventeen words for white as applied to different snow conditions. Similarly, in Chinese there are "more than 30 single characters describing different kinds of red. Red of wine, red of silk, red of wood, red of meat… And even more phrase (*sic*) are used to describe different levels of red".[73] Furthermore, all these different terms for red indicate how the meaning of colours evolves from daily life, not just for a single colour.

Hypertextuality—intertextuality. The concept of hypertextuality has been presented in detail earlier. Here a couple of examples will be used to illustrate the ramifications of external links as they may be indicators, on the one hand, of connectedness, association and/or co-operation and, on the other hand, of disapproval, criticism and condemnation. For example, the Religious Tolerance site connects itself to the Om Sakthi Spiritual Movement, to Tolerance for All and to John WorldPeace and appeals to its visitors to visit these sites for "they promote religious understanding and tolerance". However, one could question why Religious Tolerance prefers to link itself to these sites and not to other sites such as the International Foundation for Human Rights and Tolerance. A possible answer might be that Religious Tolerance does not wish to be associated with the Church of Scientology which is behind the Foundation. On the other hand though, it would be interesting to find out why Religious Tolerance connects itself to John WorldPeace, which is an individual's site, and not to the Global Dialogue Institute that also shares and promotes the same goals. Perhaps the answer may lie in competing conceptualizations and strategies or in hidden financial gains. For instance, Religious Tolerance defines itself as a "large religious site" that "promotes religious freedom, tolerance and diversity as positive cultural values". Furthermore, in the opening page the main concepts are defined and the site's mandate and motto are presented. For the owners of the site religious tolerance means "to extend religious freedom to people of all religions, even though you disagree with their beliefs and/or practices". The site's mandate is "[t]o promote religious tolerance and freedom. To describe religious faiths in all their diversity. To describe controversial topics from all points of view"; and its motto proclaims that

> [n]o peace among the nations without peace among the religions.
> No peace among religions without dialogue between the religions.
> No dialogue between the religions without investigation of the
> foundation of the religions.

The John WorldPeace site's motto is "WorldPeace is one word! Until we write WorldPeace as one word, World and Peace will continue to be two things". Regarding conceptual clarifications, John WorldPeace interprets religion as

> man created bureaucracy consisting of all the corruption that exists
> in every large corporation. Religion is not God. Spirituality can
> flourish without religion. Religion is an institution whose bureau-

crats allege that they represent God for the purpose of controlling the minds of their true believers [...] No one can deny that
Judaism, Christianity and Islam all have a long history of promoting racial and religious genocide as well as the subordination of
women.

For John WorldPeace, peace is so important that he changed his name
to show his "commitment to both peace and WorldPeace". John
WorldPeace ran for governor of Texas in 2002 (as a Democrat); in 2003
for Mayor of Houston (as a Republican); in 2004 for President of the
United States (as a Republican).[74] John WorldPeace in his mission declaration states:

> ...based on the fact that I am the only person who embraces all
> human beings and all peace initiatives yet affiliates with none;
> based on the fact that I am the only peace activist who has been
> willing to change his name for the cause of peace; based on the
> fact that no other person has a commitment to end the worldwide
> atrocities of religion, racism, nationalism and sexism as opposed
> to concern about limited violations of morality and the law; based
> on the fact that I advocate peace and WorldPeace as opposed to
> exclusively endorsing any specific peace initiative; I ask for the
> support of all peace activists and peace organizations worldwide
> to support me in my pursuit of increasing the peace on the planet.

As it appears, from this short presentation the two sites share neither
the same objectives nor similar ideological frameworks; the motives,
therefore, behind Religious Tolerance's decision to grant a link to John
WorldPeace remain unanswered.

Temporal Category(ies)

Synchronic

Because of the idiosyncratic nature of the Web—that is, its ephemerality, temporality and unpredictable capacity for shifting in multiple
directions—and also because of the spontaneous and impulsive actions
and reactions of its users, a synchronic analysis of cyberreligious utterances makes possible the identification of current trends in the field
of e-religion, as well as the subjectivity of each religious expression, as
represented within the domain of its website. The synchronic analysis,
when focused on a particular issue, aspect and/or concept, enables the
investigation of the dialectic dynamics arising from events that provoke
controversy and tension between social forces and religious doctrines;

between religions and between their followers; between Church and state; between religion and politics to mention but a few. A synchronic analysis enables the ontological investigation—the systematic account of the existence of different discourses—at a given moment in time. It could be suggested that the subject of the synchronic investigation is Web ephemerality itself. Examples of e-religious existences and controversial occurrences may include: abortion; homosexuality—especially in the context of clergy; the Cassie Bernall case; the notion of religious freedom (in various settings); the issue of the European ID cards and the Church of Greece; the Taliban regime; 9/11; the war prayer and the war on Iraq and the Buddha sculptures of Bamiyan in Afghanistan. It should be noted that each of these examples has been discussed, presented, analysed, debated and investigated within diverse social, cultural and/or political contexts in which the religious dimension is brought either as their supporter or as their polemic.[75]

9/11

While the key words "9/11 terrorist" in 2000 returned no results, between September 9 and 16 there were 171,990 unique URLs. A keyword research for "World Trade Centre attack" in October 2001 returned a seven-digit number of hits. Today (May 2004), the number of hits for "9/11 terrorist" is 123,000 and for "World Trade Centre attack" is 52,800.

Reports estimated that the traffic on the Web increased at exponential rates causing the Internet service providers to reach the point of collapse. According to Google search statistics from 9/11:

- Among the top 200 queries on Tuesday, news-related searches were 60 times greater than the number of news-related searches conducted the previous day.
- More than 80 per cent of the top 500 queries conducted on Tuesday were related to the terrorist attacks.
- At 6:51 a.m. on Tuesday, more than 6,200 queries for "cnn" were conducted on Google. Between 6:26 a.m. and 7:06 a.m., the number of searches for "cnn" averaged approximately 6,000 queries per minute.

Within the Web, the first reaction to the events of 9/11 was the updating of a large number of American sites with expressions of grief, patriotism and religious rhetoric. The most commonly used symbols were the American flag and the American eagle accompanied by the mottos "God Bless America" or "In God's Hands Now". Further, some updated sites offered comments, photographs, prayers and presentations of Islam. Cases such as the Virgin Mary's End-times Prophecies site included a page entitled "How to save your home and loved ones from terrorist attacks and war" devoted to 9/11, in which it is revealed that "[the] Lady of the Roses sadly foretold the terrorist acts that would come to New York City and the United States". In addition the page informs that "the Blessed Virgin Mary also told us how to protect ourselves and our loved ones from these terrorists' attacks". The page incorporates a number of pictures of the World Trade Centre before and after the attack and an animated airplane that flies between the two pictures. The page also analyses the numerous occurrences of the numbers "eleven" and "seven". The page offers "Heaven's Home Protection Packet" and "Heaven's Personal Protection Packet" (for $8.00) among other prophetical booklets and crucifixes. The hypertextuality of the page is defined by links such as: The Sudan-Iraq-Afghanistan Alliance: and the Russian connection; Warning: More Attacks, Use of Weapons of Mass Destruction Possible and a number of links to articles related to 9/11. Also on the page "Save America from terrorism and war" it is explained how the Rosary Crusade aims to stop terrorism and war.

The attack generated feelings of hatred, revenge, mistrust, intolerance and bewilderment among the American population. Illustrative examples could be the site of Muslim Women's League, a non-profit Muslim American organization that among issues of concern, issues of civil rights, to mention but a few, also addresses the 9/11 events and their effects on Muslim women; and the FRONTLINE (part of PBS news) site "devoted to 9/11". The page, which is very impressive in its design and its cover story "Faith and Doubt at Ground Zero", addresses questions related to God's existence, the nature of evil and includes interviews with officials from religious traditions, scholars, artists and intellectuals. The page also conducts a poll about people's religious beliefs and the effects of 9/11 on their beliefs. The Pew Forum on Religion and Public Life offers an extensive article on 9/11 and its effects. Here too a poll of "post 9/11 attitudes" is available, as well as religious responses to the "war on terror".

The religious rhetoric that surrounded the events is demonstrated in an article, entitled "Angel or Devil? Viewers See Images in Smoke", in the "Click on Detroit" site. The article presents images in which people reported that they "saw" faces (Satan's) and angels.[76] The images have appeared on a number of news sites, blogs and pages all over the world, including Japan and Finland. The "American Atheists" site, however, adds to the 9/11 event a different dimension. In response to the discussions on the 9/11 memorial, the American Atheists opposed the cross as a permanent ground zero memorial, questioning the appropriateness of a "sectarian memorial".

After the initial emotional responses to the shock of the attack, sites addressing the events in a more reflective way began to appear. For instance, academic resources on 9/11 such as "The Events of 9/11 and Islam, the Taliban, and Bin Laden" offer diverse analyses either from religious or political points of view. Additionally, the 911 Respond to the Call site is about community spirit, interfaith respect and co-operation. The site announces that the

> Homeland Ministries of the Christian Church (Disciples of Christ) and the Islamic Society of North America,… have created an opportunity for you to respond to the call. The Islamic Society of North America has invited our congregations to contact their affiliate members for partnerships on Sept. 11 work projects. Take this opportunity to meet your Islamic neighbours and work together to create a project in your neighbourhood and make a difference!

The site's theme for this year's (2004) action is "World Unity Begins in the Community".[77] The site's objective is to bring together different faith communities in an effort to develop unity, co-operation and to build relationships.

The 9/11 events generated the creation of sites which reflected people's diverse responses to an unprecedented situation. Religion is the most prominent issue on all 9/11 sites and the approaches, attitudes and perceptions range widely in character (non-religious, religious) and in volume (from mild to extreme religious zealotry). Today (May 2004), some of the sites that soon after the attack included in their front pages American symbols have returned to their original appearance. Furthermore, mega-sites, such as the September 11 Digital Archive (it may be seen as the "official" website of the events of 9/11); the September 11, 2001-The Day the World Changed; the Coping with the 9.11.01 Aftermath; the 9/11 Heroes; and September 11 Terrorist Attacks, 2001, more or less exist as historical records of the 9/11 events, containing contemporary eye-witness accounts, videos, photographs and recordings of victims' telephone calls.

Diachronic

The diachronic category refers to a critical analysis of archived material (in this case websites) in order to discover possible changes in both conceptual and contextual content, intertextuality, aesthetic and symbolic representation. Diachronic examination reveals a number of issues such as: the extent to which usage of the Web and other communicative forms of ICTs (i.e. email, BBs, forums, blogs, e-shops) are added or extended; the extent to which a site evolves in terms of content development or remains inactive; the employment of multimedia; updating the site and incorporating new features made available by software advancements.

In other words, diachronic investigation provides a historical presentation of an e-religious discourse—a "moving picture" through time—which offers the opportunity for monitoring, examining and analysing it in-depth, thus revealing its history and its possible changes. To explore adequately the research topics presented by such an examination, a dynamic method of investigation, which would extend the field of enquiry, is needed. For instance, passive observation of the changes of a website does not provide information about: the reasons behind the changes, or the interaction between participants and creator(s), or between participants themselves and the outcomes of that interaction. Furthermore, certain issues such as membership, relations, tensions and possible disagreements are not reflected on the site. Therefore, as stated previously, informant ethnography (Bainbridge 2000) is considered here as better serving the scope of diachronic analysis. Some examples that demonstrate the usefulness and effectiveness of diachronic examination are: Digitalism, the Jehovah's Witnesses, and the Church of Virus.

Digitalism

Digitalism appeared in 1996 in Denmark. Its founder is an IT and VR specialist which may explain the discourse's name. The term "digitalism" embodies a number of technical, religious and philosophical meanings which ascribe to it a number of diverse qualities. In particular, "digitalism" is not only a term that refers to all expressions of digital culture, but also a

> "scientific paradigm that postulates that the universe itself is the ultimate supercomputer". Philosophical digitalism is most commonly expressed through the simulated reality argument while religious digitalism is a modern form of Deism or Pantheism whereby God is recast as a "Divine Programmer" or Creation as a "Divine Computer". The Omega Point hypothesis is a popular but dubious synthesis of both philosophical and religious digitalism.[78]

The creation of Digitalism's site, according to its founder,[79] was "to make people think for themselves. To follow themselves". Digitalism's amalgamation of Buddhist and computing concepts is reflected in statements such as "[d]eath is only a return to the body itself, [a] return to real life" and creation, seen as part of a "program", is "just a graphical illusion". Digitalism's cosmotheory is based on "the unity of mankind; the freedom to think, speak, act and to access information". People responded positively to Digitalism's ideas and some discussion forums were created[80] which the founder observed, but did not participate in. Digitalism attracted academic attention and it was included as an example of cyber-religious expression in a number of works presented in conferences focusing on religion and ICTs. However, examining Digitalism's site over a period of three years reveals that Digitalism (as a site and as a religious utterance) has remained inactive since 2000 when it was last updated; its site, though, is still available.

Jehovah's Witnesses

The Jehovah's Witnesses site is a characteristic example of "change without change". The official site since 2000 appears to change every month. The main layout of the front page of the site remains the same but the issues seem to alter. The permanent contents of the site appear to be: who are the JWs; the issue of the Trinity; what does God require and the issue of blood. The changing topics in 2000, for example, included: sickness and its relation to the devil; blood and medicine; when a loved one dies. In January 2001 there was a personal story related to a health condition; blood and medical care. In February 2001 the new topics were safe air travel, the Enchanting Hue of Koryo Celadon and the Bible's power; 2002 who really rules the world, organic gardening and about the Occult; 2003 who is God, about genes, the resurrection of Jesus—fact or legend and about Yoga. In 2004 (between March and May) the topics were about fashion (dark side of glamour, credit cards, money and real life); medical care and blood; religious persecution; American Indians and the importance of neighbours and community, among others. The site of the Jehovah's Witnesses, although it changes its appearance, remains always the same in content, in the sense that the themes that define JWs discourse are readdressed, albeit in different contexts, from month to month.

Church of Virus

The last example to be presented briefly here is the Church of Virus (CoV). The Church of Virus was created in Canada in 1995. Its founder is an electrical engineer and computer scientist who has been an active member of online communities since the eighties and who also is involved in the development and maintenance of websites. The inspiration for the CoV was its founder's newly acquired knowledge of memetics, resulting from his studies of artificial life. Deciding that "the world needs a memetics based religion to spread the memes of rationality and science",[81] he uploaded the CoV. The name "virus" was "chosen to be deliberately antagonistic, to put people on their guard and let them know this idea was designed to infect them. Call it truth in advertising". The initial design of the site was dominated by a black background, two symbols and words warning that "Closed irrational minds may be offended". CoV exists exclusively online, but there have been a few face-to-face gatherings of members over the years. Virus was defined as:

- a forum for rational discourse
- a memetically engineered atheistic religion
- a synthesis of religion and evolution
- the best possible conceptual framework for living and thinking
- a neo-cybernetic philosophy for the twenty-first century
- an extended phenotype of the Virion Council.

The content of the site consisted of: Introduction, Questions, Virian Sins and Virtues, Philosophy, Virus' views on philosophers, philosophies and other religions, Virian Saints, Memes Virus Lexicon, reading list and alt. memetics. Its hypertextuality was defined by links to: atheism pages, weird religions, sites of the Damned, other religions and a number of links compiled by individuals. The overall design (colours and symbols) and the content of the site reflected an ambiguous identity (it has been perceived as a satanic cult).[82]

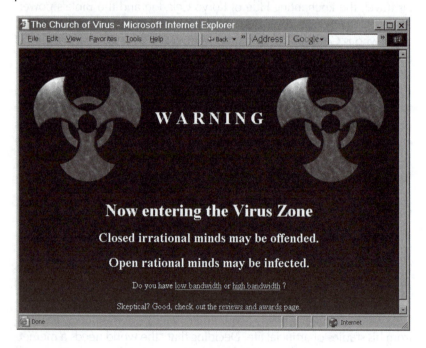

However, in August 2000 the Church of Virus' updated site was launched. The new design, far more elegant and sophisticated, changed totally the appearance of the discourse. The site and, as it appeared, the Church of Virus, were transformed.

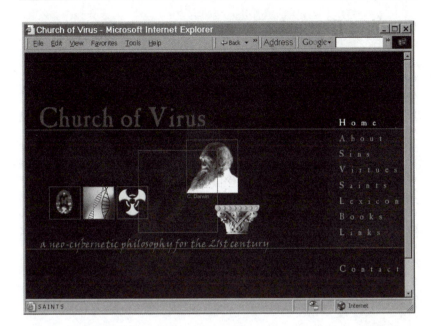

For instance, the CoV's leadership has evolved over the years. In 2003 the leadership was in the process of formalizing a Virian Council of seven members that would act like a Board of Directors. The redesigned site incorporates all initial themes and the new additions are demographics about the current membership[83] and a more extensive and informative list of external links that includes: the Principia Cybernetica Project; the International Society of Artificial Life; the Humanist Association of Canada and the Church of Scientology.

2003 was for the CoV a year of transition and changes. For instance, one result of the changes was the development of a new system called Meridion which is "a reputation/voting system unique to the Church of Virus to develop new doctrine and policy. One of the first things we did with the new system was to vote in our second saint, St. Hypatia".[84] Another event of the 2003 period was that there was a "schism at the CoV and a new religion/philosophy was born—the Meta Virus". Although "metavirus" has an allocated domain name (http://metavirus. net/), its site is not available yet. In fact the "coming soon" message that still appears on the screen, when the "metavirus" URL is activated, is the only sign that indicates the existence of "metavirus" as a cyberspatial entity. The latest from CoV is its shop which sells T-shirts, mugs, hats and baby bibs with the logo of the church. The BBs, chat room and mailing list are thriving, showing that CoV is a dynamic presence that an increasing number of people find appealing.

Closing Remarks

The division of the methodological apparatus in spatial and temporal categories enabled the exploration and investigation of e-religious discourses from different perspectives which, in turn, revealed a number of presences, expressions and aspects of e-religion that may have remained unnoticed. The small-scale implementation of the proposed methodology demonstrates that there are a number of research avenues for studying e-religious utterances and occurrences. For instance, all types of sites provide a wealth of diverse materials for investigating and analysing possible differences among either church/synagogue/mosque/temple/centres within the same religious system, or between different systems. The synchronic and diachronic approaches also offer exciting opportunities for exploring and monitoring both NCRMs and MEMs.

7 Conclusions

"By changing space, by leaving the space of one's usual sensibili-
ties, one enters into communication with a space that is psychically
innovating... For we do not change place, we change our nature".
Gaston Bachelard 1969, 206

Most people have a favourite place, a place that evokes powerful and
distinct feelings. For some, such a place may be one that feels timeless;
that has a special significance; that is exciting, adventurous and peace-
ful all at once; a place in which, and most importantly, one can experience a sense of belonging and a sense of connection. Places have an
identity which is subject both to their natural and distinct characteristics
and to the discursive practices of their inhabitants/visitors.

ICTs in general, and the Web in particular, have become the favourite
place of many people; they have been seen as the ultimate place for the
manifestation of true democracy; the empowerment of all; the inclusion of all; for citizens from any corner of the world to exercise their
right of free speech; humanity to be freed from the constraints and the
control of time and distance; the world's inhabitants freely to communicate with each other creating a "global village". Do these claims reflect
the reality of ICTs?

Although there was no central question that this study had to answer,
there were some preconceived ideas and assumptions that my involvement with ICTs, prior to this work, had generated. This study and the
snapshot of websites, as of 2003/4, confirm some of my assumptions,
dispute others, and reveal several avenues for further investigation.

I started this research assuming that:

(a)   the number of cybernauts was by far larger than what it actually
      was

(b)   having a website was a matter of choice of a religious body; there-
      fore all religious bodies could/would exist on the Web;

(c)   a deeper understanding of my research field was essential for the
      construction of a methodological approach;

(d)   techno-religious theories, in particular, the utopian perceptions
      and promotions of ICTs, were generated by the novelty of the
      technology;

(e)   a methodological set of tools would enable multiple ways of explo-
      ration, investigation and study of e-religion in its different forms;

(f)   no predetermined research question would offer more freedom and flexibility to recognize and explore emerging concepts and issues.

a) the number of cybernauts was by far larger

The first three assumptions were contested and proved invalid by the epistemological examination of the Web. For instance, contrary to my estimation regarding the number of netizens, and despite the practical difficulties arising from the Web's size and fluidity for accurate measures, the fact is that, today (May 2004), only 10 per cent of humanity is actually connected.[1] The statements that dominate the utopian discourse surrounding the Web's development and mass adoption imply that the technological infrastructure that supports the Web and secures its universality is neutral. Technology, however, can be considered as neutral only when it is available universally without any restrictions.

When it is conditioned and its applicability depends on a number of contingencies which can restrict its accessibility and/or usage, then its universality becomes partiality, carrying the biases of its creators, designers, developers and initial users. Although the issue of accessibility is in the agendas of international political and financial bodies and although at national levels every effort is made to minimize or eliminate the hurdles, netizenship is still far from being universal. Thus, it appears that Castells' (1996, 341) statement "**[w]e are not living in a global village, but in customized cottages globally produced and locally distributed**" (original emphasis) is still applicable.

b) having a website was a matter of choice of a religious body

As has been discussed in the chapter on epistemology, the provision of hardware and Internet connection do not resolve the issue of "global access". Cultural, educational and economic differences play a key role in the processes of people's effective use of ICTs. To date, the evidence suggests that Castells' (1996, 371) prediction that the "multimedia world would be populated by two essentially distinct populations: the *interacting* and the *interacted*",[2] seems to be almost a certainty, at least for the foreseeable future.

ICTs still carry the biases of an elite[3] since their availability depends on specific contingencies found at both national and international levels. Therefore it is plausible to suggest that e-religion represents the religious expressions and activities of this elite. Notwithstanding the millions of sites devoted to religion, they still account for the religious, spiritual and philosophical *Weltanschuung* of a minority within a minority of the human population. On that account, the creation and publication of an e-religious discourse, although it appears to be a matter of choice, is also a matter of capability which is closely related to affordability and, in particular cases, to freedom of speech.

c) a deeper understanding of my research field was essential for the construction of a methodological approach

Knowing how the Web is structured and how it operates, especially regarding storage and dissemination of information, highlighted close interconnections between infrastructure and Web presence, thus enlarging my list of issues-to-be-considered. The multidimensionality of the issue of access and its repercussions on the Web's subjectivity played a crucial role in the process of constructing and developing the methodology.

For instance, updated information regarding the status of ICTs in different geographical locations and the issue of restricted, or censored, or no access, introduced another aspect of e-religion. In particular, it indicated that the absence of site(s) *of* a religious discourse as opposed to sites *about* is closely related to the issue of accessibility. For example, the cases of Huhan Pai (also known as "shouters"), Mentu Hui (Disciples association), Lingling Jiao (Spirit church), the Quanfanmian Jiao (the Holistic church), and the Zhongguo Fangcheng Jiaohui (China Fangcheng Church) could be characterized as typical examples of sites *about* religious expressions. Searching Google, via keyword query for each of these groups, produced a number of hits leading to the sites of Amnesty International, Human Rights Watch and Apologetics Index among others, that present these groups in the context of religious freedom in China. Taking into account the issues raised in epistemology, it could be plausible to suggest that the control of the Internet by the Chinese government is one definite factor behind the absence of sites of these Chinese Christian expressions. Another example could be the Amish. Some may argue that the Amish sites are *about* Amish and not *of* Amish. However, Google returns 1,050,000 hits, one of which is the Amish Country that advertises Amish products, Amish farms, Amish lodging and links to other Amish sites. It would be very interesting to find out how many, if any, of these sites are indeed *of* Amish and how many are *about* the Amish; thus informant ethnography over the Web, focusing on the Amish and their interaction with cyberspace, may prove illuminating.

Knowledge of the operational properties of the Web and the ways in which information is processed, stored and searched indicated that my Web research had to include multiple search techniques. As a result, the search for e-religious discourses was broad and took advantage of hypertextuality of sites, search engines enquiries, directories' entries, Web rings, blogs, BBs, discussion forums and personal contacts.

d) techno-religious theories, in particular, utopian perceptions and promotions of ICTs, were generated by ICTs' novelty

The examination of the theoretical approaches to technology in general and to ICTs in particular and the different conceptions of communication provided a broad and comprehensive understanding of the influential role of technology and ICTs in shaping social development and the notion of communication. The exploration of the relationship between religion and technology revealed a historical continuation of the religious and spiritual rhetoric that has circumscribed technological innovations for almost one thousand years. Contemporary "technological mysticism" (Stahl 1999)—religionization and spiritualization of ICTs—therefore does not derive from the novelty of an unknown technological advancement, but rather follows a historical Western tradition, based on scriptural interpretations (Newman 1997; Noble 1997). Past and present techno-metaphysical discourses, on the one hand, highlighted the issue of interaction between the employed technology—i.e. the Web—and the publisher—i.e. the creator/owner of a site and, on the other hand, offered a valuable insight into the process of identifying the diverse ways in which different religions perceive ICTs and how these perceptions are materialized through their websites.

e) a methodological set of tools that would enable multiple ways of exploration, investigation and study of e-religion in its different forms

The versatility of the medium and the innovative ways in which it is used by its netizens confirmed that the methodological model had to meet these needs. The division of methodology into spatial and temporal categories provides a basis from which a wide variety of concepts and issues can be addressed and analysed. The spatial categories, apart from providing a typology of e-religious discourses, also offers a plurality of contexts each of which could be the starting point of in-depth investigations of a number of questions, such as implementation of multimedia, hypertextuality, aesthetics, ideological associations and collaborations. The temporal categories, by incorporating the notion of time, allow the investigation of different aspects of e-religious discourses such as evolution, development, schisms, disappearances and appearances.

For instance, when the Vatican silenced French Bishop Jacques Gaillot for his liberal views, the Bishop found a global voice and now preaches his progressive Gospel from Partenia—a virtual diocese in cyberspace.

In 1999 in the USA, Greek Orthodox dissidents carried on an acrimonious challenge to the authority of their appointed Archbishop Spyridon, challenging his authority in a movement that has made an impact around the world and which led to the Archbishop's resignation. Utilization of ICTs by Falun Gong resulted in an impressive demonstration on April 1999. Similarly, Jediism or Jedi, following a massive campaign in 2001, was included as a religion in the 2001 England and Wales census.[4]

f) no predetermined research question would offer more freedom and flexibility to recognize and explore emerging concepts and issues

Understanding my field—the Web—and realizing its fundamental features, its peculiarities and its interdependency with the physical world, allowed the development of a holistic comprehension which in turn confirmed the value of having no-predetermined question/argument. The point made here is that having no particular focus to follow, develop, study and analyse, I had the ability, on the one hand, to build my methodological model progressively and, on the other hand, to recognize and consequently to include ideas and issues as they were emerging.

Despite the fact that the Web volume is the product of only 10 per cent of the human population, its sites present a plurality of understandings, interpretations and usages, including some unique discursive formations that have been explored, investigated and monitored.

This examination, albeit concise, raises a number of questions such as:

(a) Has cyberspace evoked totally new and original religious/spiritual/philosophical discourses?
(b) What, if any, fundamentally new religious activities has cyberspace generated?
(c) How may technology, in this case, the Web, have altered the conditions of religious life?

(a) has cyberspace evoked totally new and original religious/ spiritual/philosophical discourses?

The cases of Cosmosophy, Digitalism, Technosophy, and the Church of Virus, among others, show that there is an emerging phenomenon of techno-religious, techno-spiritual, techno-metaphysical or techno-philosophical constructions. Do these emerging phenomena qualify to be termed New Cyberreligious Movements (NCRMs)? Some of these utterances, such as Digitalism, that have become a static presence defined by inactivity and changelessness, may be thought of as not being a NCRM. Others, such as the Church of Virus that, to date, demonstrate a dynamic existence, characterized by evolution, constant development and activity whether constructive/positive (new design and new interactive features in the site) or negative/destructive[5] (schism) may be seen as a typical NCRM. Perhaps the best course of action would be to monitor these phenomena, thus giving time for scholars to reflect on their further development or disappearance.

(b) what, if any, fundamentally new religious activities has cyberspace generated?

Cyberspace has provided the platform for a number of virtual religious practices and rituals among individuals and groups belonging to both traditional religions and New Age/neo-pagan ones. They range from textual descriptions and analyses of rituals, their significance and symbolism, to active performances of various rituals from either individuals or groups. The most widely spread cyberpractices and cyberrituals[6] are those of cyberprayer,[7] cybermemorials[8] and grieving support,[9] meditation,[10] cyberpilgrimages[11] and rituals of the Pagan and Wiccan[12] communities, such as Samhain[13] and "healing rituals"[14] (Karaflogka 2004, 36).

(c) how may technology, in this case, the Web, have altered the conditions of religious life?

In the section "Mainstream E-religious Manifestations" (MEMs), a number of cyberspatial expressions of established religions demonstrate that traditional religions have started to perceive the Web as an advantageous environment that offers almost unlimited opportunities for religious devotion, practice, teaching and interaction. The Church of Fools, the first 3D church to perform Sunday service, accompanied by the Zen Online Meditation, the Buddhanet and the Alpha Church, may be seen as exhibiting Levy's (2001, 8) notion of "points of irreversibility". In other words, these sites show that their owners realized that the Web provides them with opportunities for constructing activities which fully capitalize on the potentialities and actualities the Web carries. The extent to which such activities will progress and be widely adopted could be the subject of future research.

Closing Remarks

ICTs have changed pre-existing norms in all areas of human communication and interaction, whether social, professional, educational, political or commercial. The area of religion could not remain unaffected. From the concepts, points and issues raised, and from the examples presented in this study, it appears that ICTs, especially the Web, have transformed religious norms and created new ones as a result of the following factors: (a) the transcendence of time and space. When connected, people leave their physical time-space singularities and enter into cyberspace and cybertime (Strate 2003), where the notions of where (locality) and when (past/present/future) become altered, thus constituting new planes of existence. When in these planes, the users, liberated from the constraints of the physical, become and act as netizens. As such they are faced with (b) an unprecedented freedom to express themselves and to communicate this expression to the entire world. Netizens, as both individuals and groups, are enabled (c) to create and/or participate in new forms of communities, to form affiliations and collaborations, which in the offline world would not have been possible.

As with the printing press in the past, so (d) the Internet has nowadays changed the prevailing notion of traditional religious authority. Before the wide expansion of ICTs, religious authority was solidly anchored in the leadership of the scriptures and of the "clergy-people"[15] of the different religious traditions. The definition of what was accurate and in accordance with the norms, in both beliefs and practices, and what constituted unacceptable behaviour and/or heretical belief was decided by these religious authorities (Karaflogka 2004, 35).

Accessibility to ICTs enables people (e) to raise their voices in protests, which may be provoked by a political body against a religion or by the actions of a religious regime, or by the perceptions, views and attitudes held by some religions toward particular issues. Examples of such protests include the cases of Falun Gong; the Buddha sculptures in Afghanistan; the Diocese of Partenia; and the cases of human sexuality, celibacy of priests and anti-cult movements.

ICTs have contributed to humanity (f) a unique location for public gatherings on a worldwide scale. The global character of the medium gives the opportunity to millions of people to express themselves in one vehicle all at once. A community struck by disaster had never before had the opportunity to express grief, anger and support, and to be able to mourn collectively on such a scale as happened in the case of American society after September 11th. Along with prayers for the victims and their families posted on online bulletin boards, memorial sites, in photographic journals, relief funds and all kinds of different political and religious analyses of the events, there are "Light a Candle" sites from other countries[16] demonstrating their support.

Cyberspace, a blessed[17] space, is perceived as a socio-cultural, a political, a sacred and a spiritual space. As such, it not only carries institutionalized religions, new religious movements, alternative spiritualities and every voice within all these, but also (g) generates original and innovative religious phenomena, in both theoretical and practical terms. Moreover, cyberspace, as well as ICTs as a whole for that matter, may be seen as deconstructing the notion of globalization from a signifier of socio-political and economic changes to a signifier of socio-political, economic and spiritual connectedness. As technological advancements progress and new interfaces become available to the public, so the "points of irreversibility" will progress. The extent of the progress and its direction remain to be seen.

Glossary of Terms

This glossary of terms is by no means exhaustive but indicative. Any technical term and Internet concepts can be found in http://www.pcwebopedia.com/ and http://www.nottingham.ac.uk/cyber/Gloss.html. Also key phrase query (e.g. "define ISDN") in Google provides a considerable number of definitions and explanations from various sources.

ADSL
Short for *asymmetric digital subscriber line,* a new technology that allows more data to be sent over existing copper telephone lines (POTS). Source: http://www.webopedia. com/TERM/A/ADSL.html.

Alt.
Alt. is a type of newsgroup that discusses alternative-type topics. The alt. groups are not official newsgroups, but lots of people read them anyway. Source: http://www.zianet.com/ NetDNS/webonics.htm.

AVI
AVI stands for Audio Video Interleave and is currently the most common file format for storing audio/video data on PC. This file format conforms to the Microsoft Windows Resource Interchange File Format (RIFF) specification, which makes it convenient for sharing the file with law enforcement authorities and others that may need to view the video. AVI files (which typically end in the .avi extension) require a specific player that may be included with your Web browser. Source: http://www.integraltech.com/terminology.cfm. Accessed 14 February 2006.

Back links
Back links is the term used when discussing other sites that link to your website. To find your website's back links use the following syntax in the search box of your favourite search engine. Source: http://www.yoursiteurl.com.

BBS
Bulletin board system: an electronic message centre. Most bulletin boards serve specific interest groups. They allow you to dial in with a modem, review messages left by others, and leave your own message if you want. Bulletin boards are a particularly good place to find free or inexpensive software products. In the United States alone, there are tens of thousands of BBSs. Source: http://www.pcwebopedia.com/ TERM/b/bulletin_board_system_BBS.html.

B-ISDN | A standard for transmitting voice, video and data at the same time over fibre-optic telephone lines. Broadband ISDN can support data rates of 1.5 million bits per second (bps), but it has not been widely implemented. ADSL is more widely used.

Blog | Short for *Web log*, a blog is a Web page that serves as a publicly-accessible personal journal of an individual. Typically updated daily, blogs often reflect the personality of the author (http://www.webopedia.com/TERM/b/blog. html). However, the definition of blog is constantly evolving, because thousands of new blogs are being created every day, for all sorts of purposes. Apart from existing to record someone's personal life, many blogs serve as discussion communities about particular issues. Therefore, Susan Ward of About offers an alternative definition in which a blog is a regularly updated online journal of information and opinions. The difference between blogs and other online writing is their dynamic nature (as opposed to static Web pages) and their voice (style). Source: http://sbinfocanada. about.com/cs/blogarticles/f/blogdef.htm.

Browser | A program or "viewer" that allows Internet users to access pages available across the World Wide Web. The two dominant browser packages remain Microsoft's *Internet Explorer* and *Netscape Navigator*. Source: http://www.nottingham. ac.uk/cyber/fullglos.html.

CMC | Computer mediated communication. CMC refers to human communication via computers and includes many different forms of synchronous, asynchronous or real-time interaction that humans have with each other using computers as tools to exchange text, images, audio and video.

Cookie | Cookies are small data files stored on a user's PC or other Internet access hardware device when they visit and interact with certain websites. Cookies are created so that when a user returns to the same site in the future it can "remember" any details they have entered (such as their name, address and account number). Source: http:// www.nottingham.ac.uk/cyber/fullglos.html.

Deep/Invisible Web | The term refers to either Web pages that cannot be indexed by a typical search engine or Web pages that a search engine purposely does not index, rendering the data "invisible" to the general user. One of the most common reasons that a website's content is not indexed is because of the site's useof dynamic databases, which opens the door for a potential spider trap. Web pages can also fall into the invisible Web if there are no links leading to them, since search engine spiders typically crawl through links that lead them from one destination to another. Data on the invisible Web is not inaccessible; the information is out there—it is stored on a Web server somewhere and can be accessed using a browser—but the data must be found using means other than the general-purpose search engines, such as Google and Yahoo!. http://www.pcwebopedia.com/TERM/I/invisible_Web.html.

Digerati	The digital version of literati. It refers to the digital elite who form the Internet intelligentsia. For more information see: http://www.edge.org/digerati/ and http://www.edge.org/documents/digerati/a-Cover.html.
Domain name	The unique identifier associated with each particular computer attached to the Internet. Domain names typically consist of "www" followed by a "host name" followed by a "top-level category" (such as .com or .co.uk). Domain names hence usually appear in the form www.mycompany.com. Source: http://www.nottingham.ac.uk/cyber/fullglos.html.
Dynamic Web page	This is a page that contains content that has been gathered from a database, which changes constantly as the information changes (e.g. stock market, weather maps, statistics etc.) while a static Web page is a page that once produced remains the same, and it can be changed only by a computer specialist. For an extended analysis of dynamic and/or static Web pages see http://searchnetworking.techtarget.com/sDefinition/0,,sid7_gci348104,00.html.
e-commerce	This term is usually taken to encompass consumer-based electronic trading.
e-velopment	Electronic development.
GUI	Graphical User Interface. A computer terminal interface, such as Windows, that is based on graphics instead of text. Source: http://www.arl.org/scomm/subversive/glossary.html.
Hacktivism	This is the writing of code, or otherwise manipulating bits, to promote political ideology. Taking Lessig's message to heart, hacktivism believes that proper use of code will leverage effects similar to regular activism (or civil disobedience). Fewer people can write code, but code affects more people (Source: http://en.wikipedia.org/wiki/Hacktivism). Hacktivism is the fusion of hacking and activism; politics and technology. More specifically, hacktivism is described as hacking for a political cause. In this context, the term hacker

is used in reference to its original meaning. As defined in the *New Hacker's Dictionary*, a hacker is "a person who enjoys exploring the details of programmable systems and how to stretch their capabilities" and one who is capable of "creatively overcoming or circumventing limitations". By metacOm (December 2003): http://www.thehacktivist.com/ hacktivism.php.

ICTs   Information communication technologies. ICT is an umbrella term that includes any communication device or application, encompassing: radio, television, cellular phones, computer and network hardware and software, satellite systems and so on, as well as the various services and applications associated with them, such as video-conferencing and distance learning. ICTs are often spoken of in a particular context, such as ICTs in education, health care, or libraries. Source: http://whatis. techtarget.com/definition/0,,sid9_gci928405,00.html.

IDSL   ISDN Digital Subscriber Line, a method of providing DSL technology over existing ISDN lines. Even though the transfer rates for IDSL are about the same as ISDN (144kbps v. 128kbps), and IDSL circuits typically only carry data (not voice), the major benefits of switching to IDSL from ISDN are always-on connections, thus eliminating call setup delays; flat rate billing, instead of per minute fees; and transmission of data over the data network, rather than the PSTN.

Internet   *Inter*national *Net*work is a global network connecting millions of computers. More than 100 countries are linked into exchanges of data, news and opinions. Unlike online services, which are centrally controlled, the Internet is decentralized by design. Each Internet computer, called a *host*, is independent. Its operators can choose which Internet services to use and which local services to make available to the global Internet community. Remarkably, this anarchy by design works exceedingly well. The *Internet* is not synonymous with *World Wide Web*. Source: http:// www.pcwebopedia.com/TERM/I/Internet.html.

ISP   Internet service provider. A company or organization that connects end-users and businesses to the public, global Internet. ISPs often provide other services such as storing and forwarding email, and hosting websites for their customers. Source: http://www.euro-ix.net/glossary/.

IP   Internet Protocol is a unique identifier for a device on the Internet, usually expressed as four sets of numbers in the range 0–255 separated by dots (known as "4 octets in 'dotted decimal' notation" e.g. 192.254.166.25). Source: http://www. euro-ix.net/glossary/.

Memetics   Meme: an information pattern, held in an individual's memory, which is capable of being copied to another individual's memory. Memetics: the theoretical and empirical science that studies the replication, spread and evolution of memes.

MUD/MOO   MUD (Multiple User Domain) is an interactive, real-time environment for communicating with a group of users on the Internet. A MOO (MUD Object Oriented) allows users to create a virtual world with a variety of objects and manipulate those objects with commands. MUDs and their variations began around 1980 as network games (from the Dungeons and Dragons game), but many are now used as teaching tools. Source: http://www.qcc.mass.edu/booth/142/142gloss.html.

Nanotechnology A field of science whose goal is to control individual atoms and molecules to create computer chips and other devices that are thousands of times smaller than current technologies permit.

NTSC format   A specification for colour television, defined by the NTSC, which meets or exceeds the following criteria: (a) 525 scan lines, (b) broadcast bandwidth of 4 megaHertz, (c) line frequency of 15.75 kiloHertz, (d) frame frequency of 30 frames per second, and (e) colour subcarrier frequency of 3.58 megaHertz. Source: http://www.absoft.com/Products/Compilers/C_C++/XLC/docs/glossary/czgn.htm. Accessed 14 February 2006.

Portal   A website aiming to be a first "port of call" for Internet users. Most portals are search engines (such as Yahoo!, Excite, Google, Lycos or HotBot) offering news and other content facilities in their attempt to become *the best place to start* (and remain!) when browsing the Web. Successful portals are likely to be able to sustain high Internet advertising revenues. Source: http://www.nottingham.ac.uk/cyber/fullglos.html.

Static website A website that is static can only supply information that is written into the HTML and this information will not change unless the change is written into the source code. When a Web browser requests the specific static Web page, a server returns the page to the browser and the user only gets whatever information is contained in the HTML code. Source: http://www.pcwebopedia.com/TERM/s/static.html.

Technoscience   This is a portmanteau term that indicates the gradual implosion in recent years of science and technology (Wolmark and Gates Stuart 2002). http://www.herts.ac.uk/artdes/research/papers/wpades/vol2/wolmark.html. For a detailed analysis of the term see Haraway (1997).

URL   Uniform Resource Locator: the name given to the unique combination of a network communications protocol (for example HTTP or WAP) and Internet address (domain name) that a browser can use to access a particular website. For example, a typical full URL is in the form http://www.mycompany.com even though most browsers no longer require the user to type in the "http://" element. Source: http://www.nottingham.ac.uk/cyber/fullglos.html.

VR   Virtual Reality: a representation of the real world, encoded in computer software, with which computer users may freely interact. The term virtual reality is most commonly used to refer to immersive VR systems whereby peripherals such as head-mounted displays (HMDs), datagloves and bodysuits are used to allow people to become enveloped in a 3D computer-generated graphics world. Source: http://www.nottingham.ac.uk/cyber/fullglos.html.

World Wide   A system of Internet servers that support specially formatted
Web   documents. The documents are formatted in a markup language called HTML (HyperText Markup Language) that supports links to other documents, as well as graphics, audio and video files. This means you can jump from one document to another simply by clicking on hot spots. Not all Internet servers are part of the World Wide Web. There are several applications called web browsers that make it easy to access the World Wide Web; two of the most popular being Netscape Navigator and Microsoft's Internet Explorer. Source: http://www.pcwebopedia.com/TERM/W/World_Wide_Web.html.

For terms and concepts related to ICTs and computing see:
http://www.pcwebopedia.com/
and http://www.nottingham.ac.uk/cyber/Gloss.html.

Notes

1 Introduction

1. Although the term ICTs refers to a number of different communication devices, here it is used as an inclusive term that incorporates the Internet and its different parts, thus it may be regarded as a single entity.

2. In theory everyone on the planet has the capability to be part of the network; however, as discussed in the chapter on epistemology, this capability is controlled by a number of factors some of which are related to users' individual abilities, while others are totally independent from the users themselves.

3. For a detailed analysis see: http://www.hrc.wmin.ac.uk/theory-californianideology.html, accessed 10 January 2003.

4. Jeffersonian democracy advocated freedom of speech and opposed centralized government. For presentations of Jefferson's political views see: http://www.madbbs.com/~rcw/US_History/jeffersonian_democracy.htm, accessed 10 September 2003.

5. The following, which is from *Mondo*'s first editorial, is an example of the magazine's rhetoric: "We're talking Cyber-Chautauqua: bringing cyberculture to the people! Artificial awareness modules. Visual music. Vidscan Magazines. Brain-boosting technologies. William Gibson's Cyberspace Matrix—fully realized! Our scouts are out there on the frontier sniffing the breeze and guess what?… There's a new whiff of apocalypticism across the land. A general sense that we are living at a very special juncture in the evolution of the species" (Queen Mu and R. U. Sirius 1993, cited in Sobchack 1993). Although this kind of rhetoric has been minimized, if not completely abolished, it has nevertheless defined the era of the Internet's expansion in particular political and commercial terms.

6. Well-known examples are the Zapatistas: http://www.zmag.org/chiapas1/; Falun Gong: http://www.falundafa.org/.

7. These three key factors are seen as such only within the sphere of the Western world, where they have reached a point of advancement. For example the cost of Internet connection has been minimized by the development of broad bandwidth, newest software and cheaper, faster computers. Those factors are not yet applicable to the rest of the world where technical infrastructure is underdeveloped and in some cases in its infancy (for details see "Access to the Web" in Chapter 3).

8. The word "design" here refers to the software (the hypertext markup language HTML; the hypertext transfer protocol HTTP; and the system for addressing the documents also known as universal resource locator URL) that Berners-Lee developed, which are the technical foundations of the Web.

9. Berners-Lee's original design was particular software which could be used as both a browser and an editor. Such an option would enable the users to intervene in the material of a visited (via the browser) website by adding (via the editor) their views, opinions, suggestions and/or critiques, arguments and so on. This software offered seamless connections between documents, some of which could be open and editable by the public, while others could remain private and closed remaining thus uneditable. The fact that today's Web is the way it is, Berners-Lee attributes to "an accident of fate", in that the first commercially successful programmes were browsers and not editors (Wright 1997).

10. As is well known, the term cyberspace first appeared in William Gibson's novel *Neuromancer* (1984), where it is presented as a computer-generated world within which one could interact by connecting oneself to it via electrodes implanted in the brain. This cyberspatial world appears real and concrete enough, and the connected individual is able to interfere and manipulate it as easily as if it existed in the physical world.

11. Michael Hauben in 1992 coined the term netizen to describe the people inhabiting the "electronic commons" of the Internet. For a detailed account of the term see: http://www.december.com/cmc/mag/1997/feb/hauben.html, accessed 28 September 2000.

12. The term "cyburbia" is defined as: "conceptual space constituted from an invisible net of interconnections and telecommunications that substitutes the traditional physical urban environment". This definition is attributed to Sorkin 1992. Source: http://parole.aporee.org/work/hier.php3?spec_id=2713&words_id=205, accessed 29 December 2003.

13. Pope Pius XII in the encyclical *Miranda Prorsus* of 1957, in the Message of the Holy Father for the XXIII World Communication Day 1989 with the theme: "Religion in the Mass Media". Available online: http://www.vatican.va/holy_father/john_paul_ii/messages/communications/documents/hf_jp-ii_mes_24011989_world-communications-day_en.html, accessed 28 December 2002.

14. Ibid.

15. This number refers to groups that exist in the religion categories, i.e. from Agnosticism to Zoroastrianism. It does not include the "additional categories" such as: angels, discrimination, magic, mythology and folklore. An examination of a small number of random groups revealed that the number of members varies between 200–400. This indicates that if the number of groups is multiplied by 200 or 300 then an estimated 20,340,600 to 30,510,900 people respectively participate in those groups. These numbers are offered here only as indicators of the volume of e-religious activity, for definite number or volume of online activity is impossible to be measured accurately.

16. Alt. is a type of newsgroup that discusses alternative-type topics. The alt. groups are not official newsgroups, but lots of people read them anyway.

17. Charles Henderson "…In the prologue of St. John's Gospel we read: 'In the beginning was the Word and the Word was with God'. The Word really… refers to the wisdom. It is the structure of truth that ties the whole cosmos together. And we say that that is part of God or it is God. Now, the whole idea

of the World Wide Web is that ultimately all of human knowledge could be tied together through the links of hypertext. Now if you achieve that and you had all human wisdom tied together in an interconnecting web, or a structure, this would be analogous to the Biblical concept of the Word. So couldn't you say, in the beginning was the Web?" (Henderson 2000).

18. For examples of different interpretations of the term in different historical periods see Smith's work (1998) "Religion, Religions, Religious".

19. For an example see Beckford's work "Scientology, Social Science and the Definition of Religion".

20. For an in-depth analysis of the problems deriving from defining "religion" and their implications see Gunn (2003).

21. The categories presented here, concisely, are not exhaustive but indicative, as the purpose of this discussion is solely for conceptual clarity.

22. For extensive analyses of the different definitional approaches and their strengths and weaknesses see: Kirkland Russell, *Defining "Religion"* (1976), http://www.arches.uga.edu/~kirkland/rk/pdf/guides/RELDEFINE.pdf, accessed 14 February 2005; also Russell T. McCutcheon *Religion* (2004), http://www.as.ua.edu/rel/pdf/rel237definitionofreligion.pdf, accessed 14 February 2005.

23. Source: www.cogsci.princeton.edu/cgi-bin/webwn.

24. Source: www.tearsofllorona.com/jungdefs.html.

25. Source: www.teachingaboutreligion.org/MiniCourse/glossary.htm.

26. Source: www.oregonstate.edu/dept/anthropology/glossary2.htm.

27. Source: www.muslimphilosophy.com/mih/tech/dict.htm.

28. Source: www.jdar.org/dico/dico/R.htm.

29. Credited to Malinowski, source: http://www.religioustolerance.org/rel_defn.htm.

30. Source: http://www.religioustolerance.org/rel_defn.htm.

31. Source: http://www.gslis.utexas.edu/~palmquis/courses/discourse.htm, accessed 27 November 2004.

32. The sub-categories included cyber-churches, cyber-sanghas, cyber-synagogues, and cyber-mosques, each one of them giving the opportunity to their followers to participate in and be part of the "community" when physical contact, for whatever reason, is neither possible nor desirable. There were religious meta-networks, and bulletin boards, newsgroups, chat rooms and discussion forums which had reached a five, if not six, digit number. Additionally there were different forms of religious practices online such as prayer, rituals and pilgrimages. For a detailed account of the practices see Karaflogka 2003, 283–84).

33. Newtech '98 <www.sni.net/archden/dcr/1998100101.html>, accessed 21 September 1999.

34. ECIC conferences were launched in 1996 and have taken place every year since. The rationale behind the establishment of such annual meetings was that the Internet, having "immense networking capabilities", offers a "unique opportunity for ecumenical and inter Church networks, teachings, learning pastoral care and other services" (ECIC: http://www.ecic.info/).

35. ECIC 1999, Pastoral Care Workshop <www.ecic.org/ecic4/workshop-develop. html>, accessed 21 September 1999.

36. The term "snail mail" was coined by Jim Rutt in 1981 to refer to the time consumption of communication via the postal services, especially the delay of time that occurs between dispatch of a letter and its receipt in contrast to the email which is almost instantaneous. Source: http://www.ketupa.net/timeline6.htm, accessed 20 September 2001.

37. The US Senate Special Committee on the Year 2000 Technology Problem was disbanded on 29 February 2000, after having finalized its report on the much anticipated computer crash in both the US and the rest of the world. For an analytical report of the Y2K problems and issues see: http://www.senate.gov/~y2k/documents/final.pdf, accessed 17 June 2001.

38. That is by employing either a utopian or a dystopian approach to the question of technology and the Internet in particular.

39. The "Internet-as-frontier" metaphor first appeared in Gibson's book *Neuromancer* and has been used excessively by various writers since to denote the genesis of a new territory that waits to be explored.

40. For an analytical presentation of these works see Chapter 2, Literature Review.

41. A small sample has been presented in the Introduction. See also Chapter 6, Methodology.

42. For more on the parts of the Internet and how they work see: J. Quarterman and Smoot Carl-Mitchell *What is the Internet Anyway?* (1994) Available online: http://www.mids.org/what.html, accessed 22 November 1999. For a detailed historical account of the Internet and its development see Gregory Gromov, "The Roads and Crossroads of Internet History", http://www.netvalley.com/intval.html, accessed 22 May 2002; also http://www.isoc.org/internet/history/brief.shtml, accessed 20 November 2002.

43. TCP is an abbreviation of the term Transmission Control Protocol. TCP is "one of the main protocols in TCP/IP networks. Whereas the IP protocol deals only with packets, TCP enables two hosts to establish a connection and exchange streams of data. TCP guarantees delivery of data and also guarantees that packets will be delivered in the same order in which they were sent". Source: Webpopedia online: http://www.webopedia.com/TERM/T/TCP.html, accessed 4 April 2003.

44. For more on the Web, its historical development and its applications see: http://www.internet101.org/web.html, accessed 10 March 2002.

45. Although Sterling has defined cyberspace as the " 'place' where a telephone conversation appears to occur. The place between the two phones. The indefinite place out there, where the two of you, two human beings actually meet and communicate" (1992, xi–xii, cited in Jordan 1999), this interpretation of the term is often credited to John Barlow and it is defined as Barlovian to differentiate it from the Gibsonian cyberspace (Jordan 1999, 55–56; Featherstone and Burrows 1995a, 5).

46. At least the cyberspace (in the Barlovian sense) of the Internet network.

47. Jacques Derrida coined the term "technoscience" when he declared: "One can no longer distinguish between technology on the one hand and theory, science and rationality on the other. The term techno-science has to

be accepted" in his paper "Full Speed Ahead, Seven Missiles, Seven Missives", *Diacritics* 14, no. 2 (Summer 1984), 12. Bruno Latour (1988, 29) is also considered as the inventor of the term.

2 Literature Review

1.   In "Studies on Religion and the Internet" in the Introduction.

2.   Because this study is focused on religion an extensive reference on other subjects is not included. However, the issue of ICTs has also been investigated in relation to economics, education, health, social policies, organizational relationships and so on.

3.   For a short presentation of Silver's model see the Introduction. For an extended version see the sub-section "Introducing Cyberculture".

4.   For instance, Gary Bunt who is British and Babin who is French.

5.   Margaret Wertheim is the writer and host of the PBS TV programme "Faith and Reason". She has two science degrees: a Bachelor of Science majoring in pure and applied physics, and a Bachelor of Arts majoring in pure mathematics and computing.

6.   Jeff Zaleski is an editor at *Publisher's Weekly* and a consulting editor to *Tricycle*, the Buddhist review.

7.   Eric Davis is a regular contributor to *Wired* and has written for a number of magazines.

8.   Hammerman is a rabbi in Connecticut, a journalist and the spiritual leader of the Beth El temple.

9.   Unfortunately the site "goodvsevil.org" does not exist anymore.

10.   For a detailed account of the experiment of the "goodvsevil" site and the results of a poll between the two poles see Hammerman 2000, 138–47.

11.   Groothuis is Associate Professor of Philosophy of Religion and Ethics at the Denver Seminary.

12.   In his analysis virtual reality sex, pornography and virtual sexual abuse are used as examples of the different ways which cyberspace offers for sexual exploration and experimentation.

13.   Groothuis is an Evangelical Christian, denomination unknown.

14.   For instance, Grootuis is highly recommended in the Apologetics site; in the Christian Countercult Movement; Apologetics Ministries and in the Gospelcom site. Hammerman is advocated in Christianity Today; in Spirituality and Health; in Temple Beth El and in the Jewish Bulletin. Babin and Zukowski are included in the Computer Aided Ministry Society; in the Glenmary Home Missioners; in the Institute for Pastoral Initiatives of the University of Deyton; in the FaithFirst Cobb is recommended in Online Journalism Review; in Spirituality and Health; in the science and religion reading list compiled by the Pastor of the First Congregational Church.

15.   Cobb is a Union Theological Seminary graduate and communications consultant.

16.   An example could be: "within a holoarchy, holons emerge holoarchically" (Cobb 1998, 104).

17. Arlene H. Rinaldi, *The Ten Commandments for Computer Ethics in the Net: User Guidelines and Netiquette* (1996). Available at: http://www.fau.edu/netiquette/net/index.html, accessed 22 October 2001.

18. Electronic sources do not have pagination systems.

3 Web Epistemology

1. The specific term "Web epistemology" was coined by Rogers (2000) in his excellent *Preferred Placement*, which critically analyses the politics of search engines, profiling, cookies and the geography of Web pages.

2. The invention of the WWW by Tim Berners-Lee in 1990 simplified Internet use by combining different information transfer systems. The Mosaic browser (1992) was developed into Netscape Navigator and spread with other graphic user interfaces (e.g. Microsoft Explorer and software for email and dial-up connections). Such user-friendly programmes resulted in the exponential growth of Internet use in the developed western countries in 1993.

3. An in-depth investigation of accessibility would include statistical data, literacy data at national and international levels, governmental policies on the implementation of ICTs for public sectors, etc. Johnson 1997; Turkle and Papert 1990; Jordan 1999; and Warschauer 2003a, b have explored access and its relation to gender, cost, cyberpolitics, race, education and so on.

4. See for example www.grayday.org.

5. The concept, understood in a poststructuralist context which sees the subject or self to be incoherent, disunified, and in effect "decentred", so that it is subject to such structures as language, culture and institutions, is used here to signify that the "self" or "subjectivity" of the various religious phenomena of the Web is a mere conveyor of the ideologies of the users. In other words, as the "self" of a human being is shaped by various cultural constructs and discursive patterns, so the subjectivity of cyberreligious discourse finds itself in, and structured by, the discursive patterns of the users.

6. Figures up to May 2002. Sources: for Iceland http://www.nua.ie/surveys/; for Afghanistan http://www.meilb.org, accessed 28 September 2002.

7. The discrepancy between people who access new ICT tools such as the Internet, and people who cannot. Source: Webopedia: http://www.Webopedia.com/TERM/d/digital_divide.html. Warschauer (2003a, b) attributes the term to the US National Telecommunications and Information Administration under the Clinton administration. Yu (2002) points out that although term's origin is unknown, a Lexis-Nexis search traced the term back to Moore's "The Emperor's Virtual Clothes: The Naked Truth about Internet Culture" (1995).

8. http://www.w3.org/WAI/, accessed 12 November 2002.

9. For an extensive report on accessibility see: http://www.ncddr.org/du/researchexchange/v06n03/emphasis.html, accessed 20 November 2002.

10. http://www.soundlinks.com/

11. Home Page Reader costs £125 plus VAT; additional user licences are £55 per user. For the visually impaired there is a concessionary price of £95.

12. Adaptable computer interfaces, ergonomic keyboards, portable devices, voice recognition and artificial speech were all first developed for or adopted by people with disabilities. "The technologies we are developing today to accommodate people with disabilities are the future of the high-tech industry" (Microsoft PressPass, July 1999): http://www.microsoft.com/PressPass/features/1999/07-26access.asp, accessed 29 September 1999.

13. Microsoft describes assistive technologies as "specially designed products chosen specifically to accommodate an individual's disability or multiple disabilities". Such "accessibility aids" include e.g. a pointing device in place of a mouse and a Braille display and screen reader. See: http://www.microsoft.com/enable/at/default.htm, accessed 20 November 2002.

14. NUA, founded in 1996 in Ireland, offers statistical information about Internet demographics and trends worldwide. Its sources are mainly news agencies.

15. Source NUA, May 2002. See http://www.nua.com/surveys/index.cgi?f=VS&art_id=905357944&rel=true, accessed 20 November 2002.

16. The examples used are indicative, not representative, of wider social, political and economic trends. Extensive qualitative research is needed to address gender bias in relation to accessibility in different regions.

17. For several projects and analyses on women and ICT see: http://www.developmentgateway.org/node/133831/browser/?keyword%5flist=277008&country%5flist=0, accessed 10 May 2003. For seniors see: http://www.developmentgateway.org/node/133831/browser/?keyword-%5flist=466165&country%5flist=0. For a wide collection of reports, statistics and analyses on ICT globally see: http://www.developmentgateway.org/node/133831/?, accessed 10 May 2003.

18. For full report see: http://www.statistics.gov.uk/pdfdir/inta1202.pdf, accessed 10 May 2003.

19. http://www.statistics.gov.uk/STATBASE/xsdataset.asp?vlnk=4090&More=Y. Laurence Chiles, lead producer of BBC WebWise, estimates that ICTs' abundant choices and people's inadequate education result in people believing that they are incapable of understanding the Internet. BBC News, 2000, Bridging the Digital Divide: http://news.bbc.co.uk/1/hi/uk/1078047.stm, accessed 10 May 2003. It would be interesting to find out the extent to which political, cultural and/or religious issues/views deter people in the UK from engaging with computers and ICTs.

20. On race and access see D. L. Hoffman, T. P. Novak and A. Schlosser (2000) "The Evolution of the Digital Divide: How Gaps in Internet Access May Impact Electronic Commerce". *Journal of Computer-Mediated Communication* 5.3. Available: http://www.ascusc.org/jcmc/vol5/issue3/hoffman.html, accessed 10 September 2001.

21. For a slide analysis of Katz and Aspden's research see: http://www.communitytechnology.org/aspden/aspden_slides.html, accessed 5 June 2002. Full article: http://www.communitytechnology.org/aspden/aspden_talk.html, accessed 5 June 2002.

22. Full report: http://www.mediamanage.net/Beyond_Access.pdf, accessed 5 June 2002.

23. OECD Information Technology Outlook 2002, http://www.oecd.org/pdf/ M00030000/M00030907.pdf, accessed 10 May 2003. Reports, surveys and statistical information about the digital divide in the USA (1995 onwards): http://www.ntia.doc.gov/ntiahome/digitaldivide/, accessed 10 May 2003.

24. http://www.dpg-hv.de/english/ibfg_durban.html, accessed 5 June 2003.

25. 80 per cent of the world's population lacks elementary telecommunication facilities.

26. BBC news review on Internet connectivity worldwide (2000): http://news.bbc.co.uk/1/hi/sci/tech/843160.stm, accessed 10 May 2003.

27. See for example NUA's methodology in: http://www.nua.ie/surveys/how_many_online/methodology.html, accessed 20 November 2002.

28. Source: http://www.commerce.net/research/stats/wwstats.html, accessed 10 May 2003.

29. According to the UN Human Development Report cited in Global Information and Communications Technologies Department (GICTD), World Bank Group 2000, 14: http://www.infodev.org/library/WorkingPapers/ NetworkingRevolution.pdf, accessed 20 May 2003.

30. Source: NUA: http://www.nua.ie/surveys/how_many_online/index. html, accessed 20 November 2002.

31. On November 20, 2001, Secretary General Kofi Annan officially launched the UNICT (United Nations Information and Communication Technologies) Task Force at the UN in New York. The Task Force comprises an unprecedented mixture of worldwide representatives from governments; the private sector; non-governmental organizations (NGOs); foundations and UN bodies in a cooperative effort to build digital opportunities and leverage the many efforts to bridge the digital divide. See: http://www.unicttaskforce.org/.

32. Source: Reuters, in NUA.

33. Source South African Technology Vanguard (SAVANT): http://www.savant. co.za/home.asp?pid=11, accessed 20 May 2003.

34. ITU Telecom: http://www.itu.int/AFRICA2001/press/presskit/backgrounders/ overview.html, accessed 20 May 2003.

35. Organisation for Economic Cooperation and Development (OECD) Information Technology Outlook 2002. Available online: http://www.oecd.org/pdf/ M00030000/M00030907.pdf, accessed 20 May 2002.

36. Announcement of the first conference on "WIFI: UNIVERSAL BROADBAND INTERNET ACCESS FOR THE DEVELOPING WORLD" at UN HQ June 17, 2003, organized by The Wireless Internet Institute (private sector) and the UNICT Task Force to search for "strategies necessary to overcome those obstacles and develop environments favourable to the broad deployment of WiFi infrastructures". http://www.w2i.org/pages/wificonf0603/PressRelease. html, accessed 20 May 2003.

37. Several stories behind the headline "Digital Empowerment" establish the advantages of access and the socio-economic repercussions on both individuals and communities, as the article presents: "Every evening, Govardhan Angari lights a joss stick and offers a silent prayer to a computer in a poky 20-sq-ft room, Dehri Sarai, Pradesh's Dhar district. Beside the Pentium II machine

on a creaky table, there is a modem, a sheaf of white paper and a battery back-up. This unremarkable paraphernalia has changed the life of the 21-year-old boy, a landless Bhil tribal and son of a daily wage labourer, who takes home Rs 40 on days when he finds work. These days, Govardhan earns up to Rs 3,500 a month ferreting out crop market rates, emailing villagers' grouses, generating caste and land certificates out of this rural cyberkiosk". Additionally, the article concludes, he teaches "some 16 village children the basics of computing". Source: Outlook India.com: http://www.outlookindia.com/full.asp?fodname=20010409&fname=Cover%20Story%20(F)&sid=1%20, accessed 10 January 2003.

38. American Assistance for Cambodia, an aid organization, funded the project of equipping Rovieng's school with computers, solar panels and the remaining parts necessary for connecting the village's school to the Internet. Source: Washingtonpost.com: http://www.washingtonpost.com/ac2/wp-dyn?pagenam e=article&node=&contentId=A16336-2001May11&notFound=true.

For more case studies see: http://www.bridges.org/casestudies/index.html, accessed 24 February 2003. It should be noted that as early as 1998 employment of ICTs in rural areas in Guatemala proved quite successful in developing e-commerce.

39. Warschauer defines social capital as "the capacity of individuals to accrue benefits by dint of their personal relationships and memberships in particular social networks and structures" (Warschauer 2003a, 6).

40. For example, studies conducted in California report that those who had acquaintances/contacts with other computer users were more likely to gain access to ICTs while those who did not found the whole process of getting computer literate overpowering (Warschauer 2003a). Similar results were drawn from Stanley in the San Diego survey in which technical help and support in community technology centres proved influential in people's decision to become PC users. Stanley, in her conclusions, demonstrates that the need for culturally sensitive, adult-centred, community technology centres could provide the basic framework for social capital (Stanley 2001). Additionally, Warschauer emphasizes that the results of ICT projects, which provided only physical access to ICT equipment, in three different social settings such as India, Ireland and Egypt, clearly demonstrate that the acquisition of a variety of skills, necessary to meaningful utilization of ICTs for social, educational and economic inclusion and development, is contingent on "human and social systems that must [also] change for technology to make a difference" (Warschauer 2002).

41. The UN E-Commerce and Development Report, 2002. Online: http://r0.unctad.org/ecommerce/ecommerce_en/edr02_en.htm, accessed 20 November 2002.

42. Source: United Nations Statistics Division, Indicators of Literacy: http://unstats.un.org/unsd/demographic/social/illiteracy.htm, accessed 20 November 2001.

43. Source: VilaWeb.com as quoted in http://www.global-reach.biz/globstats/refs.php3, accessed 10 October 2002.

44. Pandia: http://www.pandia.com/sw-2001/57-Websize.html.

45. Source Pandia 2001: http://www.pandia.com/sw-2001/57-Websize. html. An analysis of the functionality of search engines and their positioning systems is presented later in this section.

46. Pandia, devoted to effective Internet searching and search engine optimization, is a Norwegian site which is solely in English.

47. For instance, while in the mid-1990s 80 per cent of the websites were in English (Cyberspeech 1997, cited in Warschauer 2002), as the chart shows this has dropped to 69 per cent in 2002.

48. A study conducted by the Organization for Economic Cooperation and Development found that while "some 78 per cent of websites in OECD countries were in English, 91 per cent of websites on 'secure-servers' were in English, and a fully 96 per cent of websites on secure servers in the .com domain were in English" (The Default Language, 1999, cited in Warschauer 2002). The importance of this is obvious because secure servers are used for e-commerce.

49. M-commerce refers to trade via wireless communications which are seen to open wider opportunities for economic development especially to developing countries, because it does not depend on wired communication infrastructure. The UN E-Commerce and Development Report, 2002. Online: http://r0.unctad.org/ecommerce/ecommerce_en/edr02_en.htm, accessed 20 November 2002.

50. As a matter of fact, a United Nations World Intellectual Property Organization (WIPO) conference in Geneva focusing on multilingual domain names reports that it is predicted that by 2007 Chinese would be the most used language on the Internet (Williams 2002, cited in Yu 2002). For a detailed account of the growth of the non-English netizens since 1995 see Global Reach: http:// global-reach.biz/globstats/evol.html, accessed 30 October 2001.

51. See for example Warschauer 1997, 1998, 2000, cited in Warschauer 2002.

52. See Warschauer et al., 2002 for an ethnographic survey on the usage of English in online communication among young Egyptian professionals. Also, for an investigation of linguistic variations among Usenet newsgroup soc.culture. punjab, a forum chartered for discussion of the culture of the Punjab region of India and Pakistan, see Paolillo 1999.

53. There are many numbers of examples of machine translated phrases which prove that even after 40 years of research this domain is far behind in reaching appropriate standards.

54. Bridges.org is an international non-profit organization with a mission to help people in developing countries use information and communications technology (ICT) to improve their lives. For the report: "Spanning the Digital Divide: Understanding and Tackling the Issues 2001" see: http://www.bridges. org/spanning/pdf/spanning_the_digital_divide.pdf, accessed 8 May 2002.

55. A characteristic example of the importance of policy-makers' socio-economic and political standpoint is that of the Republican-appointed chairman of the Federal Communications Commission (US)—whose purpose is the formulation of regulations affecting broadcasters, telephone companies,

cable operators and Internet service providers. Holding opposite views from his Democrat predecessor regarding deregulation of the companies, Mr Powell sees the term "digital divide" as "dangerous because it could be used to justify government entitlement programs that guaranteed poor people cheaper access to new technology, like digital television sets or computers" (cited in Yu 2002). The chairman understands the digital divide to be "a Mercedes divide. I'd like to have one; I can't afford one. I'm not meaning to be completely flip (sic) about this. I think it's an important social issue. But it shouldn't be used to justify the notion of essentially the socialization of the deployment of the infrastructure" (Yu 2002). His views on the issue of digital divide were perceived by the consumer groups as reflecting a "deeper ideological move to the right than they had expected" (Labaton NYT 2001 cited in Yu 2002). For policies related to Web accessibility in different countries see: http://www. w3.org/WAI/References/Policy.html, accessed 2 January 1999.

56. For example, there are variable levels of access in US urban and rural areas; in African cities and villages; in European and Asian countries, which require different approaches and solutions. For detailed accounts see: Wresch, cited in Kraidy 2001; Yu 2002.

57. www.prb.org.

58. Some predict that one billion people will be using the Internet by 2005. However, although there are positive signs that the less technologically advanced countries and groups of people within countries are, through various programmes, getting involved with ICTs, some regions and some groups of individuals within countries will continue to be excluded from the Internet (Wresch, cited in Kraidy 2001). (Projections' Source: http://www.digitalplays. com/key_stats.htm#How%20Many%20are%20On%20Line%20Globally, accessed 17 April 2003; also http://www.medialifemagazine.com/news2002/ aug02/aug12/5_fri/news4friday.html, accessed 17 April 2003.

59. See for example the cases of Clipper Chip, Lotus Marketplace (Gurak 1999) and the demonstrations against the G7 summits. For a history of Clipper Chip see: http://www-cse.stanford.edu/classes/cs201/current/Projects/clipper-chip/history.html; also see Wired's call for action against Clipper Chip: http:// www.boogieonline.com/revolution/express/techno/crypto/escrow/wired.html, accessed 25 March 1995. For a brief account of Lotus Marketplace, see: http:// catless.ncl.ac.uk/Risks/10.79.html, accessed 25 March 1995. For examples of usage of the Internet for socio-political inclusion and development see Warschauer 2003a and b.

60. For different views on and definitions of hacktivism see: http://www. collusion.org/Article.cfm?ID=109; http://www.thehacktivist.com/hacktivism. php.

61. For examples see Cynthia L. Webb (2003), "Religious Groups go Online for Peace". Online: http://www.washingtonpost.com/ac2/wp-dyn?pagename=ar ticle&contentId=A19961-2003Mar13&notFound=true, accessed 10 May 2004. A number of protests were made against the French government's decision to ban religious symbols in schools (available on keyword search in all search engines); for related articles see: http://yaleglobal.yale.edu/display.article?id=3242. Also,

on the formation of institutes for dialogue such as the TODA see: http://www. toda.org/index.html, and so on.

62. These two examples have been used excessively within this study, and in other works, for they characteristically illustrate several aspects of ICTs.

63. Partenia came into being through the following set of circumstances: In the early 1990s the Catholic Bishop Gailot of Evreux in Normandy expressed his views on controversial issues including priestly celibacy, homosexuality, women's ordination and homelessness. What the Bishop said was not in accordance with the Church's teachings as proclaimed by the Vatican. By January 1995 the Vatican had heard enough, but for constitutional reasons the Church had to give Bishop Gailot a place where he could still be bishop. So Bishop Gailot was taken from Evreux and transferred to the diocese of Partenia. Where is Partenia? In fact it is nowhere. The diocese of Partenia is in Algeria, on the slopes of the Atlas Mountains, covered by the Sahara desert and home to lizards and scorpions; in effect it is a virtual diocese (Zaleski 1997, 3). Leo Sheer, a French media philosopher and the Bishop's friend, thought that Gailot should embrace that virtuality: Why not put Partenia online? His argument was: "Instead of a metaphysical idea of a bishop, attached to a real place, we would have a metaphysical idea of a place attached to a real bishop" (Cobb 1998, 75). Partenia.org was born.

64. For the history and the activities of Falun Gong, as well as the responses of the Chinese government, a great number of sites are available. The official site is www.falundafa.org.

65. http://www.clearwisdom.net/eng/2001/Jan/11/EWA011101_3.html, accessed 15 April 2001.

66. "China Internet Users Double to 17 Million" announces CNN's report on technology and computing in China. Web posted 27 July 2000 by Reuters. Available online: http://www.cnn.com/2000/TECH/computing/07/27/china. internet.reut/, accessed 14 April 2001.

67. For an analysis of the status of the Internet and its political implications in Asia see: Kloet de Jeroen, "Digitisation and Its Asian Discontents: The Internet, Politics and Hacking in China and Indonesia". *First Monday* 7.9 (2002). Online: http://firstmonday.org/issues/issue7_9/kloet/index.html, accessed 22 October 2002.

68. For a critical analysis of the Singapore case see Garry Rodan (1998), *The Internet and Political Control in Singapore*. Online: http://www.sfdonline.org/ Link%20Pages/Link%20Folders/Political%20Freedom/rodan.html, accessed 15 May 2002. For a more up-to-date account about inequality of access, and control see Warschauer 2000, *Does the Internet Bring Freedom?* Available online: http://www.gse.uci.edu/markw/freedom.html, accessed 19 June 2002. For the status of freedom internationally, including that of religion, press and media see: www.freedomhouse.org.

69. Electronic Frontier Foundation (EFF) is a non-profit group of passionate people—lawyers, volunteers and visionaries—working to protect your digital rights. If America's founding fathers had anticipated the digital frontier, there would be a clause in the Constitution protecting your rights online, as well.

Instead, a modern group of freedom fighters was necessary to extend the original vision into the digital world. (Taken from EFF's opening page.) In its mission statement EFF state that "Just as Patriots fought for liberty and freedom, we fight measures that threaten basic human rights. Only the dominion we defend is the vast wealth of digital information, innovation, and technology that resides online". For further information see: www.eff.org.

70. As for example navigational tools, browsers, portals and so forth.

71. Although an in-depth analysis of the different stages of the Web's evolution would be quite intriguing, for it would present in detail the various parameters, agents and factors that influenced the Web's growth, and their socio-economic consequences, here a succinct presentation of the two phases would be sufficient to illustrate the points discussed in the following sections.

72. For an introduction to the Semantic Web see Tim Berners-Lee, James Hendler and Ora Lassila's article, "The Semantic Web: A new form of Web content that is meaningful to computers will unleash a revolution of new possibilities". Available online: http://www.scientificamerican.com/article. cfm?articleID=00048144-10D2-1C70-84A9809EC588EF21&catID=2, accessed 10 February 2003.

73. The difference between the indexed Web and the Web is that the indexed Web contains pages while the Web contains sites. For example, while search engines announce the number of pages they have included in their databases (e.g. FAST 2.1 billion in 2001), the actual size of the Web itself was 8.4 million unique sites (PANDIA, 2001). That designates the importance of the role of search engines in searching and researching the Web for specific information.

74. Search Engine Watch, 2001.

75. An estimated 83 per cent of sites contain commercial content (Lawrence and Giles 1999).

76. For years databases on the Web were referred to as speciality databases, subject-specific databases, virtual libraries, and other similar terms. The term "Invisible Web" was coined in 1994 by Jill Ellsworth and these databases were referred to (and still are) as the invisible Web. However, Bergman quite rightly indicates that the term "Invisible Web" is inaccurate because it is the incapability of the search engines that makes the database content undetectable. When the correct search engines are used and the required fees, in most cases, are paid, then the "deep content" becomes apparent.

77. For an extensive list of databases stored in the deep Web see http://www.invisibleWeb.com/main.asp?sessionid={350D7BF3-64E7-459F-B59B-4 F81EC6B92FD}&action=SETTAB: 3,6,17#7, accessed 10 February 2003.

78. Public information on the deep Web is currently 400 to 550 times larger than the commonly defined World Wide Web. The deep Web contains 7,500 terabytes of information compared to 19 terabytes of information in the surface Web and nearly 550 billion individual documents compared to the one billion of the surface Web. The deep Web also appears to be the fastest growing information component of the Web (Bergman 2001; Lyman and Varian 2000). For a comprehensive description and analysis of the size of terabytes

see: http://www.jamesshuggins.com/h/tek1/how_big.htm, accessed 16 February 2003.

79. There are a number of sites offering detailed information about the deep Web and the current database search engines. See for example: http://www.lib.berkeley.edu/TeachingLib/Guides/Internet/InvisibleWeb.html; http://www.powerhomebiz.com/vol25/invisible.htm; http://www.completeplanet.com/, accessed 16 February 2003.

80. In the computer community the pre-browser period is presented as: "In the beginning was the Word, and the Word was *ascii* encoded, typically displayed in monochrome courier on a black screen". Source: www.dejavu.org, the "timeline" link, accessed 9 November 2001.

81. In 2000 it was calculated that there were 704 Web browsers offered by different companies. Some indicative examples are: AOL, AOL-Netscape, Apple Safari, IBM Web browser, Microsoft Internet Explorer, iCab, Konqueror, Lynx, Mozilla, OmniWeb, Opera, and W3C Amaya. Source: http://www.upsdell.com/BrowserNews/, accessed 31 January 2004.

82. Microsoft's control is the result of a commercial war between Netscape and Microsoft during the pre-expansion period, which Microsoft won by offering its browser for free by integrating it within the Windows software package. The domination that Microsoft established in the computer software and its control over the Internet is one example of the desire of transnational corporations to preside over the Web by monopolizing its operationality via their own products.

83. Source: www.learnthat.com. Accessed 17 September 2000.

84. Microsoft's packaging of its browser (Internet Explorer) with its Windows software is a well-known case of enterpreneurial dominance.

85. That is how their formatting details are designed. Theoretically each browser can interpret the HTML language in its own way and place it in a configuration of its own. That means that while the information the browsers read is the same, the representation of the information is different (Altena 1999).

86. The use of colours here is purely metaphorical, offered as an illustration of this point. Yet, it may be literal in cases where the browser's configuration is to present the colour blue more strongly than any other colour.

87. For example, setting the "Homepage" of their own preference; creating their own "Favorites" and so on. There are a number of both online and offline guides that teach users step-by-step how to perform these configurations. Of course the most available is the "Help" key that exists in all computer applications.

88. Source: www.cogsci.princeton.edu/cgi-bin/webwn, accessed 17 February 2004.

89. Source: http://cfdccariboo.com/glossary.htm, accessed 17 February 2004.

90. Source: www.i-stt.com/resources/glossary/P.html, accessed 17 February 2004.

91. Source: www.mediafederation.org.au/glossary.html, accessed 17 February 2004.

92. Source: www.daleen.com/company/glossary.htm, accessed 17 February 2004.

93. As Patelis explains, "the concept of structuration adopted here is described by Mosco as a process that, among other things, constructs hegemony, defined as the taken-for-granted, common way of thinking about the world, including everything from cosmology, through ethics, to social practices that is both incorporated and contested by everyday life". Mosco 1999, cited in Patelis 2000, 51.

94. This research was conducted using the "Recall Archive": http://recall. archive.org.

95. A random example of the companies focused solely on search engine optimization is Search Engine Goldmine.com, which guarantees to increase the ratings and traffic of "your site".

96. Examples of such services can be found in: http://www.abakus-internet-marketing.de/en/directories/directories.htm; http://searchenginewatch.com/webmasters/article.php/2167881, accessed 10 February 2003.

97. For a detailed history of Yahoo's development see: http://docs.yahoo. com/info/misc/history.html, accessed 10 March 2003.

98. Some directories are: The open directory project; Google's directory; About.com; Omniseek; Linkopedia; Direct Hit; InstantSeek.

99. Source: http://www.anybrowser.com/DirectoriesvsSearchEngines.html, accessed 12 March 2003.

100. Source: http://www.iWebdesign-inc.com/promotion/, accessed 10 February 2003.

101. Yahoo! Express Service Agreement: http://docs.yahoo.com/info/suggest/terms.html, accessed 12 March 2003.

102. For the whole list of criteria see: http://docs.yahoo.com/info/suggest/terms.html.

103. http://dmoz.org/.

104. Source: Gerhart (2002), Open Directory Project Search Results and ODP Status, in: http://www.pagepromoter.com/dmoz, accessed 22 August 2002.

105. The survey was published on the company's site: http://www. iprospect.com/, but it is no longer available. However, it can be found at: http://www.clickz.com/stats/markets/advertising/article.php/5941_ 1500821, accessed 13 May 2004.

106. An estimated 7.3 million unique pages are uploaded every day (Cyveillance, 2000).

107. An algorithm is "an explicit effective set of instructions for a computing procedure (not necessarily numerical) which may be used to find the answers to any of a given class of questions". A. G. Hamilton (2000), "Logic for Mathematicians, Cambridge". In: http://www.geocities.com/n_fold/algo.html, accessed 27 December 2003.

108. For a short explanation of robots' functionality see: http://101registerme. com/robots_and_spider.htm and http://www.wdvl.com/Location/Search/Robots. html. Accessed 13 November 2002. For a more detailed account of the practical, technical and ethical problems that are incorporated in the use of robots for information finding see: Koster 1995.

109. For detailed and in-depth descriptions of search engines' operationality see: http://www.monash.com/spidap4.html; http://searchenginewatch.com;

http://www.searchengineworld.com/. For a detailed tutorial on search engines' ranking system see: http://library.albany.edu/internet/second.html.

110. For more information see: http://searchenginewatch.com.

111. Link farms are a group of websites that link to each other. If there were 50 websites and they all link to each other, this would be considered as a link farm, especially if their content is unrelated to each other.

112. http://www.itadvanced.co.uk/

113. Source: http://www.lotusboy.com/essays/analysis/, accessed 12 March 2003. For a detailed and updated list of search engine collaboration see "Who Powers Whom? Search Providers Chart", at: http://searchenginewatch.com/reports/article.php/2156401#lycos, accessed 11 May 2004.

4 Theory

1. As for example the claims about the Internet's unprecedented impact on global economies, which was the dominant theme of economic analyses during the second half of the nineties, especially regarding the explosive development of e-commerce.

2. Some argue that the initial hype about the Internet is in decline and their claim is supported by the failure of some of the e-companies and also by the results of some studies that show that fewer people are now actively interacting via CMC. However, these claims are contested by the increase of e-commerce which shows no signs of decline.

3. See for example the advertisement of the British government with its aim to have the whole country online by 2005.

4. The last years have seen a considerable increase in the number of courses on cyber studies; also the number of conferences on theoretical and methodological issues regarding the impact of the Internet on social and cultural interaction and so on; as well as the number of scholarly works. For example courses on religion and cyberspace, modern spiritual movements, modern christianity, religion, technology and cultural studies and Christian thought from modernity to post-modernity, to mention but a few. As far as I am aware such courses are offered in a number of American universities as well as European ones. Conferences include: European Christian Internet Conference (ECIC) Network (every year since 1996); Religious Encounters in Digital Networks, Denmark 2001; Sacred Media, Finland, 2003.

5. For a complete presentation of the 249 distinct theories of communication see Anderson 1996.

6. This is, at least in theory, accurate, for the preservation of information through time in computer networks can be quite problematic, as explained in Chapter 6, p. 159.

7. There are also the possibilities of teleconferencing and voice over IP (VoIP).

8. Mark Poster, *The Mode of Information: Poststructuralism and Social Context* (Chicago: University of Chicago Press, 1990). Cited in Aoki 1994.

9. For examples of such analytical presentations see Chapter 6, Methodology.

10. Kellner's work cited here is available online. There are no pagination or paragraph numbers.

11. US Department of Commerce, National Technical Information Service in *The National Information Infrastructure: Agenda for Action*. Washington, DC: The National Telecommunications & Information Administration, 1993 (no page no.), cited in Birdsall 1996.

12. For a detailed account of the Third Wave society, see A. and H. Toffler, *Creating a New Civilisation: The Politics of the Third Wave* (Atlanta: Turner Publishing, 1995).

13. T. Blair (1999) "The Knowledge Economy", speech of PM Blair in Cambridge (Silicon Fen). Available online: http://www.number-10.gov.uk/output/Page1456.asp, accessed 30 January 2001.

14. For an in-depth analysis of Ellul's discourse, the literature about his work and an account of the "religious antitechnological movement" see Newman 1997, 8–27.

15. These references have been taken from the electronic versions of Ellul's work: http://jan.ucc.nau.edu/~jsa3/hum355/readings/ellul.htm, accessed 29 October 2001.

16. Taken from Rheingold's collection of Ellul's technology quotes available online: http://www.rheingold.com/texts/techpolitix/techquotes/ellul.html, accessed 29 October 2001.

17. For a detailed presentation of the relation of technology to progress in both socio-economic and moral/intellectual terms see Newman 1997, ch. 3.

18. In Genesis 6:14–16 the construction of Noah's ark.

19. The chapters 20 to 24 are devoted to religious and moral guidance and from 25–28 are the instructions for the building of the Temple.

20. See for example Exodus 25:9: "...I show you concerning the pattern of the tabernacle and of all its furniture, so you shall make it".

21. "In the beginning when God created the heavens and the earth, the earth was a formless void..." (Genesis 1:1).

22. See Exodus 11:1–9.

23. See Exodus 32:1–4.

24. "And God said, Let us make man in our image...and have dominion... and over every living thing that moveth upon the earth" (Genesis 1:26).

25. For a detailed list of theologians who have been engaged with the question of technology and Christianity see Newman 1997, 122–33.

26. Exodus 31:18; 32:15–16.

27. The commonly held Christian belief up to the fourth century was that of the Church elite in which technology existed for humankind in its fallen state and had no significance nor value in the process of redemption, which was achievable only and exclusively through the grace of God gained by rigorous mental activities such as acquiring knowledge and contemplation (Noble 1997, 9–12); Mumford (1946, 29) also stresses the unimportance of the physical world and the objects of living, which were seen as "accessories" to "Man's pilgrimage through eternity".

28. Psalm 63, written by David when he was in the wilderness of Judah, expresses the intimate relationship between God and the worshipper. The Psalm can be found online in in the Bible Gateway , in the Library of Hebrew Songs and in numerous other sites and versions.

29. For an extensive bibliography on the subject see Noble 1997, ch. 1.

30. For instance, for a historical account of the invention and development of the clock see Mumford 1946, 12–18.

31. The "useful arts" was the term which referred to arts and crafts such as cloth-making, silversmithing, navigation and so on. The lack of an all-inclusive generic term for the arts and crafts is demonstrated in the writings of St. Augustine who used expressions such as "innumerable arts and skills", "astonishing achievements" and "contrivances" when referring to various forms of craftsmanship (St. Augustine in Noble 1997, 12, 15). Although these terms express some kind of admiration, it should be noted that Augustine did not perceive technology as related to transcendence. In fact, Augustine, as Walton (2003) highlights, perceived the arts and crafts as anti-Christian, for they aspired to gain control over nature which was understood as distorting God's design.

32. The early Christian fathers such as Aquinas and Augustine were much influenced by both Aristotelian and Platonic thinking, in which the manual arts were perceived as being inferior to intellectual activities. This perception derived mainly from the social stratification of both ancient Greek and Roman societies, in which the craftsmen and manual workers were primarily slaves and those belonging to lower classes (Walton 2003). For quick references on Augustine see the online Catholic Encyclopaedia: http://www.newadvent.org/cathen/02084a.htm, and for Aquinas see: http://www.newadvent.org/cathen/14663b.htm.

33. The seven "liberal arts" that, in Capella's work, Mercury gave his bride Philology were: Grammar, Dialectic, Rhetoric, Geometry, Arithmetic, Astronomy and Harmony. Capella excluded Medicine and Architecture, which being relevant to "mortal subjects" could not be placed alongside the "celestial deities" (Capella in Noble 1997, 16).

34. In Erigena's version of the allegory, Philology, after receiving Mercury's gifts (the liberal arts), offers to him, as her wedding gift, the seven mechanical arts, including Medicine and Architecture. For an analysis of the seven mechanical arts and the development of their status see Walton 2003; for an extensive account of the liberal arts see the online Catholic Encyclopaedia: http://www.newadvent.org/cathen/01760a.htm.

35. Daniel (12:4): "many shall run to and fro, and knowledge shall be increased".

36. Lewis Mumford has indicated that for Bacon science always meant technology (Mumford 1964, in Noble 1997, 49).

37. For bibliographic details of these writings see Noble 1997, ch. 7, 88–100.

38. In fact, the very first message transmitted via the telegraph was the passage from the Bible "What hath God wrought" (Carey 1989, 94).

39. For a detailed account of project "Adam" see Encyclopaedia Astronautica: http://www.astronautix.com/craft/adam.htm.

40. For Artificial Life see: http://www.alife.org/.

41. The human Genome Project can be found at: http://www.doegenomes.org/.

42. Eve, according to the Church fathers, being not created directly by God, but from Adam's rib, not only does not share the original divine likeness, but being prone to temptation she destroyed man's original perfection. Therefore, technology, as a means of soteriological recovery, was bound to be for men only, as the existence of women was perceived as incompatible to the process of restoration (Noble, 213–14).

43. The Christmas 1968 voyage of Apollo 8 was the first space flight in which astronauts left the earth's vicinity to orbit the moon and it was characterized as a "millennial event" by Pope Paul VI (Noble 1997, 138).

44. The term is used here as the three-dimensional representation of information that flows on ICTs.

45. For a detailed historical analysis of cyberspace from its early days—mid sixties up to the beginning of the nineties see Stone 1991, 85–99.

46. The whole text of the Declaration can be found at: http://www.eff.org/~barlow/Declaration-Final.html.

47. Gibson, *Neuromancer* (1984). A science-fiction work that presents a future of corporate hegemony and urban decay. Yet, it also creates a new world, a new concept, a new sense of social space within which humanity and human culture may evolve into something completely different from what is known.

48. Source: NetLingo.com—The Internet Dictionary: http://www.netlingo.com/inframes.cfm.

49. Source: Webopedia: http://www.webopedia.com/TERM/c/cyberspace.html.

50. Source: http://www.advanced.org/jaron/general.html, accessed 10 November 2003.

51. Novak's understanding of cyberspace reflects the vision of cyberspace as a synthesized conceptualization of space "spanning the entire Internet, a spatial equivalent of the Web" (Pesce, Kennard and Parisi 1994), which was the aim of the designers of Virtual Reality Markup Language (VRML). The unified representation of "space" across the Internet was achieved by VRML which enabled data to be presented in three dimensions.

52. Popper (1972 in Benedikt 1991, 3–4) understood the whole of the world to consist of three interconnected worlds. World 1 is the objective world of material and natural things. World 2 is the subjective world of consciousness and World 3 is the world of objective, real, public structures, which are the products of the minds of living creatures interacting with each other and with the natural world. Many World 3 structures are abstract, that is, they are purely informational: forms of social organization, or patterns of communication.

53. For example, "language, mathematics, law, religion, philosophy, arts, the sciences and institutions of all kinds and their by-products such as temples, marketplaces, courts, theatres, books, music, performances...are all physical manifestations—or the physical components—of objects of World 3. In other words they are patterns of ideas, images, sounds, stories...patterns of pure information" (Benedict 1991, 4).

54. Stenger (1991, 50) refers here to the mental, spiritual i.e. the non-material part of the human being.

55. The Gutenberg project entails the uploading of all books ever written. For more information see: http://promo.net/pg/.

56. "A silver tide of phosphines boiled across my field of vision as the matrix began to unfold in my head, a 3-D chessboard, infinite and perfectly transparent... Ice walls flick away like supersonic butterflies made of shade. Beyond them the matrix's illusion of infinite space. It's like watching a tape of a prefab building going up; only the tape's reversed and run at high speed, and these walls are torn wings... The core data tower around us like vertical freight trains, color coded for access. Bright primaries, impossibly bright in that transparent void, linked by countless horizontals in nursery blues and pinks" (Pesce 1997).

57. In Hinduism, the last of the four yugas (ages) that make up one cycle of creation. The Kali-Yuga, in which Hindus believe we are now living, is characterized by wickedness and disaster, and leads up to the destruction of this world in preparation for a new creation and a new cycle of yugas. For a number of descriptions of the Age of Kali see: http://www.indiadivine.org/predictions-kali-yuga1.htm.

58. See also Dawson and Hennebry 1999.

59. The San Francisco Chronicle, in Herman and Sloop 2000, 78.

60. *Time's* magazine cover story in Herman and Sloop 2000.

61. Katz 1997 in *Hot Wired*: http://hotwired.wired.com/netizen/97/13/index0a.html.

62. Katz 1997 in *Hot Wired*: http://hotwired.wired.com/netizen/97/13/index0a.html.

63. For Zaleski (1997, 249), those most susceptible to a cult's message are "the lonely, shy, misfits [and] outcasts" who are attracted to the opportunities for communication within the safety of anonymity provided by ICTs.

64. The source of this statement is identified as "one UCLA professor", but Herman and Sloop (2000, 80) do not provide any further details.

65. For a detailed historical account of ICTs' creation and development see Jordan 1999, 33–48. Also: http://www.isoc.org/internet/history/.

66. For a visual representation of the notion of noosphere see: http://ecumene.org/noogenesis.html.

67. Teilhard's work *The Phenomenon of Man* was first published in French in 1955. The first English translation was published in 1959. Therefore while the idea of the "Noosphere" appeared in 1955, the citations used in this work correspond to the 1959 publication of the English translation.

68. Carey and Quirk attribute this quotation to Emerson, but they do not provide detailed bibliographical information; however, the first part of the quotation is in the Journal, May 18, 1843, found by the author online: http://www.wisdomportal.com/Emerson/Emerson-Journal.html.

69. Kerckhove (1998, 145) indicates that each phase of the development of communication apparatuses produces new features that merge with those of the previous phase, adding thus another layer on to the communication system.

70. For more information about Open Source see: http://www.opensource. org/. Also for the whole analysis and discussion on Open Source see E. Raymond (1998), "Homesteading the Noosphere", at: http://www.catb.org/~esr/writings/ cathedral-bazaar/homesteading/.

71. A detailed report on the history and activities of CBCPNet can be found in: http://ph.fujitsu.com/fpi/success/telecoms/telecoms18/, accessed 9 May 2004.

72. Drees (2002, 646) cites the cyber-Psalm 139 but the original author is not known.

5 Research Process and Method

1. See Introduction.
2. For a detailed discussion on these issues see Chapter 3, Web Epistemology.
3. These circumstances are presented in detail in Chapter 3, Web Epistemology.
4. The differences of updated technical infrastructures as opposed to out-dated, and the impact they have in finding information, the presentation of the information and the speed by which the information is retrieved, are discussed in various points in the study.
5. See Introduction.
6. See Chapter 3, Web Epistemology.
7. For a detailed analysis of H-links and time see Chapter 6, Methodology.
8. Because of the way the database is organized an exact count is not possible. However, an estimated number of the sites is in the region of thousands.
9. See, for example, in Chapter 6 on Methodology the sections on: NCRMs, Digitalism, and the Church of Virus.

6 Methodology

1. This point has been made earlier and it is a repeated one, for it is a fundamental issue which decisively determines the methodological approach.
2. See Introduction: Issues and Considerations.
3. This invented term is a combination of the words Internet and the plural of the Greek word "topos", namely "topoi" which denotes place.
4. For a detailed analysis of the term religion and its historical development see Smith 1998.
5. The term refers to all different religious expressions as they appear within the various applications of the Web.
6. This can be seen on the website of Biblenet that he offers as an example (217) which in its menu provides links to chat rooms and forums. Also Helland himself points to Usenet discussion forums (2000, 222 n. 9).
7. As for example: http://www.dcn.davis.ca.us/~vctinney/LDS.htm; http://www.mormons.org/.

8. Each state of affairs has its own email address. For the whole list and email addresses see: http://www.tldm.org/email/vatican_emails.htm, accessed 20 May 2004.

9. Source: http://news.bbc.co.uk/1/hi/world/europe/218500.stm. Other sources reported that the Vatican's intranet searcher is called Seraphim and that the whole process of Vatican's wiring was dubbed, "Father, Son and Website Host" (Internet News, December 1998. The link is no longer available).

10. Some examples are: Laura Italiano "launch[ed] the Pope into cyberspace" during his 1995 visit to the USA. The URL of Italiano's site is: www.nj.com/popepage (the site currently is available via the Internet archive); http://www.wf-f.org/02-3-Bishops-Scandals.html, a site reporting Catholic clergy's scandals; http://catholiccitizens.org/platform/platformview.asp?c=12459, site of American Catholics on American politics; http://www.cath4choice.org/, the Catholics for Choice site.

11. For an extensive analysis of identity see Turkle 1995.

12. See Chapter 4, Theory: Techno-religious Responses.

13. An extended analysis of the notion of "shifting realities" is in Chapter 4, Theory.

14. As it has been stated in the Introduction, the website has been defined as the field of this study.

15. The inclusion/exclusion of hypermedia and links and the effect of time is presented in the Topography section.

16. For bibliographic details see notes 22 and 23.

17. Bearing in mind the limitations of this diversity presented in Chapter 3, Web Epistemology.

18. WorldNet Dictionary online: http://www.hyperdictionary.com/dictionary/hypertext, accessed 9 November 2000.

19. For detailed explanations about hypermedia and the Web see Webopedia: http://www.Webopedia.com/TERM/h/hypermedia.html, accessed 10 August 2003.

20. This sound is usually part of the computer's different operations such as when an email is received, or when a command such as closing a file that needs saving is performed and so on.

21. Both text and images can be found either still or animated.

22. Hypertext/hypermedia has been the subject of a number of works that investigate and analyse: the term (Bornman and von Solms 1993; Landow 1992; Bolter 1991); the effects of hypertext on writing (Joyce 1991; Burbules 1997); on reading (Kaplan 2000; Bolter 1991); on typology of hypermedia (Hoffman and Novak 1995) and text–hypertext theory (Titon 1995).

23. Apart from specific works focusing on H-links, almost all studies related to the Web address the issue of H-links to either a greater or lesser degree. See for instance: Shields 2000; Burbules 1997; Harrison 2002; Rogers and Morris 2000; Mitra and Cohen 1999; Tosca 2000.

24. Whether that act is through a default Web browser, or a directory or via the result pages of a search engine, the unquestionable fact is that the user has to click somewhere.

25. This point has been discussed in Chapter 3 especially with reference to directories, search engines and Web rings.

26. Taking into account the role of H-links in the search process it should be mentioned that excessive use of H-links, especially incoming ones, does not necessarily imply only affiliations and collaborations; they may imply a strategy, probably mutually agreed by the different linked parties, to achieving a higher ranking.

27. The notion of time within the domain of ICTs can be investigated in great depth and detail as a metaphysical, sociological and a methodological issue. The focus here is on time and its methodological repercussions; however, short references to some metaphysical and technological aspects of it will be used as aids to establish an understanding of time as a methodological issue and its importance to the investigational process. For detailed accounts of time see Castells 1996; Strate 2003; Cooper 2002; Finnegan 2002.

28. The term fps stands for frames per second, a "measure of how much information is used to store and display motion video". The term applies equally to film video and digital video. Each frame is a still image; displaying frames in quick succession creates the illusion of motion. The more frames per second (fps), the smoother the motion appears. Television in the US, for example, is based on the NTSC format, which displays 30 interlaced frames per second (60 fields per second). In general, the minimum fps needed to avoid jerky motion is about 30. Some computer video formats, such as AVI (Audio Visual Interleave), provide only 15 frames per second.

29. The term literally means "occurring immediately". It is also used to describe a "number of different computer features. For example, real-time operating systems are systems that respond to input immediately. They are used for such tasks as navigation, in which the computer must react to a steady flow of new information without interruption. Most general-purpose operating systems are not real-time because they can take a few seconds, or even minutes, to react. 'Real time' can also refer to events simulated by a computer at the same speed that they would occur in real life. In graphics animation, for example, a real-time program would display objects moving across the screen at the same speed that they would actually move" (Webopedia 2002). Available online: http://www.Webopedia.com/TERM/r/real_time.html, accessed 12 December 2003.

30. For a detailed genealogical analysis of time in different contexts, such as social, economic and cultural, see Castells 1996, 429–68.

31. For example e-shopping, e-banking, chatting online and so on.

32. For instance the live broadcast of the fall of the Berlin wall; the images of the collapsing twin towers in New York; the blowing up of the Buddha sculptures in Afganistan and so on.

33. Internet Time is a " 'new' way to tell time invented and marketed by the Swiss watch company Swatch. The current Internet Time is the same all over the World (no time zones or daylight-saving time adjustments). The current Internet time can be found on the World Clock just below the long list of cities there. ('Internet time: @xxx .beats')". Source: time and date. com: http://www.timeanddate.com/time/internettime.html. As an illustra-

tion, the world's clock was as follows on Monday 29 December 2003: Current UTC (or GMT)-time used: Monday, December 29, 2003, at 13:00:50. UTC is Coordinated Universal Time, GMT is Greenwich Mean Time. Internet time: @583.beats.

34. See Chapter 4, Theory.

35. The term "discourse" is defined in a number of ways, one of which is "an extended communication (often interactive) dealing with some particular topic". Source: www.cogsci.princeton.edu/cgi-bin/webwn, accessed 28 November 2003.

36. Some of the most characteristic metaphors for ICTs are those of: "Information Superhighway", which emphasizes the speed by which information moves; as a "noosphere", which emphasizes the collective intelligence of users and computers connected by the global network; "cyberspace", which pictures networked information as an immense space through which one can "surf"; as a "Virtual Global Mall", which emphasizes the commercialization of the network, and so on.

37. This process, especially regarding the religious character of technology, has been explored in detail in Chapter 4, Theory. For statistical information related to users and the metaphors they employ see L. Ratzan, "Making Sense of the Web: A Metaphorical Approach". _Information Research_ 6.1 (2000). Available online: http://informationr.net/ir/6-1/paper85.html, accessed 11 November 2003.

38. Sharot conducts a sociological comparative analysis of world religions' penetration into the religious framework of the rural masses of agrarian or preindustrial societies. Focusing on the differences, conflicts and interrelationships between "religious elites and lay masses", he proposes a distinction of the different interpretations of the religious messages and practices, in which he incorporates categories such as: the "great/little traditions", the "official/unofficial" and the "elite/popular". Sharot (2001, 15) explains that while the "elite/popular" distinction is the prevalent one in his work, occasionally he also uses the terms "great/little traditions" and "official/unofficial", for this enables him to "distinguish religion as practiced, as proclaimed and as prescribed".

39. More specifically, Sharot investigates the interaction of "elite" and "popular" religion in the context of religious action and he examines the topic within Buddhism, Hinduism, Islam, Judaism, Catholic and Protestant Christianity, and Chinese religions.

40. It should be noted, though, that this applies in theory and as long as the politics of the search engines and directories are put aside.

41. Source: www.cogsci.princeton.edu/cgi-bin/webwn.

42. Multilingual content and information about TM's issues of concern in different countries.

43. TM's definitions of "Positive Trends", "success" and "flops" are given at http://www.globalgoodnews.com/about-this-site.htm. Accessed 12 March 2005.

44. The list provided is indicative and by no means exhaustive.

45. "Cult" here means "pattern of devotional practices" rather than implying anything more sinister.

46. Source: http://www.corrymeela.org/Who_we_are/who_we_are.html, accessed 30 March 2005.

47. Source: http://www.catholicsforchoice.org/lowbandwidth/indexhealth.htm, accessed 5 May 2005.

48. Web Missiology is "the systematic study of the evangelizing activity of the Church and of the ways in which it is carried out in cyberspace. It is the scientific study of the missionary reality of the Church in which scientific discipline, missionary charism and cyberspace enrich each other". Source: http://nuntia.cs.depaul.edu/webmissiology/concept.htm, accessed 30 November 2003.

49. The term "sponsored sites" usually refers to sites whose prominence is due to financial incentives from the source of the site to the "host" that includes them.

50. http://members.xoom.com/gecko23/moo.

51. Personal correspondence with the founders of Digitalism, Technosophy, and the Church of Virus, between 2000–2001 and 2003.

52. Every computer connected to the Internet is assigned a unique number known as an Internet Protocol (IP) address. Since these numbers are usually assigned in country-based blocks, an IP address can often be used to identify the country from which a computer is connecting to the Internet. Source: https://adwords.google.com/select/glossary.html, accessed 9 November 2002.

53. Javascript is used to make neat little effects on pages, like animations and interactive features, enabling Web authors to spice up their sites with dynamic content. Sources: www.denow.com/6gloss/; http://www.webopedia.com/TERM/J/JavaScript.html, accessed 15 June 2003.

54. In an experimental stage, as it is stated in the main page, which is sponsored by the Methodist Church and by the Christian Resources Exhibition.

55. It should be noticed that a particular software is needed for the church to be launched. The software enables the appearance of the 3D environment and activates the "characters" from which the visitors have to choose in order to enter. For instance, one may choose to enter either as male or female, and for each category there are a number of options which include different skin colour, hair colour, clothes and so on. Once in, the "character" is offered: a number of specific movements that may be performed (kneel, wave, walk, sit on the available pews); different places to go such as the crypt or the sanctuary and a selection of gestures such as bless, cross self, wave, shake hands, point and so on.

56. See Chapter 4, Theory: Information Communication Technologies.

57. The term "text" is used by Mitra and Cohen in a broad sense and refers to both the traditional meaning of text as written word and text as multimedia. Since a website embodies both text and multimedia, the author here suggests that the term "text" can be replaced by the term "site".

58. Amber's photographs are of her family and best friends; the monastery's photographs are of various masters, other monasteries, ceremonies and temples.

59. Here only a concise description of the pages is offered. However, it should be noted that colour, as well as the overall "feeling" of the sites, is almost impossible to describe accurately.

60. Brief information about him can be found only if one visits his personal writings in which he offers the "about the author" part.

61. First-level is the home page, or the index page of a site. The term "second-level" refers to pages whose links appear on the home page. If those pages incorporate links to other pages, then these are labelled as "third-level", "fourth-level" and so forth.

62. The term here refers to the domain space that can be bought from Internet service providers.

63. For example, sites of elite, formal, subjective, NCRM, MEM and/or personal orientation.

64. The studies were conducted in the USA.

65. The report is available online: http://www.christianitytoday.com/yc/9y4/9y4072.html, accessed 19 January 2002.

66. For a comprehensive analysis and statistical information on church attendance and ICTs and denominations and ICTs among others see: http://www.hartfordinstitute.org/internet.html, accessed 17 January 2003.

67. The Global Good News site offers "good news" from around the world related to agriculture, education, business, science and government that present "the rise of a better quality of life dawning in the world and highlights the need for introducing Natural Law based—Total Knowledge based—programmes to bring the support of Nature to every individual, raise the quality of life of every society, and create a lasting state of world peace" (taken from: http://www.globalgoodnews.com/environmental-news-a.html?art=10880983931709538).

68. For a variety of types of interpretive textual analysis see Daniel Chandler's excellent mass media site: http://www.aber.ac.uk/media/Documents/S4B/, accessed 19 November 2003.

69. Semantics is the branch of linguistics which studies meaning in language. One can distinguish between the study of the meanings of words (lexical semantics) and the study of how the meanings of larger constituents come about (structural semantics). Source: www.essex.ac.uk/linguistics/clmt/MTbook/HTML/node98.html, accessed 22 March 2003.

70. The rules that govern and describe how language is used in different contexts and environments. Source: www.beyond-words.org/definitions.htm, accessed 22 March 2003.

71. This has been proposed by Babin and Zukowski (2000, 64), Venerable Pannyavaro (1998), Fajardo (2002) and others and was discussed in the "Techno-religious Responses" section of Chapter 4.

72. For instance, Google returned 73,700 hits for the query "colour symbolism in web design". For more information about technical and aesthetical issues of colour in Web design see: http://graphicdesign.about.com/od/color/a/colormeanings.htm; http://www.creativity-portal.com/howto/artscrafts/design_color.html and http://www.websitetips.com/color/.

73. Taken from the bulletin board of the Color Matters site: 30 varieties of Red in China, accessed 23 November 2003.

74. For updates on John WorldPeace see: http://www.johnworldpeace.com/ Accessed 12 February 2006.

75. For instance, the Cassie Bernall case is a characteristic example of the polarized discourses and the controversy they generated, especially regarding the extent to which Cassie Bernall should be considered a "martyr". Cassie Bernall was one of the pupils of Columbine school killed in the 1999 massacre. Even today (May 2004) Google returns 5,970 hits for "Cassie Bernall". For details on this case one may start from the extensive entry of Wikipedia: http://en.wikipedia.org/wiki/Columbine_massacre, accessed 19 May 2004.

76. For an excellent article on image and its significance in sharing a moment of catastrophe see R. W. Smith, "The Image is Dying". *M/C: A Journal of Media and Culture* 6 (2003). Available online: http://www.media-culture.org.au/0304/09-imageisdying.html, accessed 11 March 2004.

77. For current activities of the 9/11 Respond to the Call site see: http://www.respondtothecall.org/index.html. Accessed 12 February 2006.

78. Source: Encyclopedia.WorldSearch: http://encyclopedia.worldsearch.com/digitalism.htm, accessed 19 September 2002.

79. Personal correspondence, 14 May 2001.

80. Personal correspondence, 14 May 2001.

81. Personal correspondence with the founder, 6 October 2003.

82. Personal correspondence with the founder, 6 October 2003.

83. According to the founder's estimation: "Over 1600 have contributed to the discussions over the years. There is usually a 10:1 ratio between 'lurkers' and contributors so I would guess over 16,000 have joined the mailing list over the years". Personal correspondence, 6 October 2003.

84. Personal correspondence, 6 October 2003.

7 Conclusions

1. For the latest statistics, trends and patterns see NUA.

2. By "interacting", Castells refers to those who can choose "their multidirectional circuits of communication" and by "interacted" he refers to those "who are provided with a restricted number of prepackaged choices" and he points out that the members of each category would be "largely determined by class, race, gender and country" (1996, 371).

3. Active use of and participation in the digital domain is the privilege of a minority whether this is located in a Western country or not.

4. For details see BBC news: http://news.bbc.co.uk/1/hi/uk/2757067.stm; BBC results: http://news.bbc.co.uk/1/hi/uk/2756993.stm; The Register: http://www.theregister.co.uk/2003/02/14/jedis_reach_the_stars/.

5. Of course the Church of Virus may not interpret the schism as destructive.

6. Although thousands of sites are devoted to virtual/cyber marriage, the vast majority, if not the totality, are parodies. At the moment only one legal cybermarriage has taken place, in 1995 in the US. The wedding's site is: http://www.terwillegar.com/cyber__wedding_.html.

7. Perhaps the most active prayer group online is the Prayer-Warriors: http://www.prayer-warriors.org/.

8.   Sample sites of cybermemorials: http://www.e-memoriam.com/; the JFK memorial rose garden: http://www.jfkfoundation.org/rosegarden/.

9.   For online grief and loss counselling see: http://www.angelfire.com/hi5/memories0/id12.html.

10. In fact a "meditation guidelines" research in August 2003 offered 120,000 hits. A couple of examples are: http://dharma.ncf.ca/introduction/meditation.html; http://www.buddhanet.net/v_guide.htm.

11. Although most of what have been defined as cyberpilgrimages are no more than virtual tours of religious places such as Cathedrals, the Holy Land, monasteries, and shrines of different religions.

12. See: http://www.angelfire.com/folk/wiccasinovess/Main2.html.

13. See Zaleski 1997, 262.

14. The keyword search "Healing ritual" returned (in 2003) an impressive number of 228,000 sites. Some sites refer to academic works on the subject, such as: http://www.museum.state.il.us/exhibits/changing/journey/healing.html; other sites include confessional approaches, such as Jewish views: http://www.beliefnet.com/story/35/story_3569_1.html; guidelines on how to set up a healing ritual according to occultist practices are available on: http://realmagick.com/articles/11/1311.html; pagan ritual: http://www.paganspath.com/magik/grimoire/healing.htm.

15. The term is used here in a broad sense to signify the authority figures that exist in all diverse religious institutions, NRMs, organizations, groups and so on.

16. For example the Danish site: http://lightacandle.sol.dk.

17. A blessing of cyberspace was performed by the monks of the Namgyal Monastery, the personal monastery of the Dalai Lama, who thought that the Kalachakra Tantra, believed to have been first taught by the Buddha, would be highly appropriate as a blessing vehicle because it especially emphasizes space itself (along with consciousness), as one of the six constituent elements of the universe, in addition to the more familiar elements of earth, air, fire and water. The blessing was performed on February 8, 1996. It can be accessed at http://www.namgyal.org/blessing.html.

Bibliography

Agre, P. E.
    1998   "Designing Genres for New Media: Social, Economic, and Political Contexts". In Jones 1998a.

Altena, A.
    1999   "The Browser is Dead; Long Live the Browser". Translation Laura Martz. *Mediamatic* 9.4/10.1. Available online: http://www. mediamatic.net/cwolk/view/2554. Accessed 13 April 2000.

Altintas, K., T. Aydin, and V. Akman
    2002   "Censoring the Internet: The Situation in Turkey". *First Monday* 7.6. Available online: http://www.firstmonday.dk/issues/issue7_6/ altinta/. Accessed 14 February 2006.

Anderson, J.
    2000   "New Media & Globalization in the Internet Age". Keynote address in MEViC Online Inaugural Conference, "People Across Border", August 2000. Available online: http://www.mevic.org/. Accessed 19 November 2000.

Aoki, K.
    1994   "Virtual Communities in Japan". Paper presented to the *Pacific Telecommunications Council 1994*. Available online: http://www. uni-koeln.de/themen/Internet/cmc/text/aoki.94.txt. Accessed 10 October 2000.

Anderson, J. A.
    1996   *Communication Theory: Epistemological Foundations*. New York: Guilford Press.

Arquilla, J., and D. Ronfeldt
    1999   "The Emergence of Noopolitik: Toward an American Information Strategy". *A RAND Publication*. Available online: http://www. rand.org/publications/MR/MR1033/#contents. Accessed 29 September 2000.

Arthur, C. (ed.)
    1993a   *Religion and the Media: An Introductory Reader*. Cardiff: University of Wales Press.
    1993b   "Learning from Failure: Towards a Rationale for Religious Communication". In Arthur 1993a.

Aycock, A.
    1995   "'Technologies of the Self': Foucault and Internet Discourse", *Journal of Computer Mediated Commmunication* 1.2. Available online: http://jcmc.indiana.edu/vol1/issue2/aycock.html. Accessed 9 December 2002.

Babin, P., and A. A. Zukowski
    2002   *The Gospel in Cyberspace: Nurturing Faith in the Internet Age*. Chicago: Loyola Press.

Bachelard, G.
1969   *The Poetics of Space*. Boston: Beacon [orig. 1958].
Bainbridge, W. S.
2000   "Religious Ethnography on the World Wide Web". In Hadden and Cowan 2000.
Barbrook, R., and A. Cameron
1995   *The Californian Ideology*. Available online: http://www.hrc.wmin. ac.uk/hrc/theory/californianIdeo/main/t.4.2.1#. Accessed 22 October 1998.
Bard, A., and J. Soderqvist
2002   *Netocracy*. London: Pearson Education.
Barker, E.
1992   *New Religious Movements: A Practical Introduction*. London: HMSO.
Barlow, J. P.
1994   "The Economy of Ideas: A Framework for Patents and Copyrights in the Digital Age. (Everything you know about intellectual property is wrong.)" *WIRED* 2 (March 3). Available online: http://www.wired. com/wired/archive/2.03/economy.ideas.html. Accessed 22 October 2000.
Bauwens, M.
1997   "Deus ex Machina vs. Electric Gaia". *CMC Magazine* (April 1997). Available online: http://www.december.com/cmc/mag/1997/apr/ last.html. Accessed 17 November 2000.
Bauwens, M., and V. Rossi
1999   "Dialogue on the Cyber-Sacred and the Relationship Between Technological and Spiritual Development". *Cybersociology Magazine* 7. Available online: http://www.socio.demon.co.uk/magazine/7/rossi. html. Accessed 25 November 2000.
Beaudoin, T.
1998   *Virtual Faith: The Irreverent Spiritual Quest of Generation X*. San Francisco: Jossey-Bass.
Beckford, J. A.
1980   *Scientology, Social Science and the Definition of Religion*. Available online: http://www.humanrights-germany.org/experts/eng/ beckford01.pdf. Accessed 10 February 2005.
Bedell, K.
1998   "Religion and the Internet: Reflections on Research Strategies". Annual meeting of the Religious Research Association Montreal, Quebec. Available online: http://www.religion-research.org/ rrapaper.html. Accessed 10 October 1999.
2000   "Dispatches from the Electronic Frontier: Explorations of Mainline Protestant Uses of the Internet. " In Hadden and Cowan 2000.
Benedikt, M. (ed.)
1991   *Cyberspace First Steps*. Cambridge, MA and London: The MIT Press.
Bergman, M. K.
2001   "The Deep Web: Surfacing Hidden Value". *The Journal of Elec-*

tronic Publishing. 7.1. Available online: http://www.press.umich. edu/jep/07-01/bergman.html. Accessed 5 November 2001.

Berland, J.
2000   "Cultural Technologies and the 'Evolution' of Technological Cultures". In Herman and Swiss 2000.

Bieber, M.
2000   "Hypertext". In *Encyclopaedia of Computer Science (4th Edition)*, ed. A. Ralston, E. Reilly and D. Hemmendinger, 799–805. Nature Publishing Group, 2000. Available online: http://web. njit.edu/~bieber/pub/cs-encyclopedia/csencyclopedia00.pdf. Accessed 21 May 2002.

Birdsall, W. F.
1996   "The Internet and the Ideology of Information Technology". *INET96*, Montreal, Canada. Available online: http://www.isoc. org/inet96/proceedings/e3/e3_2.htm. Accessed 25 November 1999.

Blair, T.
1999   "The Knowledge Economy". Speech of PM Blair in Cambridge (Silicon Fen). http://www.number-10.gov.uk/output/Page1456. asp. Accessed 30 January 2001.

Bolter, J. D.
1991   *Electronic Signs Writing Space: The Computer, Hypertext, and the History of Writing*. Hillsdale, NJ: Lawrence Erlbaum Associates.

Bornman, H., and S. H. von Solms
1993   "Hypermedia, Multimedia and Hypertext—Definitions and Overview". *Electronic Library* 11: 4–5, 259–68.

Boulding, E.
1982   *The Family as a Small Society*. Available online: http://www. schumachersociety.org/lec-bou.html. Accessed 12 November 2000.

Brasher, B. E.
1996   "The Cyborg: Technological Socialization and its Link to the Religious Function of Popular Culture". *Journal of the American Academy of Religion* 64.4: 809–30.
2001   *Give Me that Online Religion*. San Francisco: Jossey-Bass.

Bridges.org
2001   http://www.bridges.org/digitaldivide/index.html

Brockman, J.
1997   *Digerati: Encounters with the Cyber Elite*. London: Orion Business Books.

Brown, L. J.
1996   *The Spirit of Cyberspace*. Available online: http://www.lightparty. com/Spirituality/CyberSpace.html. Accessed 28 May 1998.

Bruckman, A. S.
1992   "Identity Workshops. Emergent Social and Psychological Phenomena in Text-based Virtual Reality". *MIT Media Laboratory*. Available online: http://www.cc.gatech.edu/~asb/papers/old-papers. html#IW. Accessed 9 November 1999.

Bunt, G.
  2000   *Virtually Islamic Computer-mediated Communication and Cyber Islamic Environments*. Cardiff: University of Wales Press.
  2002   "Surfing Islam: Ayatollahs, Shayks and Hajjis on the Superhighway". In *Religion on the Internet: Research Prospects and Promises*, ed. J. K. Hadden and C. E. Douglas. New York: Elsevier Science Inc.
Burbules, N.
  1997   *Rhetorics of the Web*. New South Wales: Allen and Unwin.
Bush, V.
  1945   "As We May Think". *The Atlantic Online*. Available online: http://www.theatlantic.com/unbound/flashbks/computer/bushf.htm. Accessed 28 October 2002.
Carey, J. W.
  1989   *Communication as Culture*. Boston: Unwin Hyman.
Carey, J., and J. J. Quirk
  1989   "The Mythos of the Electronic Revolution". In Carey 1989.
Carvin, A.
  2000a   "Beyond Access: Understanding the Digital Divide". Keynote Address, NYU Third Act Conference, May 19, 2000. Available online: http://www.benton.org/Divide/thirdact/speech.html. Accessed 10 August 2000.
  2000b   "Gap: The Digital Divide as the Civil Rights Issue of the New Millennium". *Multimedia Schools* 7 (January/February). Available online: http://www.infotoday.com/MMSchools/Jan00/carvin.htm. Accessed 18 December 2000.
Castells, M.
  1996   *The Rise of the Network Society*. Oxford: Blackwell Publishers.
Cavanagh, A.
  1999   "Behaviour in Public? Ethics in Online Ethnography". *Cybersociology* 6. Available online: http://www.socio.demon.co.uk/magazine/6/cavanagh.html.
Chandler, D.
  1994   *Semiotics for Beginners*. Available online: http://www.aber.ac.uk/~dgc/semiotic.html. Accessed 12 May 2000.
  1998   *Personal Home Pages and the Construction of Identities on the Web*. Available online: http://www.aber.ac.uk/media/Documents/short/webident.html. Accessed 23 August 2000.
Charney, D.
  1995   "The Effect of Hypertext on Processes of Reading and Writing". In *Literacy and Computers*, ed. C. L. Sellfe and S. Hilligoss. New York: Modern Language Association.
Cho, J., H. Garcia-Molina and L. Page
  1998   *Efficient Crawling Through URL Ordering*. In *Proceedings of 7th World Wide Web Conference*. Available online: http://citeseer.ist.psu.edu/cache/papers/cs/23742/http:zSzzSzwww-db.stanford.edu zSz~chozSzpaperszSzcho-order.pdf/cho98efficient.pdf/. Accessed 20 November 2000.

Choo, C. W., B. Detlor and D. Turnbull
  2000   "Information Seeking on the Web: An Integrated Model of Browsing and Searching". *First Monday* 5.2. Available online: http://firstmonday.org/issues/issue5_2/choo/index.html. Accessed 21 November 2000.
Chu, H., and M. Rosenthal
  1996   "Search Engines for the World Wide Web: A Comparative Study and Evaluation Methodology". ASIS 1996 Annual Conference Proceedings, Baltimore, MD, October 19–24, 1996. Available online: http://www.asis.org/annual-96/ElectronicProceedings/chu.html. Accessed 12 November 2000.
Cobb, J.
  1998   *Cybergrace: The Search for God in the Digital World*. New York: Crown Publishers, Inc.
Codognet, P.
  1996   "The Semiotics of the Web". Paper presented at the 2nd International Summer School on Semiotics, Varna, Bulgaria, September 1996. Available online: http://pauillac.inria.fr/~codognet/web.html 2000. Accessed 25 July 2000.
Cohen, L.
  2002   *The Deep Web*. Available online: http://library.albany.edu/internet/deepweb.html. Accessed 10 January 2003.
Colon, C.
  1995   *Semiotics in Hyperspace*. Available online: http://php.indiana.edu/~ccolon/Semiotics/ccolon3.html. Accessed 4 March 2000.
Cooper, S.
  2002   *Technoculture and Critical Theory*. London and New York: Routledge.
Couch, C. J.
  1996   *Information Technologies and Social Orders*. New York: Aldine de Gruyter.
Coyne, R.
  1999   *Technoromanticism: Digital Narrative, Holism, and the Romance of the Real*. Cambridge, MA and London: The MIT Press.
Craig, R. T.
  1999   "Communication Theory as a Field". *Communication Theory* 9.2: 119–61.
Cunningham, P. J.
  1997   "Teilhard de Chardin and the Noosphere". *CMC Magazine* 4.3 (March 1). Available online: http://www.december.com/cmc/mag/1997/mar/cunning.html. Accessed 11 September 2000.
Cybernauts Awake!
  1999   *Ethical and Spiritual Implications of Computers, Information Technology and the Internet*. London: Church House Publishing. Also available online: http://starcourse.org/sciteb2/starcourse/cyber/. Accessed 6/12/99.
Cyveillance, Inc.
  2000   http://www.cyveillance.com/web/downloads/Sizing_the_Internet.pdf. Accessed 14 February 2006.

David, T. (ed.)
   2001   *Reading Digital Culture*. Malden, MA; Oxford: Blackwell Publishers.
Davidson, L.
   1995   *Cyberspace Satsang: Speculations on a Guru for the 21st Century*. Available online: http://www.collaboration.org/97/nov/text/8_ cyberspace.html. Accessed 28 November 2000.
Davies, C. A.
   1999   *Reflexive Ethnography: A Guide to Researching Selves and Others*. London and New York: Routledge.
Davis, E.
   1998   *Techgnosis: Myth, Magic, and Mysticism in the Age of Information*. New York: Harmony Books.
Dawson, L. L.
   2000   "Researching Religion in Cyberspace: Issues and Strategies". In Hadden and Cowan 2000.
Dawson, L. L., and J. Hennebry
   1999   "New Religions and the Internet: Recruiting in a New Public Space". *Journal of Contemporary Religion* 14.1: 17–39.
De Vaney, A., S. Gance and Y. Ma (eds.)
   2000   *Technology and Resistance: Digital Communications and New Coalitions Around the World*. New York: Peter Lang.
DeAngelis, T.
   2000   "Is Internet Addiction Real?" *Monitor on Psychology* 31.4. Available online: http://www.apa.org/monitor/apr00/addiction.html. Accessed 14 October 2000.
Deck, A.
   1998   *Regressive Tendencies*. Available online: http://artcontext.org/crit/ scrapbook/opensource.html. Accessed 21 October 2000.
Denzin, N. K.
   1999   "Cybertalk and the Method of Instances". In Jones 1999a.
Dodge, M.
   2000   "Mapping the World Wide Web". In Rogers 2000a.
Donath, J. S.
   1999   "Identity and Deception in the Virtual Community". In Smith and Kollock 1999.
Drees, W. B.
   2002   "Playing God? Yes! Religion in the Light of Technology". *Zygon* 37.3: 643–54.
Dreyfus, H. L.
   2001   *On the Internet*. London and New York: Routledge.
Durkheim, E.
   1965   *The Elementary Forms of the Religious Life*. Trans. Joseph Ward Swain. New York: The Free Press [1912].
Dyens, O.
   2003   "The Debate Around Reproductive Technologies: The Birth of a Godless Nature". Paper presented at the International Conference on *Transforming Traditions in the Interplay of Religion and Media*. Jyväskylä, Finland 10-13 July 2003.

Ebo, B. (ed.)
  2001a   *Cyberimperialism? Global Relations in the New Electronic Frontier.* Westport, CN; London: PRAEGER.
  2001b   "Cyberglobalization: Superhighway or Superhyperway?" In Ebo 2001a.

Ellul, J.
  1964   *The Technological Society.* Trans. John Wilkinson. New York: Knopf.

Elmer, G.
  2000   "The Economy of Cyberpromotion: Awards on the World Wide Web". In Herman and Swiss 2000.

Emery, M., and B. J. Bates
  2001   "Creating New Relations: The Internet in Central and Eastern Europe". In Ebo 2001a.

Ensenberger, M.
  1997   *Universals in Colours.* Available online: http://www.letras.up. pt/translat/i_unicol.html. Accessed 12 October 2000.

Escobar, A.
  1996   "Welcome to Cyberia. Notes on the Anthropology of Cyberculture". In Sardar 1996.

Ess, C. (ed.)
  1996   *Philosophical Perspectives on Computer-Mediated Communication.* New York: State University of New York Press.
  1998   "Cosmopolitan Ideal or Cybercentrism? A Critical Examination of the Underlying Assumptions of 'The Electronic Global Village'". *American Philosophical Association Newsletter on Computers and Philosophy* 97.2 (Spring, 1998): 48–51. Available online: http://www.drury.edu/ess/papers/cybercentrism. html. Accessed 15 November 2001.

Fajardo, A.
  2002   *Poor of the Kingdom, Popular Mission and Internet.* Available online: http://nuntia.cs.depaul.edu/webmissiology/kingdom_of_god.htm. Accessed 11 April 2002.

Featherstone, M., and R. Burrows
  1995a   *Cyberspace/Cyberbodies/Cyberpunk: Cultures of Technological Embodiment.* London: Sage.
  1995b   "Cultures of Technological Embodiment: An Introduction". In Featherstone and Burrows 1995a.

Feenberg, A.
  1991   *Critical Theory of Technology.* Available online: http://www-rohan. sdsu.edu/faculty/feenberg/CRITSAM2.HTM. Accessed 28 November 1998.
  1999   *Questioning Technology:* London: Routledge.
  2000   "From Essentialism to Constructivism: Philosophy of Technology at the Crossroads". In *Technology and the Good Life*, ed. E. Higgs, D. Strong and A. Light. Chicago: University of Chicago Press, 2000. Available online: http://www-rohan.sdsu.edu/faculty/feenberg/talk4.html. Accessed 18 December 2000.

Feenberg, A., and A. Hannay
    1995   *Technology and the Politics of Knowledge.* Bloomington, IN: Indiana University Press.
Ferre, F.
    1995   *Philosophy of Technology.* Athens and London: The University of Georgia Press.
Finnegan, R.
    2002   *Communicating: The Multiple Modes of Human Interconnection.* London and New York: Routledge.
Fisher, D. R., and L. M. Wright
    2001   "On Utopias and Dystopias: Toward an Understanding of the Discourse Surrounding the Internet". *Journal of Computer-Mediated Communication* 6.2. Available online: http://www.ascusc.org/jcmc/vol6/issue2/fisher.html. Accessed 18 November 2001.
Fitzgerald, T.
    1995   "Religious Studies as Cultural Studies: A Philosophical and Anthropological Critique of the Concept of Religion". *DISKUS* 3.1: 35–47. http://www.uni-marburg.de/religionswissenschaft/journal/diskus/fitzgerald.html
    2003   " 'Religion' and 'the Secular' in Japan: Problems in History, Social Anthropology, and the Study of Religion". *The Electronic Journal of Contemporary Japanese Studies.* Available online: http://www.japanesestudies.org.uk/discussionpapers/Fitzgerald.html. Accessed 10 February 2005.
Floridi, L.
    1999   *Philosophy and Computing: An Introduction.* London and New York: Routledge.
Fore, W. F.
    1987   *A Theology of Communication.* Available online: http://www.religion-online.org/cgi-bin/relsearchd.dll/showarticle?item_id=268. Accessed 19 June 2002.
    1993   "The Religious Relevance of Television". In Arthur 1993a.
Foucault, M.
    1972   *The Archaeology of Knowledge.* New York: Irvington Pub.
    1994   *The Order of Things: An Archaeology of the Human Sciences.* London: Routledge.
Frobish, T. S.
    2000   "Altar Rhetoric and Online Performance: Scientology and the World Wide Web". *American Communication Journal* 4.1. Available online: http://acjournal.org/holdings/vol4/iss1/articles/frobish.htm. Accessed 17 December 2000.
Garton, L., C. Haythornthwaite and B. Wellman
    1999   "Studying On-line Social Networks". In Jones 1999a.
Gauntlett, D. (ed.)
    2000a   *Web.Studies: Rewiring Media Studies for the Digital Age.* London: Arnold.
    2000b   "The Future: Faster, Smaller, More, More, More". In Gauntlett 2000a.

Gibson, W.
  1995   *Neuromancer.* London: HarperCollins [1984].
Goethals, G.
  1993   "Media Mythologies". In Arthur 1993a.
Goggin, G.
  2000   "Pay Per Browse? The Web's Commercial Futures". In Gauntlett 2000a.
Graham, G.
  1999   *The Internet: A Philosophical Inquiry.* London and New York: Routledge.
Groothuis, D.
  1999   *The Soul in Cyberspace.* Eugene: Wipf and Stock.
Gunn, T. J.
  2003   "The Complexity of Religion and the Definition of 'Religion' in International Law". *Harvard Human Rights Journal* 16 (Spring). http://www.law.harvard.edu/students/orgs/hrj/iss16/gunn.shtml
Gurak, L. J.
  1999   "The Promise and the Peril of Social Action in Cyberspace: Ethos, Delivery, and the Protests over Marketplace and the Clipper Chip". In Smith and Kollock 1999.
Hadden, J. K., and D. E. Cowan (eds.)
  2000   *Religion on the Internet: Research Prospects and Promises.* Amsterdam: JAI/Elsevier Science.
Hakken, D.
  1999   *Cyborgs @ Cyberspace?: An Etnographer Looks at the Future.* New York and London: Routledge.
Hamelink, C. J.
  2000   *The Ethics of Cyberspace.* London: Sage.
Hammerman, J.
  2000   *Thelordismyshepherd.com. Seeking God in Cyberspace.* Deerfield Beach, FL: Simcha Press.
Haraway, D. J.
  1997   *Modest_Witness@Second_Millenium.Female_Man©_Meets_ Oncomouse™: Feminism and Technoscience.* New York and London: Routledge.
Harrison, C.
  2002   "Whither Thou Goest, and Why". *First Monday* 7.10. Available online: http://firstmonday.org/issues/issue7_10/harrison/index.html. Accessed 10 October 2002.
Heath, R. L., and J. Bryant
  2000   *Human Communication Theory and Research: Concepts, Contexts, and Challenges.* Mahwah, NJ: Lawrence Erlbaum Associates.
Heim, M.
  1993   *The Metaphysics of Virtual Reality.* New York, Oxford: Oxford University Press.

Helland, C.
2000   "Online-Religion/Religion-Online and Virtual Communitas". In Hadden and Cowan 2000.
Henderson, C.
2000   "Spiritual Surfers". Interview with Scott Simon, Public Broadcasting Service program. Available online: http://www.godweb.org/transcript.html. Accessed 1 July 2000.
2002   "Religion and the Internet". *MIT Communications Forum*. Available online: http://web.mit.edu/comm-forum/forums/religion.html. Accessed 14 May 2002.
Herbrechtsmeier, W.
1993   "Buddhism and the Definition of Religion: One More Time". *Journal for the Scientific Study of Religion* 32.1: 1–17. Available online: http://ccbs.ntu.edu.tw/FULLTEXT/JR-ADM/herbre.htm. Accessed 10 February 2005.
Herman, E. S., and R. W. McChesney
1997   *The Global Media: The New Missionaries of Corporate Capitalism*. London and Washington: Cassell.
Herman, A., and J. H. Sloop
2000   " 'Red Alert!': Rhetorics of the World Wide Web and 'Friction Free' Capitalism". In Herman and Swiss 2000.
Herman, A., and T. Swiss (ed.)
2000   *The World Wide Web and Contemporary Cultural Theory*. New York and London: Routledge.
Hoffman, D. L., and T. P. Novak
1995   *Marketing in Hypermedia Computer-Mediated Environments: Conceptual Foundations*. Available online: http://elab.vanderbilt.edu/research/papers/html/manuscripts/cmepaper/cme.conceptual.foundations.html. Accessed 28 December 2000.
Holmes, D.
1997   *Virtual Politics: Identity and Community in Cyberspace*. London and Thousand Oaks, CA: Sage.
Horn, S.
1998   *Cyberville: Clicks, Culture and the Creation of an Online Town*. New York: Warner Books.
Horsfall, S.
2000   "How Religious Organizations Use the Internet: A Preliminary Inquiry". In Hadden and Cowan 2000.
Innis, H.
1951   *The Bias of Communication*. Toronto: University of Toronto Press.
Introna, L., and H. Nissenbaum
2000   "The Public Good Vision of the Internet and the Politics of Search Engines". In Rogers 2000a.
Introvigne, M.
2000   "So Many Evil Things: Anti-Cult Terrorism via the Internet". In Hadden and Cowan 2000.

Jackson, M. H.
   1997   "Assessing the Structure of Communication on the World Wide Web". *Journal of Computer-Mediated Communication* 3.1. Available online: http://www.ascusc.org/jcmc/vol3/issue1/jackson.html. Accessed 10 May 1999.

Johnson, J.
   1997   "Universal Access to the Net: Requirements and Social Impact". Conference on Human Factors in Computer Systems, Atlanta, Georgia, USA, March 22–27, 1997. Available online: http://www.acm.org/sigchi/chi97/proceedings/invited/jj.htm. Accessed 5 June 1999.

Jones, S. G.
   1997   *Virtual Culture: Identity and Communication in Cybersociety*. London and Thousand Oaks, CA: Sage.

Jones, S. G. (ed.)
   1995   *Cybersociety: Computer-Mediated Communication and Community*. Thousand Oaks, CA: SAGE Publications Inc.
   1998a *Cybersociety 2.0. Revisiting Computer-Mediated Communication and Community*. London and Thousand Oaks, CA: Sage.
   1998b "Information, Internet, and Community: Notes Toward an Understanding of Community in the Information Age". In S. G. Jones 1998a.

Jones, S.
   1999a *Doing Internet Research: Critical Issues and Methods for Examining the Net*. Thousand Oaks, CA: Sage.
   1999b "Studying the Net: Intricates and Issues". In Jones 1999a.

Jordan, T.
   1999   *Cyberpower: The Culture and Politics of Cyberspace and the Internet*. London and New York: Routledge.

Joyce, M.
   1991   "Notes Toward an Unwritten Non-Linear Electronic Text, 'The Ends of Print Culture' (a work in progress)". *Postmodern Culture* 2.1. Available online: http://www.uv.es/~fores/programa/joyce.html. Accessed 12 October 1992.

Kaplan, N.
   2000   "Literacy Beyond Books". In Herman and Swiss 2000.

Karaflogka, A.
   1998   "Religious Discourse in Cyberspace". Paper presented at the British Association for the Study of Religions (BASR) Annual Conference, University of Wales, Lampeter, September 1998.
   2000a "Religious Discourse and Cyberspace". Paper presented at the 18th Quinquennial Congress of the International Association for the History of Religions (IAHR), Durban, South Africa, August 2000.
   2000b "Cyberritual: Multivocal Evolution and Development of Religious Practice". Paper presented at the British Sociological Association (BSA), Sociology of Religion Study Group Annual Study Day, Birkbeck College, University of London, November 2000.

2002   "Religious Discourse and Cyberspace". *Religion* 32: 279–91.

2003   "Religion on—Religion in Cyberspace". In *Predicting Religion: Christian, Secular and Alternative Futures*, ed. G. Davie, P. Heelas and L. Woodhead. Hampshire: Ashgate.

2004   "CyberReligious Norms: Breaking Old Codes—Creating New Patterns". *Cyberspace 2003: Normative Framework*. Conference Proccedings organized by Masaryk University in Brno.

Katz, J., and P. Aspden

1997   "Motivations for and Barriers to Internet Usage: Results of a National Public Opinion Survey". *Internet Research: Electronic Networking Applications and Policy* 7.3: 170–88.

1998   *Social and Public Policy Internet Research: Goals and Achievements*. Available online: http://www.communitytechnology.org/aspden/aspden_talk.html. Accessed 23 October 1999.

Kellner, D.

1999   "New Technologies, TechnoCities, and the Prospects for Democratization". In *Technocities*, ed. J. Downey and J. McGuigan, 186–204. London: Sage Publications. Available online: http://www.gseis.ucla.edu/faculty/kellner/Illumina%20Folder/kell25.htm. Accessed 12 March 2002.

2001   "Feenberg's Questioning Technology". *Theory, Culture and Society* 18.1: 155–62.

Kellner, D., and S. Best

2001   *The Postmodern Adventure: Science, Technology, and Cultural Studies at the Third Millenium*. New York: Guilford and London: Routledge.

Kelly, D.

2002   *Search Engine Secrets Revealed*. Available online: http://www.search-engine-goldmine.com/. Accessed 30 November 2002.

Kelly, K.

1994   "The Electronic Hive: Two Views". *Harpers Magazine* 288 (May 1994): 1728. Available online: http://chnm.gmu.edu/courses/rr/f01/cw/hive.html. Accessed 14 August 1999.

Kemal, A., A. Tolga and A. Varol

2002   "Censoring the Internet: The Situation in Turkey". *First Monday* 7.6. Available online: http://firstmonday.org/issues/issue7_6/altinta/index.html. Accessed 22 June 2002.

Kenan, P. J.

2001   *Inclusion in the Information Age: Reframing the Debate*. Available online: http://www.athenaalliance.org. Accessed 21 July 2002.

Kendall, L.

1999   "Recontextualising Cyberspace: Methodological Considerations for On-line Research". In Jones 1999a.

Kerckhove, D. D.

1998   *Connected Intelligence: The Arrival of the Web Society*. London: Kogan Page.

King, M.

1996   "Concerning the Spiritual in Cyberspace". Paper presented at ISEA96 and published in the proceedings. Available online: http://web. ukonline.co.uk/mr.king/writings/asats/spiritcyb0.html. Accessed 22 October 2000.

Kinneya, J.
  1995   "Net Worth?; Religion, Cyberspace and the Future". *Futures* 27.7: 763–76.

Kirkland, R.
  1976   *Defining "Religion"*. Available online: http://www.arches.uga. edu/~kirkland/rk/pdf/guides/RELDEFINE.pdf. Accessed 10 February 2005

Kleinberg, J., and S. Lawrence
  2001   *The Structure of the Web*. Available online: http://www.cs.cornell. edu/home/kleinber/sci01.pdf. Accessed 29 March 2002.

Kollock, P., and M. A. Smith (eds.)
  1999   *Communities in Cyberspace*. London and New York: Routledge.

Kong, L.
  2001   "Religion and Technology: Refiguring Place, Space, Identity and Community". *Area* 33.4: 404–413.

Koster, M.
  1995   "Robots in the Web: Threat or Treat?" *ConneXions* 9.4 (April 1995). http://www.robotstxt.org/wc/threat-or-treat.html. Accessed 13 November 2002.

Kraidy, M.
  2001   "From Imperialism to Glocalization: A Theoretical Framework for the Information Age". In Ebo 2001a.

Kress, G.
  1998   *Visual and Verbal Modes of Representation in Electronically Mediated Communication: The Potential New Forms of Text*. London: Routledge.

Krol, E., and E. Hoffman
  1993   *What is the Internet?* Available online: http://nexus.brocku.ca/ rogawa/rfc/rfc1462.html. Accessed 21 March 1998.

Landow, G.
  1991   "Hypertext and Critical Theory". In *Reading Digital Culture*, ed. D. Trend. Malden, MA and Oxford: Blackwell Publishers.

  1992   *Hypertext: The Convergence of Contemporary Theory and Technology*. Baltimore: The Johns Hopkins University Press.

LaRue, J. C.
  1999   "Churches and Computers". *Your Church* 45.4. Available online: http://www.christianitytoday.com/yc/9y4/9y4072.html. Accessed 27 November 2000.

Latour, B.
  1988   *Science in Action: How to Follow Scientists and Engineers Through Society*. New Haven: Harvard University Press.

Lawrence, S., and L. Giles
  1999   "Accessibility of Information on the Web". *Nature* 400. Available online: http://wwwmetrics.com/. Accessed 15 November 2000.

Lax, S.
    2000   "The Internet and Democracy". In Gauntlett 2000a.

Lehikoinen, T.
    2003   *Religious Media Theory: Understanding Mediated Faith and Christian Applications of Modern Media.* Yyvaskyla: University of Yyvaskyla.

Leighton, H. V., and J. Srivastava
    1997   *Precision Among World Wide Web Search Engines: AltaVista, Excite, Hotbot, InfoSeek, and Lycos.* Available online: http://www.winona. msus.edu/library/webind2/webind2.htm. Accessed 4 May 1999.

Lengel, L. B., and P. D. Murphy
    2001   "Cultural Identity and Cyberimperialism: Computer-Mediated Explorations of Ethnicity, Nation, and Citizenship". In Ebo 2001a.

Levinson, P.
    1999   *Digital Mcluhan: A Guide to the Information Millennium.* London and New York: Routledge.

Levy, P.
    1997   *Collective Intelligence: Mankind's Emerging World in Cyberspace.* Cambridge, MA: Perseus Books.

Levy, S.
    1994   "The Battle of the Clipper Chip". *New York Times Magazine* (12 June).
    2001   *Cyberculture.* Minneapolis and London: University of Minnesota Press.

Liu, J.
    2001   *Meta Search Engines.* Available online: http://www.indiana.edu/ ~librcsd/search/. Accessed 25 May 2001.

Lovink, G.
    2002   *Dark Fiber: Tracking Critical Internet Culture.* Cambridge, MA and London: The MIT Press.

Lyman, P., and H. R. Varian
    2000   *How Much Information.* Available online: http://www.sims.berke-ley.edu/how-much-info. Accessed 10 July 2000.

MacDonald, C.
    1995   "The Ethics of Web Site Engineering". *CMC Magazine* (1 July). Available online: http://www.december.com/cmc/mag/1995/jul/ macdonald.html. Accessed 17 October 1999.

Mahan, Jeffrey H.
    2005   *Reporting Religion in Unexpected Places.* Available online: http:// www.facsnet.org/issues/faith/mahan.php. Accessed 10 February 2005.

Mann, C., and F. Stewart
    2000   *Internet Communication and Qualitative Research: A Handbook for Reseaching Online.* London and Thousand Oaks, CA: Sage.

Manovich, L.
    2001   *The Language of New Media.* Cambridge, MA and London: The MIT Press.

Markham, A. N.
    2003   "Metaphors Reflecting and Shaping the Reality of the Internet:

Tool, Place, Way of Being". Paper presented at Association of Internet Researchers conference, Montreal, Canada, October 2003.
Available online: http://ascend.comm.uic.edu/~amarkham/writ-
ing/MarkhamTPWwebversion.htm. Accessed 5 December 2003.

2004 "Internet Communcation as a Tool for Qualitative Research". In
Qualitative Research: Theory, Methods, and Practice. ed. D. Silver-
man. London: Sage. Available online: http://ascend.comm.uic.
edu/~amarkham/writing/silvermandraft.html. Accessed 23 January
2004.

Marks, T.
1997 *Windweavers Search Guide: Using the Best Directories and Search
Engines*. Available online: http://www.windweaver.com/search-
guide.htm. Accessed 22 September 2000.

Marres, N., and R. Rogers
2000 "Depluralising the Web, Repluralising Public Debate: The Case of
the GM Food Debate on the Web". In Rogers 2000a.

Mason, B., and B. Dicks
1998 "Hypermedia and Ethnography: Reflections on the Construction
of a Research Approach". *Sociological Research Online* 3.3. Available online: http://www.socresonline.org.uk/socresonline/3/3/3.
html. Accessed 16 February 2000.

Matheson, K.
1992 "Women and Computer Technology". In *Contexts of Computer-
mediated Communication*, ed. M. Lea. New York: Harvester
Wheatsheaf.

Mayer, J.-F.
2000 "Religious Movements and the Internet: The New Frontier of
Cult Controversies". In Hadden and Cowan 2000.

McChesney, R.
2000 "So Much for the Magic of Technology and the Free Market: The
World Wide Web and the Corporate Media System". In Herman
and Swiss 2000.

McCutcheon, R. T.
2004 *Religion*. Available online: http://www.as.ua.edu/rel/pdf/rel237de
finitionofreligion.pdf. Accessed 10 February 2005.

McKenna, K. Y. A., and J. A. Bargh
1999 "Causes and Consequences of Social Interaction on the Internet:
A Conceptual Framework". *Media Psychology* 1.3: 249–70.

McOmber, J. B.
1999 "Technological Autonomy and Three Definitions of Technology".
Journal of Communication 49.3: 137–53.

McSherry, L.
2002 *The Virtual Pagan: Exploring Wicca and Paganism Through the
Internet*. Boston, MA and York Beach, ME: Weiser Books.

Miller, V.
2000 "Search Engines, Portals and Global Capitalism". In Gauntlett
2000a.

Mills, S.
1997 *Discourse*. London: Routledge.

Mitchell, S.
1996   *General Internet Resource Finding Tools: A Review and List of Those Used to Build Infomine.* Available online: http://infomine. ucr.edu/pubs/navigato.html. Accessed 20 November 2000.
Mitra, A., and E. Cohen
1999   "Analyzing the Web: Directions and Challenges". In Jones 1999a.
Miyake, Y.
2002   *Information Technology and Religion.* Available online: http://www.relnet.co.jp/relnet/brief/r12-130.htm. Accessed 11 December 2002.
Mizrach, S.
1997   "Techgnosis, Infomysticism, and the War Against Entropy". *CMC Magazine* 4.3. Available online: http://www.december.com/cmc/mag/1997/mar/mizrach.html. Accessed 11 September 2000.
Moriarty, S.
1994   "Visemics: A Proposal for a Marriage Between Semiotics and Visual Communication". Paper presented at Visual Communication 94, Blairsden, California. Available online: http://spot.colorado.edu/~moriarts/visemics.html. Accessed 17 June 2000.
Morton, J.
1998   *Colour, the Chameleon of the Web.* Available online: http://www.colormatters.com/chameleon.html. Accessed 19 March 2001.
Mosco, V.
2000   "Webs of Myth and Power: Connectivity and the New Computer Technopolis". In Herman and Swiss 2000.
Moulthorp, S.
2000   "Error 404: Doubting the Web". In Herman and Swiss 2000.
Mumford, L.
1946   *Technics and Civilisation.* London: George Routledge & Sons.
Nakache, P.
1998   "What Is Yahoo, Really?" *Fortune* (June 22). Available online: http://www.trinityventures.com/team/articles/yahoo.html. Accessed 28 August 1999.
The New Oxford Annotated Bible
1991   New York: Oxford University Press
The New Penguin English Dictionary
2000   London: Penguin.
Newman, J.
1997   *Religion and Technology: A Study in the Philosophy of Culture.* Westport, CT: Praeger.
Noble, D. F.
1997   *The Religion of Technology: The Divinity of Man and the Spirit of Invention.* New York: Alfred Knopf.
Novak, M.
1991   "Liquid Architectures in Cyberspace". In Benedikt 1991.
O'Dochartaigh, N.
2002   *The Internet Research Handbook.* London: SAGE Publications.

O'Leary, S. D.
    1996   "Cyberspace as Sacred Space: Communicating Religion on Computer Networks". *Journal of the American Academy of Religion* 59.4: 781–808.
O'Leary, S. D., and B. E. Brasher
    1996   "The Unknown God of the Internet: Religious Communication from the Ancient Agora to the Virtual Forum". In Ess 1996.
Otto, R.
    1950   *The Idea of the Holy*. Harmondsworth: Penguin Books.
Pacey, A.
    1992   *The Culture of Technology*. Cambridge, MA: MIT Press.
Palmquist, M.
    1997   *Overview: Content Analysis*. Available online: http://writing. colostate.edu/references/research/content/index.cfm. Accessed 27 October 1999.
Pannyavaro
    1998   *The Internet and Monkhood—Should Monks Surf the Internet?* Available online: http://www.buddhanet.net/mag_surf.htm. Accessed 12 November 2000.
Paolillo, J.
    1999   "The Virtual Speech Community: Social Network and Language Variation on IRC". *Journal of Computer-Mediated Communication* 4.4. Available online: http://www.ascusc.org/jcmc/vol4/ issue4/paolillo.html. Accessed 19 October 2001.
Patelis, K.
    2000   "E-Mediation by America Online". In Rogers 2000a.
Pesce, M. D.
    1997   "Ignition". Keynote Address at World Movers Conference, San Francisco, January 1997. Available online: http://www.hyperreal. org/~mpesce/. Accessed 23 November 2000.
Pesce, M. D., P. Kennard and A. S. Parisi
    1994   *Cyberspace*. Available online: http://www.hyperreal.org/~mpesce/ www.html. Accessed 22 October 1999.
Peterson, R. E.
    1996   *Internet Search Engines*. Available online: http://www2.hawaii. edu/~rpeterso/engine_.htm. Accessed 22 October 2000.
Pokorny, G.
    1997   *Cyberspace Ministry*. Available online: http://www.rpinet.com/ml/ 2407cybr.html. Accessed 25 March 1999.
Poster, M.
    1995a   "Postmodern Virtualities". In Featherstone and Burrows 1995a.
    1995b   *Cyberdemocracy: The Internet and the Public Sphere*. Available online: http://www.hnet.uci.edu/mposter/writings/democ.html. Accessed 28 November 1997.
Pringle, G., L. Allison and D. L. Dowe
    1998   "What is a Tall Poppy among Web Pages?" Seventh International World-Wide Web Conference, April 14-18, 1998, Brisbane, Australia. Available online: http://decweb.ethz.ch/WWW7/00/index. htm. Accessed 12 November 2000.

Rappoport, A.
    2002   *Anatomy of a Search Engine: Inside Google*. Available online:
            http://www.searchenginewatch.com/searchday/02/sd1030-in-
            google.html. Accessed 12 November 2000.
Raymond, E. S.
    1998   "Homesteading the Noosphere". *First Monday* 3.10. Available
            online: http://www.firstmonday.org/issues/issue3_10/raymond/
            index.html. Accessed 12 October 200.
Reid, E.
    1995   "Virtual Worlds: Culture and Imagination". In Jones 1995.
Rheingold, H.
    1993   *Homesteading on the Electronic Frontier*. Reading, MA: Addison-
            Wesley.
    2000   "Community Development in the Cybersociety of the Future". In
            Gauntlett 2000a.
Robins, K.
    1995   "Cyberspace and the World We Live In". In Featherstone and
            Burrows 1995a.
Robinson, B., A.
    2000   "Evolution of a Religious Web Site Devoted to Tolerance". In
            Hadden and Cowan 2000.
Rodan, G.
    1997   *The Internet and Political Control in Singapore*. Available online:
            http://www.sfdonline.org/Link%20Pages/Link%20Folders/
            Political%20Freedom/rodan.html. Accessed 17 June 2002.
Rodriguez, F., and E. J. Wilson
    2000   "Are Poor Countries Losing the Information Revolution?" *InfoDev
            Working Paper*. Available online: http://www.infodev.org/library/
            WorkingPapers/wilsonrodriguez.doc. Accessed 7 July 2000.
Rogers, R. (ed.)
    2000a   *Preferred Placement: Knowledge Politics on the Web*. Maastricht:
            Jan van Eyck Akademie.
    2000b   "Introduction: Towards the Practice of Web Epistemology". In
            Rogers 2000a.
Rogers, R., and I. Morris
    2000   "Operating the Internet with Socio-Epistemological Logics". In
            Rogers 2000a.
Ronfeldt, D., and J. Arquilla
    1999   *The Emergence of Noopolitik*. Available online: http://www.rand.
            org/publications/MR/MR1033/. Accessed 12 November 2000.
    2000   "From Cyberspace to the Noosphere: Emergence of the Global
            Mind". *New Perspectives Quarterly* 17.1.
Rusciano, F. L.
    2001   "The Three Faces of Cyberimperialism". In Ebo 2001a.
Ryan, R.
    1992   "International Connectivity: A Survey of Attitudes about Cultural
            and National Differences Encountered in Computer-Mediated
            Communication". *Online Chronicle of Distance Education and*

Communication 6.1. Available online: http://www.eff.org/Net_culture/Infotopia/culture_and_comp_mediation.paper. Accessed 23 March 2001.

Salmon, G.
2000   *E-Moderating: The Key to Teaching and Learning Online.* London: Kogan Page.

Sardar, Z. R., and J. Ravetz (eds.)
1996   *Cybercultures.* London: Pluto Press.

Schlichting, C., and E. Nilsen
1996   "Signal Detection Analysis of WWW Search Engines". *Designing for the Web Empirical Studies.* Available online: http://www.microsoft.com/usability/webconf.htm. Accessed 12 November 2000.

Seabrook, J.
1995   "Home on the Net". *The New Yorker,* 16 October. Available online: http://levity.com/seabrook/homenet.html. Accessed 11 November 2000.

Search Engine Watch
1996   http://searchenginewatch.com/ Accessed 14 February 2006.

Selbach, J.
2002   *19 Common Mistakes that Prevent your Web Site from Showing up on Search Engines.* Available online: http://www.promotionworld.com/se/articles/article/19common.html. Accessed 23 February 2004.

Sharot, S.
2001   *A Comparative Sociology of World Religions.* New York and London: New York University Press.

Sherman, C., and D. Sullivan
2002   *The Search Engine "Perfect Page" Test.* Available online: http://www.searchenginewatch.com/searchday/02/sd1104-pptest.html. Accessed 12 November 2000.

Shields, R. (ed.)
1996   *Cultures of Internet: Virtual Spaces, Real Histories, Living Bodies.* London and Thousand Oaks, CA: Sage.
2000   "Hypertext Links: The Ethic of the Index and its Space-Time Effects". In Herman and Swiss 2000.

Silver, D.
2000   "Looking Backwards, Looking Forwards: Cyberculture Studies 1999–2000". In Gauntlett 2000a.

Slevin, J.
2000   *The Internet and Society.* Cambridge: Polity Press.

Slouka, M. Z.
1995   *The War of the Worlds: Cyberspace and the Hightech Assault on Reality.* New York: Basic Books.

Smart, N.
1969   *The Religious Experience of Mankind.* London and Glasgow: Collins.

Smith, J. Z.
1998   "Religion, Religions, Religious". In Taylor 1998.

Smith, M. A., and P. Kollock (ed.)
    1999   Communities in Cyberspace. London and New York: Routledge.
Sobchack, V.
    1993   "New Age Mutant Ninja Hackers: Reading Mondo 2000". South
            Atlantic Quarterly 92.4. Available online: http://66.102.11.104/
            search?q=cache: rSFctHQ0TKAJ: www.rochester.edu/College/
            FS/Publications/SobchackNinja.html+new+age+mutant+ninja
            +hackers&hl=en&ie=UTF-8. Accessed 20 November 2002.
Sorkin, M. (ed.)
    1992   Variations on a Theme Park: The New American City and the End
            of Public Space. New York: Hill and Wang.
Soukup, P. A.
    1999   A New Context for Religious Practice. Available online: http://
            www.findarticles.com/cf_0/m1321/1999_May_8/54647905/
            jhtml. Accessed 19 November 2000.
Soules, M.
    1996   Harold Adams Innis: The Bias of Communications & Monopolies of
            Power. Available online: http://www.mala.bc.ca/~soules/paradox/
            innis.htm. Accessed 12 March 2002.
Spender, D.
    1995   Nattering on the Net: Women, Power, and Cyberspace. Melbourne:
            Spinifex Press.
Stahl, W. A.
    1999   God and the Chip: Religion and the Culture of Technology. Water-
            loo, ON: Wilfrid Laurier University Press.
Stallabrass, J.
    1995   "Empowering Technology: The Exploration of Cyberspace". New
            Left Review 211. Available online: http://www.newleftreview.net/.
            Accessed 16 November 2000.
Stanley, A.
    1993   Mothers and Daughters of Invention: Notes for a Revised History
            of Technology. Metuchen, NJ: Scarecrow Press.
Stanley, L.
    2001   "Beyond Access". UCSD Civic Collaborative 2001 San Diego Digi-
            tal Divide Study. Available online: http://www.mediamanage.net/
            Beyond_Access.pdf. Accessed 21 December 2001.
Stefik, M.
    1996   Internet Dreams: Archetypes, Myths, and Metaphors. Cambridge,
            MA and London: The MIT Press.
Stenger, N.
    1991   "Mind is a Leaking Rainbow". In Benedikt 1991.
Steuer, J.
    1992   "Defining Virtual Reality: Dimensions Determining Telepresence".
            Journal of Communication 42.4: 73–93.
Stone, A. R.
    1991   "Will the Real Body Please Stand Up?: Boundary Stories About Vir-
            tual Culture". In Benedikt 1991.

Strate, L.
2003   "Cybertime". In *Communication and Cyberspace: Social Interaction in an Electronic Environment*, ed. R. L. Jacobson and S. Gibson. Cresskill, NJ: Hampton Press Inc.

Sudweeks, F., and S. J. Simoff
1999   "Complementary Explorative Data Analysis: The Reconciliation of Quantitative and Qualitative Principles". In Jones 1999a.

Sullivan, D.
2001a   *Can Portals Resist the Dark Side?* Available online: http://www.searchenginewatch.com/sereport/print.php/34721_2163861. Accessed 18 November 2001.
2001b   *The Evolution of Paid Inclusion.* Available online: http://searchenginewatch.com/sereport/01/07-inclusion.html. Accessed 19 December 2001.
2001c   *Search Engine Sizes.* Available online: http://searchenginewatch.com/reports/sizes.html. Accessed 13 November 2001.
2002a   *Pay for Placement?* Available online: http://searchenginewatch.com/resources/paid-listings.html. Accessed 12 November 2000.
2002b   *The Mixed Message of Paid Inclusion.* Available online: http://searchenginewatch.com/sereport/02/05-inclusion.html. Accessed 12 November 2000.

Svatek, M.
2002   *Searching for a Search that Works.* Available online: http://www.zdnet.com/filters/printerfriendly/0,6061,2896255-92,00.html. Accessed 15 December 2002.

Swiss, T., and A. Herman
2000   "The World Wide Web as Magic, Metaphor, and Power". In Herman and Swiss 2000.

Tate, M. A., and J. E. Alexander
1999   *Web Wisdom: How to Evaluate and Create Information Quality in the Web.* Hillsdale, NJ: Lawrence Erlbaum Associates.

Tatusko, A.
2001   *The Theological Challenge of Cyberspace and the Logic of Simulation.* Available online: www.jcrt.org/archives/02.2/tatusko.html. Accessed 25 November 2002.

Taubman, G. L.
2002   "Keeping the Internet Out? Non-Democratic Legitimacy and Access to the Web". *First Monday* 7.9. Available online: http://firstmonday.org/issues/issue7_9/taubman/index.html. Accessed 23 November 2002.

Taylor, M. C. (ed.)
1998   *Critical Terms for Religious Studies.* Chicago and London: Chicago University Press.

Teilhard de Chardin, P.
1959   *The Phenomenon of Man.* New York: Harper & Row.

Tetzlaff, D.
2000   "Yo-Ho-Ho and a Server of Warez: Internet Software Piracy and the New Global Information Economy". In Herman and Swiss 2000.

Thieme, R.
  1997   "The Future Shape of Religious Structures". *CMC Magazine* 4.3.
Thomason, L.
  2002   "Link Farms Grow Spam". *Webmaster Newsletter*, April part 1.
          Available online: http://www.netmechanic.com/news/vol5/promo_
          no7.htm. Accessed 3 December 2002.
Thumma, S.
  2002   "Religion and the Internet". Lecture for the Communications
          Forum of the Massachusetts Institute of Technology, 18 April 2002.
          http://hirr.hartsem.edu/bookshelf/thumma_article6.html. Accessed
          14 February 2006.
Titon, J. T.
  1995   "Common Ground: Keywords for the Study of Expressive Cul-
          ture". *The Journal of American Folklore* 108: 430, 432–48.
Tomas, D.
  1995   "Feedback and Cybernetics: Reimaging the Body in the Age of
          Cybernetics". In Featherstone and Burrows 1995a.
Tong, D.
  2001   "Cybercolonialism: Speeding Along the Superhighway or Stalling
          on a Beaten Track?" In Ebo 2001a.
Tosca, S. P.
  2000   "A Pragmatics of Links". *Journal of Digital Information* 1.6. Arti-
          cle No. 22, 2000-06-27. Available online: http://jodi.ecs.soton.
          ac.uk/Articles/v01/i06/Pajares/. Accessed 17 December 2000.
Turkle, S.
  1995   *Life on the Screen: Identity in the Age of the Internet*. London:
          Weidenfeld and Nicolson.
Turkle, S., and S. Papert
  1990   "Epistemological Pluralism: Styles and Voices within the Computer
          Culture". *Journal of Women in Culture and Society* 16.1.
Turner, V. W.
  1969   *The Ritual Process: Structure and Anti-structure*. Chicago: Aldine
          Publishing.
Vehovar, V.
  2001   "Prospects of Small Countries in the Age of the Internet". In Ebo
          2001a.
Vile, A., and S. Polovina
  2000   *Making Accessible Web Sites with Semiotics*. Available online:
          http://homepages.gold.ac.uk/polovina/publications/
          Semiotics4AWDshortpaper.PDF. Accessed 20 February 2001.
Virilio, P.
  1995   "Speed and Information: Cyberspace Alarm!" *CTheory*. Article:
          A030. Date published: 27 August 1995. Available online: http://
          www.ctheory.net/text_file?pick=72. Accessed 12 November 2000.
Wærn, Y.
  2000   *Networds Methodologies for Research on Internet Communication:
          Plans for Research 2000–2003*. Available online: http://www.tema.
          liu.se/people/yvowa/Networdspres.doc. Accessed 16 June 2000.

Wakeford, N.
    2000   "New Media, New Methodologies: Studying the Web". In Gaunt-
            lett 2000a.

Walton, S. A.
    2003   "An Introduction to the Mechanical Arts in the Middle Ages".
            AVISTA, Association Villard de Honnecourt for Interdisciplin-
            ary Study of Medieval Technology, Science and Art, Univer-
            sity of Toronto. Available online: http://www.chass.utoronto.
            ca/~avista/PAPERS/mecharts_walton.html. Accessed 24 August
            2003.

Ward, G.
    2000   *Cities of God*. London and New York: Routledge.

Warschauer, M.
    2000   "Does the Internet Bring Freedom?" *Information Technology, Edu-
            cation and Society* 1.2: 93–2001. Available online: http://www.
            gse.uci.edu/markw/freedom.html. Accessed 19 June 2002.
    2002   "Reconceptualizing the Digital Divide". *First Monday* 7.7. Avail-
            able online: http://firstmonday.org/issues/issue7_7/warschauer/
            index.html. Accessed 21 November 2002.
    2003a "Social Capital and Access". *Universal Access in the Informa-
            tion Society* 2.4. Available online: http://www.gse.uci.edu/markw/
            soccap.pdf. Accessed 13 December 2003.
    2003b *Technology and Social Inclusion: Rethinking the Digital Divide.*
            MIT Press. Available online: http://www.gse.uci.edu/markw/tsi-
            intro.html. Accessed 19 December 2003.

Warschauer, M., G. R. El Said and A. Zohry
    2002   "Language Choice Online: Globalization and Identity in Egypt".
            Journal of Computer-Mediated Communication 7.4. http://jcmc.
            indiana.edu/vol7/issue4/warschauer.html

Wellman, B., and M. Gulia
    1999   "Virtual Communities as Communities: Net Surfers Don't Ride
            Alone". In Smith and Kollock 1999.

Wertheim, M.
    1999   *The Pearly Gates of Cyberspace*. London: Virago.

Wiggins, R. W.
    2001   "The Effects of September 11 on the Leading Search Engine".
            First Monday 6.10. Available online: http://firstmonday.org/issues/
            issue6_10/wiggins/index.html. Accessed 13 February 2002.

Winner, L.
    1986   *The Whale and the Reactor: A Search for Limits in an Age of High
            Technology*. Chicago: University of Chicago Press.

Witmer, D. F., R. W. Colman and S. L. Katzman
    1999   "From Paper-and-Pencil to Screen-and-Keyboard: Toward a Meth-
            odology for Survey Research on the Internet". In Jones 1999a.

Wittgenstein, L.
    1963   *Philosophical Investigations*. Oxford: Basil Blackwell and Mott.

Wolmark, J. and E. Gates Stuart
    2002   "Cultural Hybrids, Post-disciplinary Digital Practices and New

Research Frameworks: Testing the Limits". Available online: http://
www.herts.ac.uk/artdes/research/papers/wpades/vol2/wolmark.
html. Accessed 12 December 2003.

Wright, R.
1997   "The Man who Invented the Web". *Time Magazine* (May 19). Available online: http://time-proxy.yaga.com/time/magazine/article/
qpass/0,10987,1101970519-13768990873267.htm. Accessed
23 December 2000.

Yoon, S.-H.
1996   "Power Online: A Poststructuralist Perspective on CMC". In Ess
1996.

Yu, P. K.
2002   *Bridging the Digital Divide: Equality in the Information Age.* Available online: http://ssrn.com/abstract_ID=309841. Accessed 18
December 2002.

Zaleski, J. P.
1997   *The Soul of Cyberspace: How New Technology is Changing our
Spiritual Lives.* San Francisco: HarperEdge.

Zanker, C.
2001   "The Global Digital Divide: Problems and Solutions". Available
online: http://www.input-consulting.com/download/berlin-dd-eng.
pdf. Accessed 14 February 2006.

Zukowski, A. A.
2002   *The New Frontier: Integrating Media and Technology in Ministry.*
Available online: www.fithfirst.com/html/catechist/proPapers/
images/T780Zukowski.pdf. Accessed 1 February 2003.

Zurawski, N.
1999   "Research Methodology Online". *Cybersociology* 6. Available online: http://www.cybersociology.com/. Accessed 6 August 1999.